BUKOWSKI

An Anthology of Poetry & Prose
About Charles Bukowski

BUKOWSKI

An Anthology of Poetry & Prose
About Charles Bukowski

EDITED BY

MELANIE VILLINES

CONTRIBUTING EDITORS

JOCELYNE DESFORGES

S. A. GRIFFIN

SUZANNE LUMMIS

DAVID ROSKOS

JOAN JOBE SMITH

EDDIE WOODS

SILVER BIRCH PRESS
LOS ANGELES, CALIFORNIA

ISBN-13: 978-0615845494

ISBN-10: 0615845495

FIRST EDITION, SEPTEMBER 2013

Email: silver@silverbirchpress.com

Web: silverbirchpress.com

Blog: silverbirchpress.wordpress.com

Book Design: Silver Birch Press

Cover Art: Charles Bukowski by Mark Erickson and Katy Zartl, ALL RIGHTS RESERVED. For more information about this portrait and other artwork by the artists, visit their websites: www.markerickson.com, www.birgitzartl.com.

Mailing Address:
Silver Birch Press
P.O. Box 29458
Los Angeles, CA 90029

*"What matters most is how well
you walk through the fire."*
CHARLES BUKOWSKI

"Love Life V"
Portrait by Dana Laina

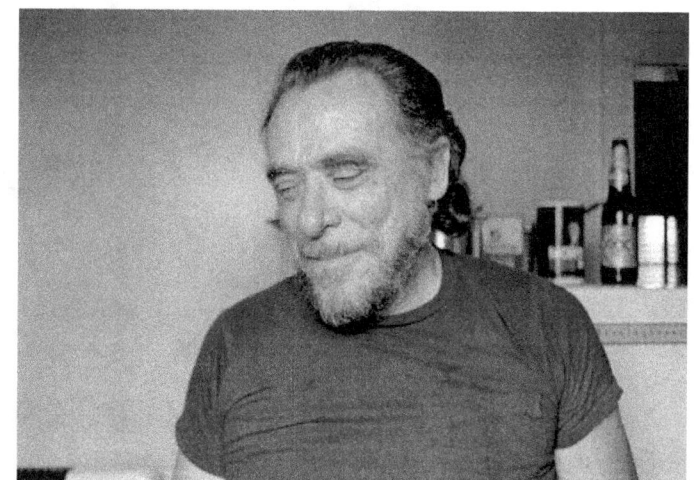

©Joan Gannij

For information about purchasing fine quality prints of
Charles Bukowski portraits by Joan Gannij,
send an email to joangannij@gmail.com.

INTRODUCTION

MELANIE VILLINES

It comes down to this: we miss Charles Bukowski. We felt better knowing he was around somewhere—East Hollywood, San Pedro, or place or places unknown. Almost twenty years after Bukowski's passing, people continue to feel his presence—not just in his words, but in his spirit. If I tried to narrow down the essence of Buk's influence to one word, I'd say, "hope." He gives people the feeling that whatever is going on, it's okay, they'll get through it, learn from it, and, if they're lucky, turn it into a story.

The point of this collection is to put our collective thoughts, feelings, and impressions together, share our stories, our poems, our portraits, and join in our joint missing of Bukowski. Now whenever we feel the pang of Buk's absence, we can pick up this book and connect with others who feel the same way.

In this volume, we've collected poetry, essays, memoirs, short stories, vignettes, book excerpts, biographies, fantasies, satires, parodies, quips, quotes, homages, and other writing about Charles Bukowski plus portraits of the great author from over seventy-five writers and artists around the world—in a celebration of the man who meant something special to so many.

My deepest appreciation to our contributors, and a special thank you to our contributing editors—Jocelyne Desforges, S.A. Griffin, Suzanne Lummis, David Roskos, Joan Jobe Smith, and Eddie Woods—who were instrumental in bringing fellow writers and artists into these pages to share their work featuring Charles Bukowski.

I can think of no other author who has affected so many people on such a deep, personal level. Why do we care so much about Charles Bukowski? Some of the reasons are inside these pages. Enjoy!

> *"That was all a man needed: hope.*
> *It was lack of hope that discouraged a man."*
> CHARLES BUKOWSKI, *Factotum*

Portrait by Germa Marquez
germamarquez.blogspot.de

CONTENTS

SILVER BIRCH PRESS

BUKOWSKI ANTHOLOGY

Prologue
Born Writer

Mr. Chinaski as seen by The Art Warriors
theartwarriors.com

SCOTT WANNBERG

Bukowski Birthday Rap, 2003 August 16

come on down the stairs now
come barefoot and let us hear you sing
for days for hours for months for seconds
the heavy hitters have been standing bare headed in the weather
making bets that you won't make it all the way down the stairs
fools, I know you built those stairs
with your heart and your brain and your blood
before you built the stairs those heavy hitters claim you can't manage
there was nothing but a big large hole in the system
come on down all the stairs now
the ones that may actually not be there as well
as the ones you damn well know for sure are beneath your feet.

the heavy hitters are getting tired from trying to prove
they can hold so much weight.

sometimes, frankly, it's okay to be wispy and float through
the clouds of ongoing.

the heavy hitters become vulnerable
lose their place in the big line of importance
someone call out for a clarifying
someone call out for edible food

you come down the stairs
barefoot
and begin to sing and dance
buck and wing

oh writer of stories novels and poems
oh writer of the moment
oh human in the moment of being human
and all the shades that thrive there
as the hot sun of ego attempts to melt you into the sidewalk
as you go outside to be yourself in the moment
the heavy hitters have melted into spring water

but here it is, summer still, August 16
and you still sing to me
and help me to find my way
through the maze.

NEELI CHERKOVSKI

Hank: The Life of Charles Bukowski (Random House, 1991)
Excerpt from Author's Introduction

...Few writers have given themselves over to the immediate world around them so completely as has Bukowski. His skill lies in taking his environment, his city, and making it universal. The particular place becomes the human city everywhere. Once, when it was suggested that he think of moving to the suburbs, Bukowski said, "Hell no! I like the anarchy of the city, the grime, the bad air, danger on the streets. I'd go mad in the country. Give me blaring car horns and dirty sidewalks."

Bukowski is a mythmaker and he has accepted his own myth. It is no accident that Henry Charles Bukowski, Jr., chose the name Henry Chinaski for the central character of his novels and much of his shorter fiction. In his books, from *Post Office*, written in 1970, to *Hollywood*, published in 1989, the reader follows the adventures of Chinaski in his role as self-deprecating saint and sinner, rarely venturing out of Los Angeles, always able to poke fun at himself...

There were no literary friends or confidantes in Bukowski's early years. The last thing he ever wanted was to be part of a literary movement. During the forties, when he was in his twenties, Hank stuck to himself, holed up in rooming houses, keeping himself together through a combination of dead-end jobs, cheap whiskey, the comfort of a succession of radios invariably tuned to a classical station, and his aspirations to become a professional writer. He spent most of his time wandering from city to city, more concerned with the next drink than with documenting his life. He doesn't even remember where he was when the war ended, nor does he recall the precise year he met Jane Cooney Baker, the woman he lived with for nearly a decade, who was the model for Wanda in his screenplay for *Barfly*. As to the cities in which he lived, he is unable to place them in accurate sequence. What he does vividly recall are the long hours he spent writing short stories that were never published.

Excerpt from introduction to
Hank: A Life of Charles Bukowski by Neeli Cherkovski
(Random House, 1991). Used by permission of the author.

Part One
Hank & Me

Portrait by Jeff Morgan

HENRY DENANDER

Accept Your Name

Henry Chesney Baker
and Henry Charles Bukowski;

if I had known about these guys when
I was young perhaps I would have liked
my own name better.

My name is OK now but I was never very
pleased with it when I was a kid.

At that time no one here in
Sweden knew about Chet or Buk
but now it's good to be able to
tell people that both of them were
named Henry.

And no one needs to know that
Buk never liked Henry
but used Charles instead.

Originally published in *Remark* (2000)

JARED CARNEY

Not Called Hank

Hank
I'm apologizing early
Hank
I know that wouldn't mean much
Hank
You hadn't done anything by my age
Except get beaten
And when that happened to me
They made a big deal of it
Hank
I'm sorry
I quite like Kerouac
Hank
I'm sorry
I quit drinking already
I went at it for a few years
But it just made everything worse
Hank
I don't mind Ginsberg either
I even went through a Rimbaud phase
Hank
Hemingway doesn't do much for me
Hank
I've never been to L.A
Hank
I think I pronounce your last name wrong
Hank
If I came to your door
Telling you I don't drink
Telling you I write poetry
In my clean shirt
And boots
I wouldn't look like much to you
And you'd be right
Hank
It's hard to explain sometimes
Hank
This repetition would probably annoy you
But I'm into it now
Hank
My assumptions

Would probably annoy you too
And look
That was nearly another trick
Hank
I can't get away with saying whore
It doesn't feel right in my mouth
Hank
At least I got Fante
And it wasn't through you either
Hank
I'm not much of a Mahler man
Hank
I'm not much of a man at all
Hank
I don't throw punches
And I do my best to avoid them
Hank
Once I saw your face on the wall of a pub
With that line about going crazy
Next to pictures of Jim Morrison
And Keith Richards
And John Lennon
Hank
I don't admire you
Hank
I don't envy you
Hank
I never knew you
Hank
I've tried not to construct you
How I'd want you
Hank
At this point it would be easy to say something like
You laid down a mean line
Or mention wine and the tapping of keys
Or Hem putting his brains to the wall
Hank
When I read you
I feel I can go
I don't even miss the drinking
I think about writing more
Hank
That's what I'm apologizing for:
Using you as the spark
For an unimpressive fire.

CATFISH MCDARIS

Out of the Mouth of Babes

When my kid was eight she
got published with Bukowski

She used to tell people she was
related to me by marriage, I was
married to her mom

I worked at the post office in Milwaukee,
near the gay district, the in place seemed
to be a bar called The Ball Game with a
big ball winking sign

When we'd drive by, my kid would start
clearing her throat & say dad I'm really
thirsty can you go inside & get me
something cold to drink.

HEATHER MINETTE

Dirty Books

I learned the hard way,
that a seventeen year old daughter,
should never mention to her father,
the name of her favorite author,
just in case
her father has read Bukowski too.

BEN TALBOT

Finding Bukowski

I first read him on the toilet in my college dorm, at twenty-three, having heard the name once or twice before but never considering who he really was. It was an anthology of his poetry, with one particular poem about camping near Bakersfield, my hometown—the last town that I suspected would ever end up in a work of art. How simple, colorful, humorous and humanistic was his voice on paper. I closed the book and never opened it again.

I forgot about Charles for the next five years. In that time, after graduating college, I was hired and fired at a restaurant, at a middle school, and at a business that sold water filtration; a life of dead romance and dead-end jobs. So I moved to Hollywood, hoping to leave the past behind, where Charles and I were to reacquaint at a 4th of July party in Lawndale. While the rest of the party was sitting drunk in the Jacuzzi outside, my friend Brendan and I were sifting through a small bookshelf in the main room, wherein he pulled out the thin motley-colored book *Hot Water Music* and wanted me to read its short stories.

"You ever read this guy?" he said.

"No," I said. I still don't know why I had told my friend this lie.

He showed me a short story about a woman being raped repeatedly in the elevator by one of her tenants. Yes, I was disgusted. But I was also captivated by how effortlessly he pulled me from the same shelf that I had been stuck in since college and drew me into the scenes; simply telling me stories, forsaking the shallow impressions of beautiful-looking prose. Brendan went back out to the Jacuzzi, but I stayed inside and kept reading story after story of this anthology; before death by a misdirected firework; before the book were to be drenched apart by a flood or burned to gray ashes in a fire. I also didn't know which was worse: Avoiding the party, putting the book away or stealing it from my coworker? Asking to borrow it would've been too awkward, nor did I care much for anyone at the party, so I decided to steal it, bring it back to Carolyn once I was done, and thank her with an apology.

After finishing *Hot Water Music* the next night, I drove to Borders on Vine (which is now closed)—ignorant then that I was standing within a few miles from Bukowski Court—and I bought every anthology of his that was there: *South of No North, Tales of Ordinary Madness, Notes of a*

Dirty Old Man...Once I read those, then what? There had to be some vault of his in the Library of Congress that preserved a collection of Bukowski's unpublished works as abundant as fortune cookies.

The only prose left of his was in his novels. In two years, I would be thirty, and I hadn't read an entire novel since junior high. What appeared to be another abused and neglected old book in the school library, wrapped in scotch tape and cellophane, was actually a crime thriller about a woman being stalked by a neighborhood pervert. How was such reprehensible literature smuggled into a junior high library? I kept looking over my shoulders in the fiction aisle for some holy teacher or librarian to bust me for reading this obscene book; she would've had me suspended and sent a shameful note to my parents. But no self-righteous adult ever appeared, nor was I ever bothered; I read the whole book on the floor.

Fifteen years after that afternoon in the library, I finished *Ham on Rye*. Bukowski enlightened me as to why some adults read authors, not books. As a young man trying to write screenplays, I studied his sentences, his dialogue, his ideas. His stories freed up and bolstered my imagination into weaving stories of my own. Brendan suggested Faulkner and Hemingway as well—with which I followed along—but I always drifted back to the tales and life lessons of Henry Chinaski. Not to be misunderstood, I respected the craft of other authors, but I couldn't rest inside anyone else's words but his. Most writers sounded too stiff (or as he used to say: intellectual). *Ham on Rye* is a novel that I will read into old age: A tragedy told in raw humor and terse honesty about his childhood; no red herrings or extensive metaphors for the readers to have to figure out. This novel taught me that literature is not some wily puzzle to endure; it is supposed to be the truth.

WIN HARMS

Feeling Like Bukowski

feeling like bukowski
here i am a lone lunatic
looking over the street
and evoking the men
i've known biblically
they were cads and
i put them out like
cigarettes in the ashtray
i am playing my music too
loud, the phone refuses to
ring, i think about
opening a beer but don't
realizing it's ten am
i light candles for
my salvation
and listen to the
wind through the trees
what a sad song they play
today i want to fly away
and forget where I was
last night

HARRY CALHOUN

Charles Bukowski and me

Forgive me in advance if I sound like an old man. As I write this, I'm a bit shy of sixty, and things were different back in the days when I read, contacted and eventually published Charles Bukowski. For one thing, when I first encountered Bukowski's work around 1975 or 1976, he was not the popular writer and cult hero he is now. Today, you can go to bukowski.net and you'll find around fifteen hundred members, including me. And most of them are totally rabid about all things Bukowski, including his rare books or videos, his life and his work in general.

Back in the mid-seventies, I was working as a bartender and going to school at Penn State. I was good friends with a fellow named Dave Dodd, who was the drummer for a group called the Keystone Rhythm Band. The band was fronted by blues legend Billy Price and they were popular at local clubs in State College, Pennsylvania. I think I first heard about Bukowski when Chuck Roethel, the band's lead guitarist, told me about him. I will always remember one of Chuck's descriptions of Bukowski. He said, "All his stories and poems are the same—I got drunk, I fucked the whore, I threw up." While that isn't exactly true, it does capture the visceral appeal (or, to his detractors, visceral dislike) that Bukowski evokes.

I remember going to the library and checking out a few Bukowski books. Of course, there wasn't much to choose from. He hadn't yet written classics such as the short story collection *South of No North* or novels like *Women*. But I was able to read *Erections, Ejaculations, Exhibitions and General Tales of Ordinary Madness, Notes of a Dirty Old Man* and a few books of poems, and I was hooked. *Erections* was the first Bukowski book I bought but it certainly wasn't the last.

BUKOWSKI, HEMINGWAY, AND MILLER

At the time I encountered Bukowski, my literary heroes were Ernest Hemingway and Henry Miller. I think a lot of writers of that era can say the same. There are similarities between Hemingway and Bukowski. Both were heavy drinkers; both were attractive to women on some level, although Bukowski never had Hem's good looks. And both had distinctive, although very different, writing styles. Today, fourteen years after Bukowski's death, a generation of young writers idolizes him. When I encountered Bukowski in the mid-seventies, it would also have been around fourteen years since Hemingway's death in 1962. In both cases, I think that writers' attitudes toward Buk and Hem go beyond worship of the dead. They also admire and try to emulate the style.

Miller also has similarities to Bukowski. While he wasn't much of a drinker, he and Bukowski both write frankly about sexual matters—so much so in Miller's case that his books were banned. While I read and enjoyed Miller, Hemingway's beautifully stark prose interested me most. I have fond memories, when I began writing in the late seventies of sitting in an upscale lounge called The Allen Room, reading Hemingway and sipping cognac by candlelight.

But Bukowski's writing style is not the neat, precise prose of Hemingway. It is littered with sometimes sloppy prose and literary fat. Yet it keeps the reader interested and reading on. It's like listening to some of the ragged Big Star songs of the seventies that seem on the verge of falling apart, yet they keep moving and keep you fascinated.

And Buk's life not like Hem's, although they both shared the tough-guy image. Bukowski talks of homelessness and living in cheap rooming houses, writing poems on the margins of newspapers, drinking and womanizing. Hemingway's stories are more polished, less rough around the edges and his lifestyle was certainly one of privilege, not of deprivation. But in their own ways, they were heroes and role models for my writing if not my lifestyle.

HOW BUKOWSKI ENTERED MY LIFE

My brush with Bukowski came in 1985. I had started a magazine called *Pig in a Poke* in 1982 and put out two issues before it became too much a burden on my income as a bartender and freelance writer. So I scaled down the format and started putting out a smaller version of the magazine and calling it *Pig in a Pamphlet*. It was in this format that I published Bukowski's work.

Even without the Internet, the small press flourished and correspondence between editor and writer—and between the editors themselves—was fast and furious. I don't remember when or where I saw Bukowski's work published in another little magazine, but by then he had been a legend to many of us for years. I remember wondering how this little magazine got Bukowski to send them some poems.

It turns out that Bukowski apparently felt warmly toward the small presses where he had gotten his start. In a move exemplary of the small press in those days—try anything—I contacted several editors that I knew and one of them gave me his address. I think it was Ron Androla, who put out a little mag called *Northern Pleasure*. So I sent Bukowski a letter asking if he would be interested in submitting some poems to my little magazine.

When Bukowski wrote back, he sent several poems with his letter. I liked the poems that he sent so much that I kept four of them. Today, the fact that I rejected some of his work still amazes me, but not even the legends get accepted all the time. And with his lifestyle, Bukowski was no stranger to rejection of all kinds. What was he like? Honestly, he seemed like a decent fellow, genuinely grateful that someone would want to publish his work. He had a good sense of humor and would frequently use it in his letters.

The pamphlet of Bukowski poems, titled *then I gave up and started drinking heavily* after a line from a poem in the collection, came out in 1985 and sold well by my modest standards. John Martin from Black Sparrow Press bought two hundred—about half of the press run—at a discount and had Bukowski sign them. So the pamphlets that I sold him at less than fifty cents a copy are now bringing two hundred dollars and upwards *each* at rare booksellers now.

I had some trouble, by the way, with John Martin. I had mentioned to Bukowski that I wanted to do another pamphlet of his work, and Bukowski apparently told Martin. I got a nasty letter from Martin, telling me to back off and that he had the rights to Bukowski's stuff. I wrote back assuring him that I had no bad intentions. When he replied he was much more pleasant than he had been before. He said he realized that I didn't mean any harm but that he had to protect his turf. He called me "a decent and honest person" (I still have the letter). And he also enclosed a check-list of Black Sparrow Press books and told me to "check off everything you'd like for yourself and let me send you the books." I took him up on that. I still have the books—by Paul Bowles, John Fante, Bukowski and others—to this day.

A final footnote to my relationship with Bukowski: I stopped publishing *Pig in a Pamphlet* around 1989 or 1990. In 1993, I left Pittsburgh for Key West, and somehow lost my signed copy of the Bukowski pamphlet. I wrote to Bukowski asking him if he would send another. Soon after, the signed copy showed up in my mailbox, but not the chatty letter that he usually sent. This was at the end of August, and a little over six months later he passed away. He must have been very sick when he got my letter but he still signed the copy and sent it back to me.

Previously published in *Abbey*

ERIK WOLTERSDORF

Justice for a Tough Guy

this Bukowski,
he was an old man,
lived in East Hollywood;
he used to drink
barrels of beer, rivers
of wine and liquor;
he often fought with his visitors,
especially those
who fancied themselves poets,
and when they overstayed
their welcome,
they often found that
he could be
hellish.

in his poems he told us
that he once inhabited
old rooms with torn shades,
that the small rooms were
often infested, and
that he sometimes shaved
at a shattered mirror;
that he usually carried steel,
and wasn't afraid to flash it;
and when he ventured into the streets,
or when he went to the track
(if you believe his stories),
that the blade actually
saved his ass.

I believed him.

I lived in Manhattan
when times were bad,
and I decided
that I should get a handgun for protection.
it was just a tiny .25 caliber, automatic,
and I had it for the same reason
that Bukowski kept his blade:

the deranged kept getting
more dangerous
and the crime rate
just kept on climbing...

I know that nobody lives in Disneyland,
and I am not complaining, but
New York used to be spooky and
Hollywood was probably similar.

you ought to believe me:
those neighborhoods were no picnic;
and there were more than just spooks
haunting our apartments;
in the shadows there were people
waiting to change you into vapor.

Buk knew this; I know it too.

humans have always been cruel to each other,
this is nothing new, but
when times get that intense
it almost becomes a necessity to
have some kind of protection.

I have no regrets—I mean,
I was not Charles Bronson—
I only wanted something small,
and the .25 caliber was
perfect for this purpose: it was
small enough to get lost in my shirt pocket
yet powerful enough to drop a hound
at a hundred paces.

I never met Bukowski, but
have always admired his toughness,
appreciated his style,
his writing,
and among other things,
that he took no shit from strangers.

but now I have grown older,
and I think to myself:

I like the way that he aged,
that he was able to mellow gracefully,
learned to be softer,
more gentle.

and I think it is good that
eventually, I softened too,
slowly, until finally, one day,
I tossed my gun into the Hudson,
thankful that I never had to fire it

and because I had recognized
that sometimes it is o.k.
to be gentle,
and that to be trespassed against
does not always call
for a reaction of vengeance.

but oddly, I am also thankful somehow
that I had been there in the bad days,
and that Bukowski
had been there before me,
and that he had been wary enough of
what was waiting out there in those shadows
that he'd had the good sense to be armed
when it counted.

that he lived to tell his story at all
should be miracle enough;
but still, he left us so much—
so many poems,

and the poems that he wrote
in those roach-infected rooms
all over Los Angeles,

they were tough poems
from hard times, from hard places
and today those words stand out—
like nails, driven into bricks…

and I am thankful for them,

but mostly, I am satisfied
that Hank was hard enough
to survive his environment,
and pleased, that he made it
to those last graceful years
of gentle living; easy,
down there by that old bridge
in San Pedro.

I suppose a tough guy like that
must have simply had it coming.

Portrait by Jocelyne Desforges

MARK ERICKSON

Bukoholic

Over the years, I have had dreams of Hank and his Volkswagens and his apartments in Hollywood. He's always been there, slightly haunting, yet always inspiring.

As a boy, I rode my bike on those very streets he lived and wandered, never knowing at the time of his existence. Sooner than later that changed.

It was an old copy of the *Free Press* I found in a record store rack in Hollywood when I was in high school that began the Bukoholic period of my life. His column jumped out at me, it was slightly dated, but I loved his sense of humor and his directness.

I wondered about folk like him, I saw them on the streets. Was one of them Bukowski?

Who is this guy that called himself Chinaski?

Buk was different, he could write and say it and it was real and direct. I still have never read anyone close that could spill it like Hank. I understood it and he was a philosopher and a poet. I first got my hands on his short story collection, *Erections, Ejaculations, Exhibitions, and General Tales of Ordinary Madness*, and I was hooked. I'd borrowed it from a friend, and when I was done reading it twice I did not want to return it. I eventually did, yet ripped off the cover, that great photo of Buk, and replaced it with my own cover art. Handed it to my friend, he was happy and I was too. Still have that original book cover somewhere.

Bukowski was the perfect channel for me to eventually move out of LA and to San Francisco. Los Angeles was great for Bukowski, but not me at the time. I needed less heat, smog, and Hollywood. In San Francisco, I found refuge in City Lights Bookstore on Columbus Avenue, next to the great bar Vesuvio's, and his books poured off the shelves, and I read all his novels and his poetry that I could get my hands on. New ones came out regularly. His straightforward style fit well with my paintings and my words. I still wondered who this guy was, but kept him close and read what I could.

I was studying painting at the San Francisco Art Institute, my first year there, when I was fortunate to catch a Bukowski reading connected with City Lights. That was something else as they say, and he did not disappoint. Loud, drunk, and he read his poems and we all enjoyed.

His books were like maps, they led us along, and we waited for more. I had drunk in his bars and walked his streets, all part of that connection I needed. I once considered heading over to his place in San Pedro and knocking on his door, but never did.

Maybe best. As we all know from his many late writings his distain for doorknockers and his objections to intruders. I felt leaving him alone and recalling, "This is the West, sir. When the legend becomes fact, print the legend." I thought how sweet it would be standing there at his door and ringing the bell, with a bottle in my hand, Buk welcomes me into his living room and tells me his stories and we would crack the bottle open and drink to old times and memories. All his words still revolve in my head, twirling images of Hollywood and New Orleans and his cross-country bus ride and in the cheap motels, apartments, and flophouses. I reread his books and his poetry collections and continue on with Hank as my wingman. The guy I used to think I saw wandering around Hollywood, and maybe I did. Maybe I walked right by him. All I know is he wanders the streets of old Hollywood still.

ADRIAN MANNING

Religion

they come to the door
peddling their manifestos
and offering their reading
material.
I am not interested.
I tell them I worship at the
Church of Bukowski
and I have plenty to read.
they look confused.
they don't understand.
but you do
don't you?

Previously published in
A Tourist, A Pilgrim, A Truth
(Bottle of Smoke Press Chapbook, 2006)

DAVID BARKER

One Match Left

Al came by, visited us in Oregon a year ago May. He brought all kinds of books and magazines to show me. Poetry stuff: color snapshots of Steve Richmond at his place in Santa Monica, pictures of Bukowski at his wedding, a wild magazine called *Pandemonium.* We drank beer and talked half the night, a good visit, and I don't get many visitors…in fact, he's been about *it* since 1982. You see, I'm fairly well isolated, like it that way. Not anti-social (though I am that too at times), just shy, reclusive.

Anyhow, one of the things he left behind was a book of matches from Bukowski's wedding. A pearly white iridescent matchbook with gold lettering on the front saying (approximately) "Hank and Linda Lee," and then a date in 1985. About half the matches were used. An interesting memento. I put it in my bookcase.

I don't smoke anymore and we don't make a habit of keeping matches around…have no use for them normally. So this Fourth of July, as I was getting ready to light the barbeque to cook up some turkey dogs and ears of corn, well, I couldn't find any damned matches. All of the big wooden kitchen ones were gone. Then I thought of the Buk matches, used a few of them.

Later that evening, getting out the fireworks, same problem. I used up all but one of them. We dedicated our fireworks to Bukowski. I told the kids if he hadn't gotten married, there'd be no show. That seemed funny.

There it sat, up on the bookcase, an almost empty matchbook. Just one left.

About a week ago, a couple of teenage girls came up and rang our doorbell fairly late at night, about ten o'clock. They wanted to borrow some matches for *their* barbeque. "Sorry," I said, "I'm all out myself. Used them all on the Fourth." I wasn't about to let them have my last Bukowski match. Not that it would matter.

Today Judy went to the store to get charcoal for tonight's barbeque. And she remembered to buy matches. A big box of those long kitchen ones. Looks like Bukowski's ass is saved again.

Hang onto that last match. You can still set the world on fire, Hank.

Written in 1987. First published in 2010 by Jocelyne Desforges and her
Purple Glow Press as a limited edition mini-chapbook
in wrappers resembling a matchbook.

JACK FOLEY

Bukowski

the mockingbird had been following the cat
there was this cat
all summer
and I only saw him
mocking mocking mocking
once
teasing and cocksure;
when he gave a
the cat crawled under rockers on porches
reading
tail flashing
and burped
and said something angry to the mockingbird
at the audience
which I didn't understand.

yesterday the cat walked calmly up the driveway
and he read this poem
with the mockingbird alive in its mouth,
about a cat
wings fanned, beautiful wings fanned and flopping,
and a bird
feathers parted like a woman's legs,
and he was both
and the bird was no longer mocking,
the cat and
it was asking, it was praying
the bird
but the cat
and he was devouring
striding down through centuries
himself
would not listen.
through the poem.

I saw it crawl under a yellow car
And I listened
with the bird
letting him die
to bargain it to another place.

summer was over.
Bukowski.

PART TWO
FIRST PERSON

Portrait by Bradley Wind
www.bradleywind.com

GERALD NICOSIA

Fourth of July with the Buk in San Pedro

He stands in a cheap plaid shirt
like some long-forgotten comedian
eyeing me sidewise
wondering what I want out of him
amazed that he's still alive
after 70 years of people coming at him
pleased by the magic he's still got
that keeps making books upstairs
on his little Mac computer
with the ancient radio blaring
the best classical music
after a day at the track
in one of the best Jap cars
money can buy
so many people coming to visit
the millionaire writer
in his fancy home and lush green yard
with self-cleaning swimming pool
don't see the lonely, troubled man
still inside
70 years haven't blunted the pain
of getting out of bed every morning
with an ugly face and a treacherous body
the horror of boredom
and the ever-nearing grave
they want to make him a hero
of the lost and down-and-out
king of the losers
what a joke
losers don't have kings
and Buk almost stumbles and falls
into the outdoor cooking grill
with wife Linda rushing to save him
though he'd already gotten his balance back
despite the dozen beers already downed
he plays with it all
the joke of holidays
celebrating your nation's independence
when your nation never gave you anything

but a big kick in the ass
and most of all the guests he invited
unaware they're foils for his madness
his need to compose their needs and hopes
into story after story
using humanity like notes in a symphony
it makes him happier than booze
and he can't figure out why
life can still be this good
when it's also so awfully
awfully bad.

Originally published in
Last Call: The Bukowski Legacy Continues
(Lummox Press, 2011)

GERALD NICOSIA

Notes on My Fourth of July with Bukowski

The Fourth of July party was not scheduled to start till six p.m. We'd been warned that Bukowski normally didn't like to socialize, but that he made this one concession to Linda's gregariousness by agreeing to participate in a party once a year on the Fourth of July. Because my wife Marcy and Linda Bukowski were friends, we were invited to come to the Bukowskis' home in San Pedro a little bit early. This was the summer of 1991.

Bukowski had been part of my consciousness for years. When I was in graduate school in 1972, the same teaching assistant who'd introduced me to Kerouac had shown me some Bukowski poems. The one that stuck in my head was "Ants Crawl My Drunken Arms." Then when I moved to San Francisco in 1979, poet Neeli Cherkovski was continually bombarding me with Bukowski stories and imitations. Recently, I had gotten to know Linda when she came to our house in Manhattan Beach a few times, and also when she read Hank's poems at an antiwar poetry reading (for the first Iraq War) that Ron Kovic and I had put on at a gallery in Venice in March 1991. I liked Linda a great deal, and figured if a gal this smart and good-hearted loved Bukowski, he couldn't be quite as bad and mean as he'd been cracked up to be.

When we walked in, we were greeted by Linda. Bukowski was standing off to the side of the living room, deliberately stationed so that he could get a look at us before we saw him. He had a wry, almost shy smile on his face—as if a little embarrassed knowing that I expected to meet the "famous writer." Maybe it helped that he'd met Marcy already several times. He was at ease and friendly shaking my hand. He looked neat enough, with a clean, crisply pressed, short-sleeve plaid shirt, and his grey cotton-polyester-blend work pants were clean too (I would have guessed Sears Roebuck), though clearly baggy and not a good fit.

One of the first things he said to us was that he was mad that he'd had to leave the track after the fourth race in order to attend Linda's party, but he said he was happy that he'd already made a profit because he'd won big on a horse called "Maroon Buck."

"I figured, I'm Buck, right?" he said, and his shirt was a maroon, blue, and green plaid. His arms weren't big any more, and his hands weren't as small as Harold Norse had told me they were. Norse used to delight in ridiculing Bukowski as a man with a big ape's body and tiny hands. Later in the day, Bukowski would take a turn at knocking Norse, as he would put down almost any contemporary writer who was mentioned in his presence. Buk later told us that Norse wrote a mean attack on him after Buk set up a reading for him where only four people came—three hundred had come to the same venue to see Buk.

"Harold said, 'It was raining,'" Bukowski laughed. "When you gotta start making excuses for yourself, you've lost it."

We talked for a while inside; then the other guests started arriving, and we moved the party to the lush green backyard, to a picnic table beside the pool. Bukowski got the grill going with a special bucket that Linda had bought him just for that purpose. The array of guests was impressive, and included filmmaker Barbet Schroeder and actor Seymour Cassel, who had appeared in several of Cassavetes' movies. There were many conversations going on simultaneously, but there was also no doubt that Bukowski was holding court, holding forth to anyone who would listen to him, which was always a substantial group of people at any particular time.

He was drinking like the Buk of old, beer after beer (Heinekins?), and wine at the end. I wasn't drinking because of my chronic esophagitis. He told me not to worry about my health problems (he had kind eyes). He related how many years ago, the Japanese doctor had told him if he had one more drink he'd die: "So I had two, three, four, five..." He'd started drinking again, he said, right after he got out of the hospital with a bleeding ulcer, where they gave him twelve pints of blood.

He said, "Drinking is better than life" (or: "more than life"). Linda said, "Gerry probably disagrees." So he asked me what else there is, and I said, "Friendship, camaraderie, conversation." He scoffed at all this: "I have no friends! Name someone you would want to be friends with! You've got to do better than that."

I caught him off guard by saying, "Linda is your friend, isn't she?"

Him: "No answer." (Although he'd claimed earlier he doesn't need the woman-mothering thing that some men do. "I've never needed that," he asserted.)

But Linda got him off the hook by saying, "The great thing about our relationship is we don't know what we are to each other—it's always changing. Sometimes we're friends for a moment."

Bukowski: "It's better to have good enemies."

Someone suggested that Hank and Linda were enemies, but neither he nor she accepted that. In the driveway later, Buk said, "A wife never knows her husband—they're too close to us—but there she is, sitting on my car."

Most of the time, though, he was cynical about almost all human relationships. He liked the line of Sartre: "Hell is other people." "Oh yeah!" he said after quoting it for us.

He kept trying to spur something to happen, urged us to jump into the pool naked, joked about how stimulating we'd find the Ray-vac pool cleaner. He also kept debating with his young friend Mike "whether there was material for a story" in the party. He said he never knew till two or three weeks later—then it all came back to him. He said he remembers too much; he wished he didn't—though when he wants to forget something, he conveniently says, "I don't remember anything."

The conversation turned to literature and writers—a topic that seemed profoundly distasteful to him. He said Beat poet Jack Micheline was limited as a writer because all he talked about was "the poet." "You gotta get beyond that," Buk said. "He never punched a time clock...I once paid him twenty-five dollars to get rid of him."

He said Neeli's biography of him, *Hank*, gave him a headache! Later, back inside, I would watch him pick it up and drop it on the floor. He said Neeli left out his best stories and only recorded himself at the interviews! "Neeli's problem," he said, "is that he freezes up when he writes, as if someone is looking over his shoulder." Someone asked him what the secret was to writing well. "I always try to write profound things as if they were simple," Buk said, "and to stick to simple language—and just to tell what I remember."

A lot of the time, Linda sat at Buk's feet as he talked, and she would call him "Papa" or "Papá." At one point, where he was pouring the live coals from his bucket into the grill, it looked like he was going to tip over and fall into the grill himself, and Linda jumped up and rushed over to grab him and pull him back out of harm's way.

He talked about how some famous French writer accused him of staging (deliberately) the drunken scene that got him thrown off a TV show in Paris, but the next day women on buses were shouting to him, and four waiters bowed to him.

He said he didn't go down to the set of *Barfly* more than once a week because "the horses were running."

He said he loves bad reviews, because if he's upsetting people then he knows he'd doing something right. "Good reviews?" he scoffed. "What's the difference? Who cares? I already know I'm good."

He said, "There's very little good literature today, most of which I've written myself."

Someone made a joke about how Hank's favorite writer is Hank. He seemed a little embarrassed to be continually dismissing other writers, but he also defended his prejudices. Micheline kept coming up in the conversation—I was a long-time friend of Jack's and I also believed (and still believe) Micheline was a very strong poet. But Buk tended to see the lacks in other writers more easily than he saw their strengths. Of Micheline he said that Jack wanted fame too much—that's why he never got it. "If you want anything too much, you'll never get it," Buk said. He said he avoids "ambition."

The conversation got round to Ron Kovic too—another friend of mine, and someone with whom I was then working on a daily basis, helping him to write a lengthy autobiography that was never published. Buk scorned Kovic for having gone willingly to war. "Only a fool goes to war thinking he won't get hurt," Buk said.

Linda quickly took up Kovic's defense. "No matter when Ron learned that war was wrong," she said, "the important thing is that he learned it."

Several more times that evening, I would notice that Linda didn't hesitate to jump in and contradict Buk when she thought he was mistaken—and he seemed to like her spunkiness in this regard.

In fact, in this instance, she made him rethink his position about young men who go to war. Buk admitted that he was "confused" and "on the verge of suicide" when he went for his own draft physical. When he was interviewed by a shrink at the examining station, Buk told the guy that he didn't believe in the war (World War II) but he claimed that he still wanted to go to it. According to Hank, "they were all trap questions," so he was trying to confuse the shrink with his answers. The shrink told Buk he was having a party at his apartment that night and asked if Buk wanted to come. Buk said no, figuring it was a test of whether he was social or antisocial. Buk just kept telling him, "I want to go, to get myself killed." At the end of the interview, the shrink said, ambiguously, "You're dismissed—you didn't think we'd understand, did you?" Buk wasn't sure what the guy "understood," but he said at that point he was smart enough to keep mum, figuring that if he started talking again, the guy would put him back in.

Barbet Schroeder was there with his lover—her name sounded like "Buehl"—but he was very tight-lipped, refused to answer my questions with more than a few words each time. The actor Seymour Cassel was much friendlier—talked about being in *Dick Tracy*, *White Fang*, and various Cassavetes' movies. Cassel impressed me with his wild, spontaneous energy. At one point, he ran across the lawn and began climbing the large fig tree, as athletic as a monkey, claiming that he wanted to get himself some fresh figs. Of Barbet, Bukowski said, "He's a great guy—he made it big, but he still likes to hang out."

Seymour had a beautiful young Asian actress with him. Mike Malone was there with his brother Steve and his third wife Cathy, who complained that they fought all the time and that sometimes he went crazy. She also talked about her jealousy of Mike's former girlfriends, especially one named "Jan," whom Buk said he liked because of her bracelets and head-beads that rattled around. "Her brains rattled around too," Cathy said. She was thirty-three, blonde and pretty, getting her MBA. Bukowski clearly liked the company of pretty women, and seemed to enjoy talking to them more than he enjoyed talking to the men.

A neighbor named Charlie was there with his wife, and they talked of Buk's other neighbor, a ninety-six-year-old guy who owned a shipping business and refused to give up his house to live in an assisted-living facility. The old guy's wife was taken away to a home, but the old guy told people he wanted a new pair of testicles!

"Like Yeats with the monkey glands?" I chimed in, but Buk didn't know the story. I told him about Yeats and his quest to remain sexually active in old age, even if he had to get monkey testicles implanted in his body.

"I never read Yeats," Buk said, maybe a touch defensively. "I only read the *National Enquirer*. It's better than Yeats."

A heavyset nurse named Crickey was there with her pretty adolescent daughter Casey. Buk was engaged in talking with them when it came time to put the chicken on. Buk acted like he'd already done his part, and let Seymour prepare and grill the chicken. It was clear he didn't dig the role of host very much. His thing was talking, telling stories, being the center of attention.

Linda talked about how Hank's lifestyle had really mellowed out. She said the first eight years they were together, she felt his lifestyle was dangerous. She also claimed that the house in San Pedro had gotten him in touch with nature for the first time in his life. It was easy to see why, since that huge backyard, filled with well-tended flowers, shrubs, and trees, was like having his own private park to go out into whenever he wanted.

He complained continually about Linda's PMS, which he thought was "more in her head than real."

"PMS gives women an excuse to act a certain way," he sneered. Then he gave us an example. "I'll say, 'Have you fed the cats?' and she'll look at me and snarl, 'What cats?!...We don't have any cats!'" Linda shook her head and said, "I never said that."

He threatened that he might take to preaching against marriage the way Ron Kovic preached against war. I told Hank that the good thing about Kovic was that he spoke an antiwar message by talking about his own experience, so that people could learn from what he'd been through. Bukowski sneered a little at me. My nature was to always take the conversation in a serious direction, when what he wanted most was to have fun with people, often at their own expense.

My wife Marcy always got cold easily, and once the sun started going down, she complained of feeling cold. Linda, always the kind host, immediately said it was time for everyone to move the party inside. Buk was clearly pissed off about this.

"It is a little cold," I said, trying to smooth things over.

"Actually I'm mildly warm!" Buk countered. That wasn't surprising, since I'd already watched him drink close to a dozen beers. But Linda was clearly going to have her way, and Buk went along with it. His pride was still at stake, though, so he added that he would "allow her" to bring them all inside—making it his decision as well.

Inside, Cathy asked him if he believed in traditional male-female roles, and he said no. He then began a surprising diatribe against sex—saying that he disliked fucking! When we all looked puzzled, he explained, "I hate doing something you're supposed to do. It's like two dogs fucking—they have no will—it's something they're driven to do." There was a little toy on the coffee table, a toy hammer that made the noise of glass shattering when you struck it against something. Someone whacked the hammer against the table, and it sounded like it had crashed through a window. "My cock is broken already," he said, astonishing us again.

But as we all looked at him, mouth agape, he apparently wanted to tack in a different direction—maybe figuring this wasn't the sort of group he wanted to make a sexual confession to. So he started another of his Bukowski pronouncements. "I hate looking at a woman's face when she's getting fucked," he began. "When you're fucking a woman—"

But here Linda angrily cut him off.

"Which woman?" she demanded.

He quickly tried to get out of trouble by saying he was talking about "Cupcakes O'Brien," someone he had written about in the past.

Just then Mike was heading back outside, and Buk yelled—maybe to make sure the last subject was forgotten: "Hey, Mike! Don't piss in my Jacuzzi!"

Buk said he always hated women confessing to him after sex about their bad childhoods.

"A man has got rid of his semen; he just wants to go to sleep," Buk provided his version of the sexual experience.

One of the women objected that most women don't talk about their bad childhoods after sex: "That's not the norm. Maybe prostitutes do that."

Buk looked a little abashed.

"I only went with prostitutes," he said. "Maybe other women don't do that. Maybe I don't know what other women do."

Linda got a nice fire going in the fireplace, and the large living room had a cozy glow. Buk had drunk enough to get his own glow going too, and now he was ready for some serious storytelling. I could see the look of relish on his face as he brought the topic of conversation back to women. He asked if I had any good stories about my wife Marcy. Talking about sexual adventures with my wife was not something I could do easily, so I just shook my head no. Buk gave me a look of displeasure—clearly I wasn't holding up my end here. Undaunted, Buk began telling us about a teacher he had had in high school named Miss Gretis, in English literature, and how much he loved looking at her silk-stockinged legs.

"I can gaze at a woman's legs for hours without getting bored," he explained. He described how the schoolteacher would routinely sit on her desk every day, letting her skirt ride up, while he and his friend ogled her legs. One day, as her skirt kept climbing higher and higher, Buk's friend whispered to him, "I think she's going for the record!" He said she had to have heard the remark, and yet she made no move to pull her skirt down. It was then that he realized she'd known all along that they were watching her, and that in fact she'd enjoyed teasing them.

"When a man looks at a woman's legs, it's all imagination what's beyond," he said. "It seems like it must be something so beautiful, something unimaginably better than a pussy, so he's disappointed when he finds it. Think about it! If we have such high hopes fantasizing from a woman's thighs, then how much more dreamlike must have been the notion of that pussy to men who only glimpsed the turn of a woman's ankle—at the turn of the century!"

From time to time, as he talked, I'd look at his face in the firelight, and he was easily the ugliest man I'd ever seen. *That face!* There were large lumps of skin on his eyelids, and his lower lip stuck out a lot farther than his upper lip, like a baboon's. There was a tuft of white hair on it and little lines of white beard stubble down the sides of his face, as if he shaved it that way on purpose. And yet there was an undeniable beauty, a kind of inner light, shining from him as well. When I went into the kitchen with Linda to help her with something, she told me he never seemed old to her; and I suddenly realized how, in truth, he did seem like a kid most of the time—the silly humor, the easy, shy smile, the perpetual hunch of shoulders, the relaxed self-assurance of someone who still believed the world could never get the better of him.

The conversation came round to movies again, and he took a crack at several of the actors in *Barfly*. "Faye Dunaway," he declared with a knowing laugh, "has a bony ass!" Barbet Schroeder had brought along videocassettes of his many-hours-long documentary on Bukowski, and Buk encouraged him to show the scene where Buk kicked Linda off the couch they were both sitting on. It was gruesome for me to watch Hank verbally and physically abusing her, but Buk laughed all the way through that scene, as if it were the funniest thing he could imagine. He was a strange man in that regard, and it made me realize how much Linda had to put up with in order to keep loving him. Linda's explanation for why she took so much abuse from Bukowski was equally strange. She claimed she had been a man in past lifetimes, and that she wanted to get more in touch with her feminine side this time on earth. One had a sense with both of them of completely unique human beings—somehow the only possible match for each other that could have existed.

When they were first together, Buk said, he'd mark down on the calendar what time she got in at night. He used to go through the roof because she would go backstage at concerts of her favorite bands, like the Who, and stay for hours. "Now if she calls and says she's getting home late," he claimed, "I figure I can spend two more hours at the computer."

(Parenthetically, I would get a very different view of this one night when Linda stayed till about three in the morning, drinking, talking, listening to music, and having a great time with Marcy and me at our house in Manhattan Beach. Every fifteen minutes Buk would phone and demand, "Tell her to come home! She's gonna have an accident if she stays there any longer!" Then he'd ask me if I thought she was still capable of driving. His frantic need of her could not have been more apparent.)

Bukowski and I kept running into conflict with each other; and because we were both big-time pissers (he with his beer, me with my coffee), we were destined to eventually bump into each other at the bathroom. There was a repeated knock on the bathroom door; and when I came out, there he was with a disdainful look on his face.

"It's the writer!" he mocked.

"There's a few of them around here," I countered.

"There's only one!" said Hank.

"With a capital *W!*" I answered. He smiled and went in.

As the evening went on, and more and more people left, I noticed that Bukowski's voice got softer, and his eyes grew softer, more tender. I could see the sensitivity in his face. He had a way of meeting my eyes occasionally and tentatively, which reminded me of my shy artist friend on Long Island, "Stasiu" (Stanley Twardowicz). Earlier, he seemed to enjoy saying things to shock or outrage people, like his demand that Los Angeles have a "straight parade," because, he claimed, "there are so few of us straights left." But now, without that big audience, he seemed to listen as much as he talked, and he showed himself equally capable of serious discussion. At one point, he asked me kindly if I was still writing, and seemed pleased when I said I was.

He began to show a lot of sadness too. He said nothing had any meaning to him now, but I told him we write because we're seeking meaning.

Buk: "But you never find it?"

Me: "Sometimes you come close—you get a glimpse."

He begrudgingly agreed—although earlier he'd said "the fairytale of God" was "too easy to believe." He said he would keep writing because it cheered him "just to see his computer screen light up." Earlier, he'd told someone that he revises less on a computer.

"With a typewriter," he said, "there was always something wrong with it after I pulled it out of the roller—I could never get it right the first time." Now, talking about how writing on a computer had changed his work, he said: "You take your words more seriously, you pick them with more care, on the computer screen, because it makes you think they're going to be 'up in lights' someday."

"Writing is more than an obsession," he summed up that discussion. "It's a madness."

I'd grown very silent listening to him. He finally asked me why I wasn't talking. I said, "I feel like I'm with Ernest Hemingway." He looked a little embarrassed by the praise. He said, "I get a good feeling about you, Nicosia. You're withdrawn, but you have a lot of juice inside you. You don't need to be talking all the time—that's all right."

Toward the end of the night, when it was just me and Marcy, Mike and Cathy, and him and Linda, he began to express some of his ambivalence about marriage itself. Picking up the bottle of Firestone Pinot Noir, his current favorite, he said that every month he had to change wines, because they got boring "just like you have to change women." He looked at Mike, as if he were expecting, or hoping, he'd take the bait—but Mike let it lie. Then Buk said, in what seemed a serious tone, that "the only way to make a marriage work is to have lots of space, not to be with each other all the time." He joked that he was proud he had succumbed to marriage only twice in seventy years.

Sounding serious again, he told Linda he was ready for them to change places. She could make the money, he said, and he would tend the garden. But she said, "I don't want to do that"—as if she were opposed to making money. This time it was Buk who let it drop.

Mike and Cathy left. Then, with just me and Marcy remaining, Buk said he wanted to show me where he worked before we went home. He took us upstairs to a small, windowless room, where his Mac computer sat on a small table, near a large, old radio. I wondered aloud how old the radio was, but Buk said he had had an even older radio, which he'd lent to Mickey Rourke during the filming of *Barfly*, and which Rourke had kept! He said he always wrote to music. What struck me was that this little room was like a replication of the tiny rented rooms where he'd first started writing. Yet he relished the fact that he'd come into the computer age, that he could write on a Mac like the new young writers just starting out. Truth be told, the past was never far away from him. He still had his old beat-up manual typewriter sitting in the dining room downstairs, and I suspected that he sometimes still wrote on that too, though I didn't ask him.

I have such a strong image of how that evening ended. It was probably about two in the morning, and we were all out in Buk's driveway, where his and Linda's matching BMW's sat side by side. It had now grown quite cool, as California near the ocean does at night. Linda was sitting on the hood of his car talking to Marcy, and I was standing behind the car talking to Buk. He was suddenly talking with a raw honesty that came up right from his gut, moving me deeply.

"I want to die," he said, "but I also want to keep writing. I want a little more, so I keep doing it. But I'm tired of living. I hate that feeling of getting out of bed in the morning, and putting your feet on the floor, one foot after the other—one more time. *Oh God!"*

I don't remember what I said to him. Probably some stupid platitude. Or maybe I was just silent. There isn't much you can say when a man who has everything anyone could want—a successful career, huge esteem from those in one's own field, a beautiful home, a beautiful and sensitive wife—tells you they want to die. But looking back at it over the years, I felt it was a gift he gave me—a bedrock honesty that he was passing along to me, and that he wanted, or hoped, I would pass along to others. To tell the truth just as it came to you. That is a gift I will always thank him for.

Portrait by David Barker

Originally published in
Charles Bukowski Spit in My Face
by David Barker (1982)

WENDY RAINEY INTERVIEWS GERALD LOCKLIN

WENDY RAINEY: *Do you ever object to being asked one more time to submit to an interview concerning Charles Bukowski?*

GERALD LOCKLIN: I do when the interviewer has not prepared for the interview and consequently asks me all and only the questions that I have been asked a zillion times before. This happens most frequently with interviewers who have little knowledge of Buk and none of me. They don't, for instance, know that I've published a book, *Charles Bukowski: A Sure Bet,* Water Row Press, 1966, in which I have said just about everything I have to say about him. Thus, the first thing they want to know is "How did you meet Charles Bukowski," which would make sense except that the first essay in *A Sure Bet* is "Meeting Charles Bukowski."

WR: *I read your book, Gerry. I know that you organized a poetry reading for Bukowski at Cal State Long Beach and that's how you met him. Not to worry. I'm not one of those annoying interviewers who would ask how bad a misogynist was he? Why did he always seem to write about sex? Why does he use so many four-letter words? Did he soil himself? If so, why? And do you have color photos of it? This is not that kind of interview.*

GL: I can, of course, try to summarize on the spur of the moment what is in the essay, but the frustration is from knowing that I've answered the question much better in the essay than I can hope to in a few sentences verbally improvised. Other lengthy chapters in the short (less than a hundred pages) volume deal with attending his sixtieth birthday party, the premiere for and reception of his film *Barfly,* and his funeral and burial. A couple of reviews of significant books summarize my critical analyses and judgments of his work. A few poems attempt to correct annoying misconceptions concerning his life, character, and relationships. There are briefer anecdotes. But basically the underpinnings of everything I have to say about Bukowski are there in that small book. Other useful sources would be the three volumes of his letters, the latter two of which contain many excerpts from his over-fifty letters to me, the originals of which are housed in the Special Collections of the Library of California State University, Long Beach, where I taught from 1965 to 2007, still enjoy access to my old, shared office, and still teach a class on occasion. Also, there are a lot of previous interviews with me easily accessible online, a couple of them on my own website and Facebook.

WR: *Does it bother you when they show little familiarity at all with your own work?*

GL: Sure, it bothers me some at times, because I've been writing my whole life and it's not hard to find a great deal of it if one is willing to make the slightest effort. But then I remind myself that Hank has earned their interest—he wrote very well for an awfully long time, and there are few writers whose works I've enjoyed and admired as much as his, and that I was immensely honored to have been admitted to his circle of friends, and that he does enjoy that tremendous advantage for a writer's reputation of his being dead. Also, I've been getting a lot of strokes myself lately, so many that the promotion of my own written works allows precious little time for writing new ones, and that, as a young writer, I, like most young writers, worried much more about whether I'd ever see even a single poem or story of mine in print, than whether my career might be overshadowed by—though at least spoken of in the same breath with—that of Charles Bukowski. And it won't be long before I join him in what I refer to as posthumidity—no antiperspirants required.

WR: *Here's one no one's asked you so far: What did you think of the Bukowski/ Sondheim musical—technically a workshop presentation—written and directed by Joanne Gordon of the Cal State, Long Beach Drama Department in a little theater on the Queen Mary in November and December of 2012? I'll tell you what I think of it first. I was floored. I would not have imagined that a pairing of Sondheim and Bukowski would work so well, but it did. I was hooked from the get go. The cast was amazing!*

GL: I thought it was brilliant and terribly intimate and moving. Of course I love Sondheim's music as much or more than I do Buk's poems—Sondheim probably has a better batting average, and it's always hard for words to compete with songs. In Joanne's play. It's assumed the two will complement rather than compete, and they generally did. The cast was outstanding and into the spirit of the material. And it was Joanne's swan song, at least as drama department chair. She was sitting right behind me the first night—and as you pointed out to me, the audience did seem more savvy to what the Bukowski portion was all about the first night than weeks later. It was the difference between an audience of Bukowski fans and one of students urged—maybe required—by their instructors to attend. When I spoke to a large class of students the week before they were going to the play, there were pockets of highly motivated students and others who couldn't care less.

Joanne had won Buk's imprimatur years ago with a review of his work she produced and directed in downtown L.A. for many performances. I think he loved that she loved his work so, and he was probably taken with her personally—she's easy to like. Later she produced a play in a now-condemned building in downtown Long Beach that was a kind of Valentine woven from his love poems—his softer, more lyrical side. It's not the side I prefer, so I did like a lot better the gritty, dirty, raunchy monologues or dialogues of the Queen Mary musical. "Fire Station," for instance, has always been my favorite of all of Bukowski's poems—and to tell the truth I like his novels best and his stories second-best of his writings, but not excluding the very best of his poems. "Fire Station" was one of the audience favorites the first night I attended—a little less so, the latter evening.

WR: *How about the posthumous works? How do they measure up to the ones published during his lifetime? Has his reputation suffered since his death, or increased?*

GL: We're talking about a world-famous writer, so generalizations are dangerous. His widow, Linda Lee Bukowski, performed a magnificent gesture—and one which must have increased his prestige exponentially—when she donated her Bukowski holdings—his papers, letters, reviews, foreign editions, etc. to the Huntington Library in San Marino, California, one of the most prestigious research libraries in the world. Widely publicized events were held there to celebrate the physical donation of the Bukowski collection and again, five years later, to celebrate the first public exhibition from the Bukowski collection. Coincidentally or otherwise, Bukowski's canonization has coincided with an official expansion of the entire American Literature collection. I cannot overestimate the significance of this enshrinement to the enhancement of Bukowski's reputation in those areas of American literary life that had for so long remained virtually impregnable to invasion by the Bukowski juggernaut: Academia, the Establishment, Respectability. The scholar/librarians/immensely human beings of the Huntington did not fear the inclusion of the most SoCal of Southern California authors: they embraced his presence warmly, intelligently, expertly, fearlessly, and, in doing so, no doubt gained increased credence and visibility for their institution in the eyes of the youthful of all ages and shades.

Was it seismically shocking? Pretty darn near close to that. But when Linda explains the genesis of the idea, it all makes common sense. She has explained how she used to drop Hank off at the nearby Santa Anita Park for the first races and return to pick him up after the last. In the meantime, she had begun enjoying lunch and relaxing and reading in the internationally famous grounds and gardens of the Huntington Estate. Inevitability she fell in love with the place and it occurred to her to offer her gift to the location she deemed the most fitting imaginable: a shrine to nature, literature and the arts. I have no idea what negotiations must have transpired. Certainly there were already Bukowski enthusiasts within the inner circle. But the immense generosity of Linda and the forward-thinking of a great institution prevailed—and suddenly it all began to make perfect sense. I myself went from an occasional visitor to a proud member.

WR: *I agree that the Huntington Library is an exceptionally good choice to house Bukowski's works. Sue Hodson, the Huntington's curator of literary manuscripts, is as enthusiastic as she is knowledgeable. And I would like to point out that she was extremely kind and forthcoming when I, as an unknown, approached her and asked several questions about the curation of Bukowski's work.*

WR: *What about the posthumous books?*

GR: Well, that's a mixed bag. For one thing I knew from Bukowski himself that he wanted every word possible of his to see print. It irked him when only a third of the poems he automatically forwarded to his publisher would make it into a volume. On the other hand, publishers can often evaluate materials more objectively (and prudently) than the authors of those works. I think many factors went into the selecting of the contents of a book during his lifetime—not excluding protecting the author from himself: the arc of his inebriation; the boiling over of personal resentments; the innate paranoia of us writers when we leave our most personal revelations vulnerable to the eyes of potentially hostile critics and readers. To my knowledge neither John Martin nor Linda Lee nor Ferlinghetti nor Marvin Malone ever castrated Bukowski's texts. But a few omissions here and there may have spared him grief. And any writer who writes as prolifically as Bukowski is going to have his share of failures of quality as well as successes.

After his death, however, I think the standards must have been lowered. The first couple of posthumous books included some of his best writing—the final poems in the elegiac mode, for instance. Even *Pulp*, which I consider the weakest of his novels—in humor and originality—was admirable in its intense acts of gratitude to his closest family and friends. In other words, what was selected during Bukowski's lifetime and published after his death was still strong—the real thing.

As for many of the pages that had been put aside from publication until after his death, supposedly as a kind of "life insurance policy," (much as Hemingway had done), they were often so worn-thin, mean-spirited, and lifeless as to render the less said of them, the better.

Major exceptions were those poems that had been published as book-issues of The Wormwood Review and never included in Black Sparrow editions until a posthumous agreement was apparently reached between the Wormwood and Black Sparrow copyright holders. Marvin Malone was a legendary editor for good reason, and those poems collectively were among the best Bukowski ever composed. And I bet he didn't reject editorial suggestions from Malone: I know I never did.

WR: *What about the films? Personally, I don't care for any of them except for The Bukowski Tapes and the Dullaghan documentary, Born Into This. I don't think Barfly did Charles Bukowski justice at all.*

GR: For me, *Barfly* remains the best. John Dullaghan did a fine job with his documentary, especially considering the pressures he apparently was operating under. All the European films misunderstand Chinaski/Bukowski as a Marxist. American workers tend to resist ideologies better than filmmakers, and Bukowski had pretty much ceased his working-class existence by the time I met him in 1970—which is when all his novels and the bulk of his stories were beginning to be published for a wider readership. The best of his novels—and his novels are the best of his works—*Post Office, Women,* and *Hollywood*—have never been committed to film or, thank God, 3-D. Film is a lesser medium by far than print, anyway—film saturates our senses and returns us to infantile pleasure states, but words are everything including intellect and subtleties. So let's be glad they haven't taken his words and our imaginations, experiences, and inner lives, away from us. So far!

HARRY CALHOUN

Rejecting Bukowski

It's like abandoning religion
and embracing God as a beautiful substitute
for whatever eternity you imagine.

When you put *you* in your dream,
you realize that even God has to rest
on his days off. Say he was a relief pitcher,

Mariano Rivera, maybe. One day he would
be tired, hung over—Mariano, not God—
but maybe injured and his strikeout pitch

would vanish. Back when I edited a poetry magazine,
I rejected some Bukowski. Not the man, his poems,
and I still don't know if he was throwing some heat

past me that I missed or if he was just due
for the showers that day. But I rejected Bukowski
and he died and I will too, but neither of us

owe that to poetry. That, my friends,
is simply what we do, and rejection

is as much a part of it as breathing.

Originally published in *Gutter Eloquence*

JOAN GANNIJ

Carl Weissner: "One Hell of an Amazing Human"

Excerpted from the author's forthcoming book *My Real Life Encounters with Charles Bukowski and Henry Miller: Mythical Dirty Old Men of the Printed Page.*

Charles Bukowski introduced me to Carl Weissner way back when—in 1976. I was a fledgling freelance photojournalist at the time and Carl was wearing multiple hats as Bukowski's friend, agent, German translator, and literary majordomo. Little did I know at the time that my relationship with Carl would evolve over the next four decades from a very long distance business relationship to a solid short-distance friendship. Let me give you some backstory.

My friend and KCET colleague Glen Esterly was going to be interviewing Bukowski for Rolling Stone and asked me to come along and take some pictures. As a young woman of the times, more humanist than feminist, I was not impressed with the Dirty Old Man's body of work in that period: his weekly columns in the LA Free Press offended my sensibility and seemed too calculated for shock value. I didn't realize that Henry Chinaski was Hank's alter ego and that he was creating a personal mythology in the spirit of Henry Miller and Anais Nin. So I told Glen to forget about it. Not interested. No way.

Glen knew I was a fan of the Beat poets and that I was studying with Sam Eisenstein, one of the top writing teachers at LA City College, where Bukowski studied English and Journalism in 1939. Glen told me not to write him off before I saw him in action; which would take place at a poetry reading later that week at Cal State LA. I went, he read, and I was convinced (if not conquered) that his was a voice to be reckoned with: a blue-collar bard, the poet laureate of Skid Row. He was leonine, eloquent, obstreperous, defiantly challenging some drunk wannabe hecklers. (See "Bukowski Reading 1976" poem). After the reading, I snapped a couple of frames, shook his hand briefly and told Glen that I was in. I joined him the next few weeks at Hank's Carlton Way bungalow and took a series of portraits, which as the fates would have it, became iconic over the next twenty years. Hank put the charm on full blast but after Glen left and I continued photographing, he adjusted the bluster and bravado and let down his guard. Those photos never got published in Rolling Stone, which it turned out had a policy of using their own "staff" shooters. I suppose you could describe my images as the "un-plugged version''; critics would later refer to them as "emotionally raw, unposed, and a jolt to the heart."

A few weeks after the Cal State reading, I dropped by Carlton Way with a box of prints for Mr. B. My mother was a glamour photographer in Hollywood in the 1950s and one of the things she taught me was when you "steal" pictures from someone, you need to give them back. Hank opened the door with a Cheshire grin and drawled, "Come on in, kid," stretching out every syllable. I made it clear that I was there strictly on business and would be departing soon to pick up my son from kindergar-ten. He got distracted by the six-pack of Dos Equis I was carrying and in-vited me to take a seat in a funky vinyl armchair that he had once at-tempted to paint. He returned with two bottles, then looked through the box of photos and didn't say a word. He didn't have to, the subtle trace of tears was enough. After gaining his composure he sighed and said matter-of-factly: "They always come and take things from me: my beer, my smokes, my women." He paused, then simply said: "Thanks, Kid. You made my day."

Hank told me that he was going to put me in contact with Carl Weissner who would arrange for my photos to be printed on his international trans-lations and for an upcoming launch of his work throughout Germany. I didn't think much about it until a couple of weeks later when I received a letter in a red, white and blue Air Mail envelope with lots of interesting stamps, postmarked Mannheim, Germany. It was from Carl Weissner, and over the next decades, I would acquire quite a collection of those en-velopes, thanks to a lively correspondence that came out of Hank's sug-gestion that Carl be my European agent and arrange that my photos would appear on all his translated book covers.

Carl's letters started out formally, strictly business and soon shifted to witty, irreverent, straightforward riffs; like a good jazz improvisation. He circulated my photographs not only to Hank's publishers around the world (from Israel to Iran, Japan to Finland, and many lands in between) but also to respected German publications like *Die Zeit* and *Der Spiegel*. He was especially enthusiastic about the soon to be infamous Hank & Georgia image, (which he said Hank called a ''high energy icon") and would soon make its German debut on a catalogue, book bag and poster for Maro Verlag, a respected publishing house in Augsburg.

A portrait from the Cal State LA poetry reading would be pasted in the best-selling hardcover of Zweitausendeins, *Stories und Romane*, and circulated on a poster promoting *"Kaputt in Hollywood"* when Hank would make his tour through Germany a few years later. Carl and I playfully referred to Hank as "our matchmaker," and I marveled that a simple act of presenting Hank with some photos had resulted in a generous gesture to jumpstart the career of a young woman in the Hollywood jungle. Over the next decades, long after his death in 1994, I still consider Hank to be a spiritual and career-enhancing godfather.

In addition to being a writer with an affinity for American culture, specifically the Jazz Age and the Beat Generation, Carl Weissner was a respected translator of William Burroughs, Allen Ginsberg, Leonard Cohen, and notably Charles Bukowski, who Carl was credited for introducing to German readers. He discovered Bukowski quite by accident when he was studying English literature at the University of Heidelberg, and had grown bored at the traditional education he was receiving. In an LA Times interview (September 1988) with Jay Dougherty, Carl explained: "American literature practically didn't exist in the university at that time, and English literature seemed to stop at Thomas Hardy. I was sitting around in cafeterias between classes, nursing a cup of coffee and reading *Naked Lunch, On the Road, Tropic of Cancer*, and so forth. And after that, you know, going back to another seminar on Blake's *Songs of Innocence and Experience*...well, that was rather discouraging."

He soon discovered the indie chapbook and literary magazine scene that was percolating in England and America and started one of his own: "Klactoveedsedsteen," after a Charlie Parker tune. This gave him the opportunity to trade copies with other small press publishers. In 1966, he got a copy of *Iconolatre* in the post, from West Hartlepool, England, with seven poems by Bukowski. "Hell, I thought, who is this guy? Here was one who apparently didn't give a damn about poetic frills and niceties. He was pissed. He was mad and he just let it hang out. Relentless. Great." Weissner got Bukowski's address from the editor and wrote to him asking for poems that he could publish. Bukowski responded with enthusiasm and thus began a significant correspondence (and unique friendship) of more than five hundred letters that Black Sparrow Press would eventually publish. In the Times article, Bukowski says: "I felt that with Carl I could say anything, and I often did. I even wrote him at times to say something like, 'Damn, man, you've saved my life.' And it was true. Without Carl I would be dead or near dead or mad or near mad, or driveling into a slop somewhere, mouthing gibberish."

In 1967, Carl received a Fulbright grant to study in the United States where he spent much of his time talking and tape-recording writers like Allen Ginsburg, Diane Di Prima, and Ted Berrigan, whose work he would end up translating years later into German. In the summer of 1968 he made his first trip to Los Angeles to finally meet Bukowski in person. According to Dougherty, Bukowski remembers the meeting like this: "I was in the Post Office…and living with a crazy and alcoholic woman and writing anyhow. All our money went for booze. We lived in rags and a rage of despair. I remember I didn't even have money for shoes. The nails from my old shoes dug into my feet as I walked my routes hung over and mad. We drank all night and I had to get up at five a.m. When I wrote, the poems came out of this. The letters from Carl had been the only good magic about…and I had pictured him exactly as he looked and acted when I met him: one hell of an amazing human." Carl responded apologetically: "I didn't have it half as bad. I had no problems except how to keep the little magazine going and scrape by somehow, working at odd jobs."

He returned to Germany in 1969 and continued working odd jobs, which included being an editor for the J. Meltzer publishing house in Frankfurt. City Lights came out with Bukowski's first full-length book, *Notes of a Dirty Old Man*, and Bukowski sent Weissner a copy. According to Weissner: "I showed it to Meltzer who sat down, read the first few pages and said: 'I want to do this. Can you get me a contract for the German rights? Will you translate it for me?" The book was not a success at first, which was attributed to poor advertising. Neither was the subsequent translation of *Post Office*. Says Weissner: "Everybody thought the publisher was nuts. Even books by well-known German poets didn't sell more than six hundred or a thousand copies. Big anthologies of the New American Poetry had flopped." He decided to challenge the German market by coming up with an extremely long title for the next poetry volume: *Poems Written Before Jumping Out of an 8th Story Window,* which in German, came out twice as long. It sold fifty thousand copies making Bukowski famous in Germany, a status that has been maintained ever since. Reflecting on the fact that he did not penetrate the mainstream bookstores in America, he mused: "I see it as a kind of poetic justice that Bukowski made his breakthrough in Germany on the strength of his poems, and entirely on his own." Why was he so connected with Bukowski? I think because he loved post-WWII American writing, and Bukowski was a refreshing, original voice without pretense; someone who wrote about the down-and-out world of the unemployed, the disenfranchised, and the voiceless everyman who was a casualty of the American dream.

Weissner continued being supportive of young writers Like Pamala Karol (aka La Loca) whose book he translated for City Lights, and would also submit some of my poems to European anthologies. After relocating from Southern California to The Netherlands in 1987, I still corresponded with him on my trusty scarlet IBM Selectric. In the next years when we grudgingly switched to computers, our communication shifted to the occasional phone call, as he was not crazy about email.

It wasn't until the mid-nineties that Carl and I would finally meet in person at The Frankfurt *Buchmesse* (Book Fair). It was thrilling to meet someone I had known only on paper for two decades. We were shy at first and then jumped into a lively conversation that was typical of a meeting of old friends.

Carl Weissner at Frankfurt Buchmesse (Book Fair)
©Joan Gannij

When he entered the booming book hall designated for German publishers, Carl got more attention than a lot of the guest authors, and I teased him about being "a rock star" or "the *Burgermeister* (Mayor) of Frankfurt. Tall and lean, with his trademark aviator specs, leather jacket, and well-worn Levis, he had the presence of a hip college professor. Everyone knew him or wanted to know him: hands got shaken, news was exchanged and deals were footnoted. He was generous in spirit and always made time to advise or introduce. When the *Buchmesse* environs got too hectic, we would flee the hall to get some one-on-one time. For the next ten years, this would be the site of our annual reunion.

Carl Weissner and Joan Gannij at Frankfurt Buchmesse (Book Fair) ©Joan Gannij.

Carl was always immersed in the latest Bukowski translation, even after Hank's death when what seemed like thousands of unpublished poems and letters were uncovered by Black Sparrow publisher John Martin. Carl was always lamenting that he needed more time for his own writing. It was good to know in the last years he was finally able to focus on his own work, with *Manhattan Muffdiver* and *Death in Paris* published the year before he died. Carl had finally taken a well-deserved sabbatical in New York, engineered by his close friends Jan and Janet Herman. During a phone call after his return to Mannheim, he spoke animatedly about his "writer's exile" and sent me a signed copy of *Manhattan Muffdiver*. We arranged to meet up at the end of 2011 or early 2012 in Amsterdam or Mannheim, rather than Frankfurt. Alas, that wasn't meant to be.

Today's technology gives us the false illusion that we are closely connected to friends around the world. We assume that information is shared but it is more the case that is withheld, usually unintentionally. I would not learn of Carl's passing until one year later, to the day. I was crushed to have missed the memorial service in Mannheim, just four hours away by train. I sit in silent regret, and suddenly remember Carl sharing anecdotes with me about Hank's funeral: the Buddhist monks, the film star (or two), some literary hangers on; the reverence, transcendence and absurdity. I feel Carl's presence, hear his trademark chuckle, as he assures me: "Don't worry, Kid, you didn't miss a thing."

Still life for Carl W. by Joan Gannij ©Joan Gannij

A.D. WINANS

Poem for Bukowski
    Inspired by Jack Micheline

He's the original
Jack the Ripper
He's the tormentor
Of John Bryan
He's the villain
Of women's lib
He's the last hope
Of the down and out
He'd be home in heaven
He'd be home in hell
He's a third Reich monster
He's a Hindu guru
He writes Harold Norse
Get well cards
He torments his enemies
He frustrates his friends
He writes poems
In the shit houses of America
He writes poems
In the ballet of his sleep
He writes Harold Norse
Get well cards
All he is folks
Is the best damn show in town
Holy priest Circus clown
The best act around
He's a Roman sonnet
He's an Irish ballad
He's the best tossed
Salad in town

He has the face
Of a moon crater
The stomach
Of a wheel barrel
The heart of a whore
Which is more than
You can say

For 90% of the poets
Around
He digs Brahms
He digs Beethoven
He's the heavyweight
Champion of Los Angeles

He's the Chaplin of San Pedro
He's stalked by the minor poets
Of San Francisco and LA
And the soft-boiled egg eaters
Of the Café Trieste
He's a rainbow of watercolors
Mixed in with one too many
Sunday morning Bloody Marys

He loves boxing
He loves his daughter
He loves his woman
He's the best relief pitcher
In town
He's an antique book
In a broken down hotel
He's a bottle of aspirin
In an empty water glass
He writes Harold Norse
Get well cards
All he is folks
Is the best damn show
In town

JOAN JOBE SMITH

Charles Bukowski: Epic Glottis Beer Bottle Zeus

Oh, Bukowski, how I'd wanted you to admire my mind when I mailed to you in 1973 my grad school thesis proposal about you, "The Colloquial Classicist," a chunk of doggerel wherein I'd called T.S. Eliot a "cyclopic windmill," Ezra Pound a "meathook," and you, Bukowski, an "epic glottis beer-bottle Zeus." Neophyte lit rubbish irrevocably rejected by my erudite, uptight Masters thesis advisor. But, you, Bukowski, loved it.

"That was one hell of a neat thesis on me," you wrote back. "I agree with you about Ezra. Sure, he taught me how to lay down the line, but damned if he had any humor. Basically the literature of the 20th century has been arid. You're touched with the knowledge, Joan Smith." Then you post-scripted: "Do you wear long silk stockings while bathing?"

Thank you, UN-arid Bukowski, for your encouragement and enthusiasm that lifted my bimbo psyche off that pilloried pedestal of my go-go girl scandaled past, dusted the barroom smoke off my body and soul, held my hand briefly, a John Lennon, while we talked Great Books—especially yours (I'd just read *The Days Run Away Like Wild Horses Over the Hills)*, during your midnight phone telephone calls, you in L.A., me in the suburbs, even though, at that time and place, I was just one more Woman to fill your boredom when you rifted with your then-girlfriend Linda King. Epic glottis, you especially liked, and laughed into the telephone receiver your approval of my neologism—har-har-har—always sounding like a trumpet amongst the gods.

Out of gratitude, I fell in love with you in spite of what the feminists thought of you. Maybe it was the five years gapping between me and most of the Baby Boomer feminists that helped me understand where you were coming from. That you had been a boy of the hard-knocked Depression roughed up by a stern, misogynist German father. To paraphrase you: "The world shaped you and you shaped what you could." You became not only my mentor but my Muse as I fell in love with your audacity, your veracity, sagacity, and especially your rugged real-life revelations of Women, good, bad, beautiful and ugly, all your Women got down on the page, the ravenous romances, pagan Pandemonia of screwball, screwed-up, wanton, weird, wild, woebegone Women. I wasn't like any of your Women. I was staid and ordinary.

One of the many times I saw Bukowski, when I attended his Laguna Beach Moulton Theatre reading August 16, 1975 (his fifty-fifth birthday),

Bukowski frowned at the cleavage heaving out of my mode-o'-day aquamarine tube top. He frowned at my ankle-length blue striped madras cloth hippie skirt. A leg man, according to his writings, liking women in short skirts and high, high heels, he said to me, "Joan, Joan Smiiiiith, you've gotten FA-AT." And I looked at him to try to find something ugly about him to insult him, pay him back. I noted the ancient acne scars on his face and neck, his beard that needed a trim, the chubby bit of beer belly pooching out his wrinkled plaid shirt missing a bottom button, the open container of cheap beer on his lap, foam dripping off the sides of the bottle and wetting the crotch of his corduroy pants. Then I saw his twinkling eyes, his big head, his thick Old Lion Zeusian salt-and-mostly-pepper hair, his confident godly grin showing off the reality that he was proudly in his prime—and he knew it, reigned supreme and basked in the Valhalla of it—and finally I said to him:

"Bukowski, you've got little hands." And he laughed. Because he really did. He held them up and wiggled his short fingers in the air to prove it. Little hands not much bigger than mine. Hands as smooth as a woman's. A writer's hands that would never hold mine nor touch me except for the one time he drunken-impulsively grabbed me to kiss me, and the times he dialed my number or wrote me a few letters. There'd never be any screams from the balcony between us, no midnight indictments. No sunrise forgiveness, no hangover promises. No clothes nor love-smacked souls thrown out an eight-story window. Maybe I was the luckiest of all his Women.

Maybe.

July 15, 2013

"I mean, what the hell, how much bacon can you eat?"
CHARLES BUKOWSKI

JOAN JOBE SMITH
FRED VOSS

The Poets, Husband & Wife, Discuss Charles Bukowski

JOAN JOBE SMITH: Fred, soon we will celebrate being together twenty-five years. Wow, how times flies when you're having fun. Remember the minister who married us Bloomsday, 1990, asking us pre-nup what we enjoyed doing together? And we mentioned watching video movies. When he blinked, I thought, uh-oh, he probably thinks we're into porn and not old Marlon Brando and Paul Newman (your favorite) and Barbara Stanwyk, Bette Davis, and Joan Crawford (mine). And one of our mutual favorite movie icons: Marilyn Monroe. Also we mentioned walks in the moonlight, watching sunsets and white herons, pelicans in Morro Bay, romantic stuff to seem normal and avoid mentioning *Poetry*. That we'd actually "met" on the pages of *Wormwood Review* when our poetry was published by editor Marvin Malone in the same issue in 1987. Nor did we mention Literature, *Moby Dick, Les Miserables, Jane Eyre.* And we dared not mention an essential ingredient of our karmic glue: a controversial uh-oh, for sure: *Charles Bukowski.* Fred, I've never asked before: *Why* do you like Charles Bukowski?

FRED VOSS: I liked Buk because he was something completely new and he spoke to me. He was adventurous, wildly lyrical, masculine, funny. His poems were crystal clear in what they said yet imaginative as hell. He was a romantic and a fighter (with his fists) and he lived what he believed, enduring hunger and poverty and danger and rejection in order to become the writer he wanted to become. Of course, he also drank a helluva lot and so did I back then, but now I relate more to the classical music he loved and the classic writers he read and the women he celebrated. His values were really classical, in line with Thoreau and Buddha and Whitman. He spoke truth to power. The best people have the worst jobs and the worst people have the best jobs, he said, and it was true. And I dropped out the UCLA PhD. Program in English Literature and went to work in a steel mill.

Bukowski helped me find the way, so in that sense he saved me. In his writing he was like a second father to me. I had a very good father, but

Bukowski gave me something else; he was a spiritual father, a writing father. And my writing saved me when I was very much on the edge at age twenty-one of the proverbial abyss, and without Bukowski who knows what might have become of me? He helped me survive because I saw he had survived loneliness, without women, without success and money and recognition, with a father who beat him and loathed him and kicked him out. He was a fighter and he survived all that so I figured I could survive, too.

Regarding that minister, today it's quite probable we'd have a younger minister who had read Bukowski and thought he was cool.

JOAN: Fred, many times since Bukowski's death, March 9, 1994, you and I have asked, when a tragic event or disturbing political coup occurs: "What would Charles Bukowski have thought of this? What would he have written?" He died two years after the 1992 Los Angeles Riots about which, in regards to Rodney King, he wrote in a letter to you: "Ow, ow, ow—they suggest we pray." My final Bukowski Question for you: I'd like to ask you: If Bukowski were alive, what would you like to ask him? Tell him?

FRED: I'd like to know what he thinks of the "Occupy Wall Street" phenomenon of 2011-2012. I think he would have been moved and encouraged by it, and angered and saddened by its quick disappearance after a huge police crackdown. And I'd ask him, "Buk do you think the Occupy Movement is dead or has it morphed into a more political movement involving debt relief the way the Latino movement of 2006 morphed from street action into political action where it is becoming a mighty force? What do you think about the ninety-nine percent versus the one percent? You chose to live in poverty and championed the underdog and the working class and the outsiders against the powerful and the rich all your writing life. Are you angered, outraged, saddened by the way the disparities of rich and poor have grown so much since your death? Do you think we're at a turning point, do you think the workingman, the common man will make a comeback? Do you think some kind of revolution or civil war might be on the horizon? Or are we headed for some kind of dystopia of a dumbed-down plutocratic tyranny in America? Or are we already there but can't see it because we're looking at our iPods all day?" In 1991, in his apocalyptic *Last Day of the Earth Poems,* he wrote in "Dinosauria, We" ...a place where the masses elevate fools into rich heroes." So I'd want to know if he would write an updated sequel?

And finally, I would tell him, "Thanks Hank for giving us your writings. No matter how bad it has gotten or will get, we have your poems. And they will get us through, and they are great, and they will live forever."

Joan, let me ask you a final Bukowski question. You've written much about Bukowski in four issues of *Bukowski Review* (2001-2005) and in a 1994 kaddish anthology *Das Ist Alles—Charles Bukowski Recollected* and a 1999 festscript *Bukowski Boulevard* (all edited by you from Pearl Editions) and, 2012, from Silver Birch Press, a literary profile *Charles Bukowski—His Art & His Women (& me)*. Buk was a confidant and mentor of yours for nearly a decade and you got to know him quite well as a human being via many telephone conversations. You were friends with many of his sweethearts, Linda King, Annie Menebroker, Frances Dean Smith (mother of his only child Marina Bukowski) and Pamela Wood Miller (aka Cupcakes, Scarlet) and recently you've made the acquaintance of Joan Gannij, one of Buk's finest photographers. Can you tell me something new about Buk you've never told me before? And what would you say to Buk if he were still alive?

JOAN: Oh, so much to say to him. I'd first ask if I captured his heart in my hand when I wrote my 2012 literary profile of him. Would he pretty-pleez write me a five-star review on amazon.com? But that would be so self-serving, wouldn't it? Though I'm sure Buk would laugh his har-har-har at me and my audacity and say, "Hell, no, kid. Find your own mockingbird to wish you luck." So I'd best stifle those neo-book-ego urges and, the diehard stereotypical nurturer that I am, ask him instead if he'd like a big bowl of my Charles Bukowski Vegetarian Chili I made yesterday, the same recipe he liked so much that I made him in 1975 when he came to my house for the disastrous party I held in his honor. He loved my chili. And my Texas-style homemade corn bread, too. Then I'd serve it to him on the same silver tray I used in 1975 and have him sit again in the same hand-carved antique oak throne chair he sat in back then that now sits next to your bookcase filled with Buk's books.

And, finally, here's that Something You Don't Know, Fred: that silver tray is the same tray I've served you your dinner on every night for the past twenty-some years.

FRED VOSS

Elegy for a Giant

First, I discovered Charles Bukowski in the university library, and it was magic—nights up smoking cheap cigars and drinking cheap booze getting gloriously drunk and enlightened with Bukowski all night, reading everything, the *Erectiions, Ejaculations, Exhibitions and General Tales of Ordinary Madness,* the *Crucifix in a Deathhand*, all the poetry and prose and that picture of him hanging onto that boxcar ladder...

It was magic and it changed me and I was never the same and though I went to PhD, graduate school at UCLA for a year I quickly dropped out and found myself filling up a boardinghouse room and then a dive apartment in Long Beach with the smell of chain-smoking and beer drinking and on-the-edge-of-suicide survival working busboy and factory jobs and knowing it was worth it, knowing it was right as I read

Burning in Water Drowning in Flame and *The Days Run Away Like Wild Horses Over the Hills,* and something he'd given me made me burn inside as I suffered and made it on not even knowing that I would be a writer, just that I was doing what I had to do and that it was right, days and nights of steel dust and furnaces and a burned-up mattress and tears in my beer listening to Hank Williams and no woman for years like Bukowski at the start of *Women* still I held on with nothing but his poems and some kind of crazy stubborn will to go on...

> and I did go on
> Bukowski
> leading me through suicide madness and bikers
> and women who threw me down into the hard asphalt of their rejection
> without my own poem, without my own voice, I had
> Bukowski
> somehow leading me out of the darkness and toward the light
> of finally finding my own voice and my own poetry
> which I owe to him
> as much as maybe my life
> and much more and so
> you see
> that for me a great great light went out of this world
> when Bukowski died

Yet
I look at my bookshelf 40 Bukowski books wide and realize that that
light can only really get brighter
and brighter
and that I will have it
always.

Originally published in
Dast ist Alles: Charles Bukowski Recollected
(Pearl Limited Editions, 1994) and
Drinking with Bukowski (Thunder's Mouth Press, 2000)

Portrait by Jeff Morgan

STEVE RICHMOND

Spinning Off Bukowski (Sun Dog Press, 1996)

Chapter 6

It's about this time he pulls out my first book of poetry, the copy I mailed him three months earlier. He starts reading the very first poem:

> i tore my nails into
> my stomach ripping a hole
> big enough to put my hand
> into me with blind fingers
> feeling between intestines
> and liver for the flower of
> me, until i found it pulling
> it out, holding it in my bloody
> right hand until my left hand
> got hold of my soul, and i
> took the two and smashed them
> together until they became a
> solid piece of total beauty
> for me to throw with all
> my strength into the
> stars

I'm watching close as he reads it through. He seems not to be hurting at all so I feel it's all working nicely and then he gets to the last word and he suddenly goes, "OOOOOHHHHHH SHIT. IT WAS GOING FINE RIGHT UP TO THAT LAST WORD—S TA R S—OHH IT'S TOO DAMN BAD—WHAT A SHAME."

I was asking myself, "What? What th'hell does he mean? Stars? What's wrong with 'stars'? Nobody's ever said anything bad about 'stars' to me in my life—hmmm."

Bukowski spoke on, "STARS is so goddamn ultra poetic. You can't use STARS. STARS STARS FUCK TH'GODDAMN STARS! What a shame, kid. You had it strong right up to the last word, then gone, ruined, all th'damn dead false sewing circle poets are forever writing STARS STARS STARS! They can't write a line without STARS in it somewhere. I'm sorry, kid."

What he was telling me made instant sense but I tried to hedge in my mind because the 1000 copies were already printed and half the run was already distributed and there wasn't any chance I could recall every copy and have Tasmania Press change the last word of the first poem to some word, any word other than "STARS."

Now it's July 11, 1994, and it's been 29 years since Hank tore his Lion's Claws into my use of STARS and I've never used the word STARS or stars or stARS even once since…since 10 minutes after I met Charles Bukowski, face to face.

Excerpted from *Spinning Off Bukowski* (Sun Dog Press, 1996)

USED BY PERMISSION

Melanie Villines

Haunts of a Dirty Old Man
The Esotouric Bukowski Tour: Charles Bukowski's Los Angeles
Hosts Richard Schave and Kim Cooper

On Saturday, July 13, 2013, I hopped onboard the Esotouric bus tour entitled, "Haunts of a Dirty Old Man: Charles Bukowski's Los Angeles." The hosts, Richard Schave (who wrote the tour) and wife Kim Cooper, are everything you'd wish for in guides: knowledgeable, enthusiastic, creative, and, best of all, passionate about their subject—in this case, the Los Angeles of Charles Bukowski.

For the in-depth journey you take in just four hours, this tour—at $58—is a super bargain. Plus you get free donuts, coffee, and an $18-dollar coupon good on another Esotouric tour. On all tours, participants are ushered from place to place in the luxurious, air-conditioned comfort of a large, modern bus.

The Bukowski tour started in downtown L.A., where Buk lived in a range of SROs (Single Room Occupancy buildings), took his meals at Clifton's Cafeteria (RIP), and worked for fourteen years at the U.S. Postal Annex Terminal.

Bukowski also spent time at the Los Angeles Central Library, the location of his fateful meeting with *Ask the Dust,* a novel by John Fante originally published in 1939—a book and an author that exerted a profound influence on Bukowski's work. During the tour, host Richard Schave informed the approximately forty Buk aficionados in attendance that in 1980, when Bukowski suggested that his publisher John Martin reissue Fante's out-of-print masterpiece, Martin couldn't locate the novel anywhere and had to borrow the one available copy from the L.A. Library and photocopy it.

The Los Angeles Central Library—a Los Angeles Historic-Cultural Monument listed on the National Register of Historic Places—is an impressive structure in the Egyptian and Mediterranean architectural style that opened in

1926. The building features fifty-foot ceilings, marble staircases, statues of various figures of wisdom and learning, and an astounding mural depicting the history of California. It was fun picturing Bukowski in these exalted surroundings searching for a book that would light a spark in him.

Regarding Bukowski's life in downtown Los Angeles, Richard Schave writes in the brochure attendees receive at the beginning of the tour: *"Charles Bukowski went to Skid Row not for lack of anything else, but because there was precisely no other choice. It was a spiritual exercise with a long buildup and huge payoff. Starvation was a warm-up to the larger trials that stood before him. Being destitute, destroying family's and friends' faith in him, was simply a prelude to destroying whatever expectations, beliefs, hopes Bukowski had for himself. Once broken, he was never more whole. He could become strong in the broken places. And begin to see what was etched in the stone of his soul."*

We then traveled to East Hollywood to stand outside the author's apartment at 5124 De Longpre Avenue—for which Esotouric founders Richard Schave and Kim Cooper assisted Lauren Everett in her 2008 campaign to landmark the De Longpre bungalow court, saving the courtyard complex from demolition. After a stop at Buk's erased residence at 5437 Carlton Way (now "redeveloped"—and not for the better), we headed to Pink  Elephant Liquors at Western and Franklin for coffee, donuts, and something stronger if we wished. On the sidewalk, I found a Pabst beer cap, part of the "deck of cards" series with playing card figures on the inside—my find was a 7 of diamonds, a great souvenir of the trip.

After stopping at the Royal Palms, a former SRO in Westlake (MacArthur Park), where Buk lived with his first love Jane, we headed back downtown.

During the tour, while the bus was in motion, the activities remained lively—with Richard and Kim offering background and anecdotes about the next location, reading Buk's letters (his letter to John Fante brought me to tears) and poetry, showing slides on a monitor of how L.A. looked back in the day, and playing video interviews with Buk, along with related movie clips.

BOTTOM LINE: I give "Haunts of a Dirty Old Man: Charles Bukowski's Los Angeles" my highest and most enthusiastic recommendation—7 diamonds! It exceeded all my wildest expectations. Thank you, Richard and Kim. To learn more or to book a tour, visit esotouric.com.

Part Three
The Poet

Portrait by Dean Marais
noonehasboundme.com

HARRY CALHOUN

Bukowski grooves

Reading on the couch
Bukowski grooves
slip into the upholstery

you know, the groove
how he's got the nuance down pat
like the cockroach

sliding into gaps
between paper plates between
the blanket and sheet

and nothing and the night
itself slips in
to a Bukowski poem

and there is nothing
a certain nothing in the air
the French would call it

je ne sais quoi
with their damned faggot language
I call it a ghost

and my man you haunt me
elusive, unattainable perfect and

hurting like the best bluesman

MICHAEL O'BRIEN

Verse 56—Old Man in the Rain

Got a copy of Bukowski
from the library.

Nice, hard
cover edition; nicer than any of the ones
I'd ever shelled out cash
for.

Just noticed that the red dye
from the binding
has bled out a bit
onto the inside
of the dust jacket.

Makes me imagine that somebody
along the line
was reading in the rain.

Not bad, old
man,
not bad.

Still there for us
when we got no place
to hide.

DAVID STEPHEN CALONNE

On Some Early Bukowski Poems: The Genius Emerges

Charles Bukowski's childhood abuse and alienation drove him towards creativity and is one source of the naked vulnerability of his responses: for example his seemingly naïve yet artistically executed cartoons exhibit innocence, sweetness, charm and openness. There is great pathos in the fact that it was only with the non-human world—the world of animals—that Bukowski found any gentleness. At the age of five the boy fed sugar to a horse, memorialized in his poem "ice for the eagles": "The horses were more real than/my father/more real than God/and they could have stepped on my/feet but they didn't/they could have done all kinds of horrors/but they didn't./I was almost 5/but I have not forgotten yet;/o my god they were strong and good/those red tongues/slobbering out of their souls." The kind courtesy accorded him by creatures larger than himself as he fed them "sugar/white oblongs of sugar/more like ice,/and they had heads like/eagles/bald heads that could bite and/did not," was something to which the young Bukowski was unaccustomed.[1] His work expresses the hurt of the child who can find no logical reason for his torment: "pain without reason," as he would later call it. His early short story "The Reason Behind Reason" (1946) can be read as an allegory of silent trauma in which a ballplayer mutely experiences the events of the game and withdraws from competition at the end with no explanation. There are no words because there are an infinite number and none is sufficient to say what needs to be said: the athlete has been rendered soundless. This experience of being a powerless victim was combated through Bukowski's power over language, through his skill as a writer. Identity was achieved in his struggle with words—as Robert Frost declared, "poetry is a momentary stay against confusion."[2]

The French psychoanalyst Jacques Lacan theorized that infants during the "Imaginary" phase of development gain a sense of identity through an early mirroring of their parents. The child must then enter the Symbolic world, which is the entrance into language. The male child learns to obey the Father, who represents the Law, the Name of the Father. In Bukowski, the struggle against the abusive Father and his fight to create his own however fragile subjectivity is continual. Indeed, Bukowski's themes and approach often are similar to many of the key ideas of post-structuralism. He understands intuitively that language is related to desire: he circles constantly around the search for a stable "center" and at the same time the realization of a fundamental "absence" at the heart of experience. As John Story remarks:

> It is in and through language that the subject becomes a subject: subject in, subject of, and ultimately subjected to, language. I can only be 'I' in and through language...Subjectivity is thus produced from the very processes of language, made and remade within its patterns and articulations, and not an essential pre-given as non-psychoanalytical accounts presuppose...There can be so such thing as an essential self. It is nothing more than a fiction we live by.[3]

So too, Bukowski found a sense of "self" through writing and his subsequent discovery of literature. He is uncannily aware from the outset of his career that he must fashion a subjectivity, must enter into the literary tradition as a means towards a kind of spiritual salvation.

Charles Bukowski's poetic development from 1946-1964 reveals the gestation, birth and flowering of his genius: during a slow process, he gradually found his own distinctive voice through experimenting with a huge variety of styles, techniques and themes. He wrote lyrical poems, love poems, surreal poems, poems based on historical events, poems inspired by Catullus, comic poems, anguished expressionistic poems. He published in scores of little magazines with quirky names such as *Matrix, Naked Ear, Quixote, Existaria, Harlequin, Semina, Approach, Compass Review, Hearse, Quicksilver, Coastlines, Epos, Flame, Galley Sail Review, Gallows, The Half Moon, Nomad, Odyssey, Views* and *Wanderlust.* One of his earliest poems—"Voice in a New York Subway" (1946)— may memorialize a monologue Bukowski overheard or imagined during his stay in Manhattan: "I regret that I have but one soul/to give to the industrial mesalliance./A cat has nine lives but I have one, /in trust of Shraft & Shraft, makers of underwear/No. I musn't bite the hand that/feeds me;/it's too well encased in an iron glove./Well, anyhow, we have Freedom from Fear/and know better than to covet our/neighbor's wife./What more can a man want than food,/shelter and clothing?/Our boys have died on battlefields./Beware of Communists." [4] The ironic, casual tone and the sudden breaks in logic as the narrator's mind jumps from one idea to the next (from a cat's nine lives to his underwear) would become typical of Bukowski's often associative/disassociative method. Two of Franklin D. Roosevelt's promises from "The Four Freedoms" wartime speech—

freedom from want and fear are invoked—as well as a prescient comment upon the future global orientation of American foreign policy as World War II ended and Soviet power emerged.

"The Look," published five years later in *Matrix* in 1951, illustrates his early dedication to the lessons of the Imagists:

I once bought a toy rabbit
At a department store
And now he sits and ponders
Me with pink sheer eyes

He wants golf balls and glass
Walls.
I want quiet thunder.
Our disappointment sits between us.[5]

The mood here is eerie, with the Imagist counsel to use the visual as much as possible rather than the cerebral ("no ideas but in things") being observed by the "pink sheer eyes" of the stuffed animal. The creature appears to symbolize the artificial, conventional desires of the bourgeoisie: "golf balls and glass/Walls," while the subject of the poem has lyrical yearnings for an oxymoron which cannot exist: "quiet thunder." Bukowski the outsider was beset with *sehnsucht*—the Romantic desire for that which lies beyond despair of daily existence.

Bukowski's sense of being an outsider propelled his genius. Gloria Anzaldua believed that the artist who does "not feel psychologically or physically safe in the world" may be gifted with intuitive powers which she termed in Spanish *la facultad*:

> *La facultad* is the capacity to see in surface phenomena the meaning of deeper realities, to see the deep structure below the surface. It is an instant 'sensing,' a quick perception arrived at without conscious reasoning. It is an acute awareness mediated by the part of the psyche that does not speak, that communicates in images and symbols which are the faces of feelings, that is, behind which feelings reside/hide. The one possessing this sensitivity is excruciatingly alive to the world.

> Those who are pushed out of the tribe for being different are likely to become more sensitized (when not brutalized into

insensitivity). Those who do not feel psychologically or physically safe in the world are more apt to develop this sense. Those who are pounced on the most have it the strongest—the females, the homosexuals of all races, the dark-skinned, the outcast, the persecuted, the marginalized, the foreign."[6]

Bukowski's health crisis of 1954 when he almost died from a bloody hemorrhaging of his stomach due to his drinking increased his already extraordinary sensitivity to the fragility, beauty and horror of life. His work began to launch into an extreme surrealistic lyricism in which his *facultad*— his mystical encounters with the cosmic depths of the psyche— began to be expressed.

Bukowski's experiences recall the *shaman*—the visionary healer of tribal societies around the world—who returns from his encounter with madness and death with healing and creative powers. As Piers Vitebsky has remarked:

> The shaman's mental strength comes from an expanded experience of mental disturbance. The initiation is a controlled disintegration which is always followed by a reintegration into someone more powerful and more whole ...It is ultimately society which distinguishes between the behavior of the shaman and that of the schizophrenic or psychotic. One becomes a hero, the other a hospital patient. The shaman lives on the brink of the abyss but has the means to avoid falling in.[7]

Bukowski's struggle with madness is constantly chronicled in his writings, yet as Vitebsky remarks, Bukowski-the-shaman was able to dance on the brink of the abyss without "falling in." This accounts for the power of his poetry, stories, novels, essays and letters. We have the sense of encountering someone who has personally experienced *the dark night of the soul* but has lived to tell the tale, has survived lacerating physical and psychological sufferings yet has in many ways been strengthened rather than weakened by his tribulations.

Bukowski's near-death experience coincided with a revolution in American poetry and Bukowski himself theorized about its beginnings in the mid-Fifties in the "Introduction" he wrote for Doug Blazek's *Skull Juices* (1970):

It is difficult to say exactly when the Revolution began, but roughly I'd judge about 1955, which is more than ten years, and the effect of it has reached into and over the sacred ivy walls and even out into the streets of Man. Poetry has turned from a diffuse and careful voice of formula and studied ineffectiveness to a voice of clarity and burnt toast and spilled olives and me and you and the spider in the corner. By this, I mean the most living poetry; there will always be the other kind.[8]

So too Bukowski's approach began to shift at the same time that *Howl* arrived on the scene—Ginsberg wrote the poem in mid-1955 and performed it at the famous Gallery 6 reading in San Francisco on October 7, 1955. Bukowski now begins to experiment more insistently with style as we see in his first European appearance in *Quixote*—printed in Gibraltar in 1956—with the two poems: "You Smoke a Cigarette" and "these things." The former begins "You smoke a cigarette in fury and fall into/neutral slumber, to awaken to a dawn of /windows and grieving, without trumpets; and/somewhere, say, is a fish—all eye and movement—/wiggling in water; you could be that/fish, you could be there, held in water,/you could be the eye, cool and hung,/non-human." Here is a surreal telescoping of human and marine imagery which ends: "scream, scream/like a trumpet, put on your shirt, your/tie, boy: grieve is a pretty word like/mandolin, and strange like artichoke..."[9] Bukowski evolves a surging lyricism featuring lines packed with oddly oblique images and metaphors: "a dawn of/windows and grieving, without trumpets." There is even the shape-shifting typical of the shamanistic journey into the unconscious in which the "you" of the poem transforms into a fish, into the eye of the fish, "cool and hung,/non-human."

"Layover," published in 1956 in Judson Crews' The *Naked Ear* is a nostalgic love poem which celebrates "making love in the sun, in the morning sun/in a hotel room/above the alley/where poor men poke for bottles;/making love in the sun/making love by a carpet redder than our blood,/making love while the boys sell headlines/and Cadillacs,/making love by a photograph of Paris/and an open pack of Chester-fields,/making love while other men—poor fools—work." Bukowski seems here to be ahead of his times, predicting the ruling theme of the *Zeitgeist* of the sixties: the placing of love above materialism and moneymaking, the injunction of "make love, not war." The use of repetition and Whitmanian cataloguing would also become a typical aspect of his poetics. At the close of the poem, the narrator passes the hotel where he made love with his lady and notices the "cats in the alleys, and bottles and bums,/and I look up at the window and think,/*I no longer know where you are,*/and I walk on and wonder where/the living goes/when it stops."[10] The counterpointing of cats, alleys and bottles recalls Hart Crane's "Chaplinesque": "we have seen /the moon in lonely alleys make/A grail of laughter of an empty ash can,/And through all sound of gaiety and quest/Have heard a kitten in the wilderness."[11] So too the yearning for love in "Layover" marks the early elaboration of a poignant Bukowskian theme: unspeakable fragile tenderness confronting the grubby realities of the quotidian world.

One of his most startling poems, "Treason" (presently uncollected) appeared in *The Beloit Poetry Journal*, Winter 1957-58. The issue had the subtitle "The Underground Movement," thus signaling the early stirrings of what was to become the literary revolution of the Sixties. "Treason" is one of the few Bukowski poems that takes a historical incident as its background: King Richard III and the political machinations surrounding his reign. "Colynbourne crossed a King with a poem/and inherited new gallows on *Tower Hill,*/and they cut him down while he still bubbled/and tore out his disenchanted bowels/and tossed them in the fire by his side/where they sputtered and curled like live snakes,/and the butcher put his hand into the hole/of his body/and moved the fingers/like a suckling red spider..."[12] Colyngbourne's poem: "The Cat, the Rat and Lovell our dog/Rule all England under an Hog" led to his death, and Bukowski perhaps again is invoking the theme of poet as martyr. This poem represents a remarkable advance in technique, control of metaphor and mastery of sound. It seems a confirmation of the theory adumbrated above that following Bukowski's near-death experience from the rupturing of his stomach, the way was opened to a fecundating area of his imagination. The enjambment of "and the butcher put his hand into the hole/of his body," the guttural noise of "a suckling red spider" speed the lines forward and the violent, twisted, gruesome images seem dredged up from some deep, wounded place in the unconscious and signal Bukowski's genius at probing the dark currents of the psyche. As Aristotle in his *Poetics* remarked: the ability to make metaphors is "the mark of genius, for to make good metaphors implies an eye for resemblances."[13]

"Some Notes of Dr. Klarstein" from *Hearse*, 1958 is composed of fractures of logic, absurd non-sequiturs and surreal causal dislocations: "Read the paper. Comb a monkey's hair. Listen to/the radio./Early in our time men walked in and out of caves,/they say, but I don't believe it. I think they/lived in palm fronds, rolled up inside of them/like banana fruits in the skins." The poem ends: "…sure I've/read Robert Frost! I wish I had a bag of peanuts and a jug of lemon juice, a 5 gallon/jug of lemon juice. All I can think of is/streetcars and buzzflies, flies sticking their feet/in people's food./I simply hate you./I hate everybody." [14] Diverse names and objects— Robert Frost, peanuts, bananas, lemon juice, streetcars, buzzflies—are comically juxtaposed. A bizarre interior monologue of a perhaps "insane" psychiatrist's (or a "sane" psychiatrist's?) notes on his "insane" patient (his name *Klarstein*— "clear rock" in German—may pun on "clearing the rocks" out of a troubled psyche), the poem demonstrates Bukowski's idiosyncratic grotesquerie. Even in a slight, improvisatory poem, he is able to conjure striking images and juggle with meaning—teasing in and out of coherence, enjoying himself as he plays.

"To the Whore Who Took My Poems," first published in *Quagga* in 1960 is a variation on Catullus 42, "*Adeste, hendecasyllabic, quot estis/omnes,*" the first of several Bukowski composed in tribute to the great Roman poet.[15] The narrator laments the fact that a prostitute has stolen his writings: "twelve poems gone and I don't keep carbons and you have/my/paintings too, my best ones; it's stifling:/are you trying to crush me out like the rest of them?/why didn't you take my money? they usually do/from the sleeping drunken pants sick in the corner." [15] These lines allude to Catullus' "*iocum me putat esse moecha turpis,/et negat mihi nostra reddituram/pugillaria, si pati potestis*"; "this vile slut seems under the impression/I'm a walking joke, won't give me back my/writing tablets—really, can you beat it?" [16] Bukowski responded to the essential modernity of Catullus and saw his own experience reflected back to him in the lines of an ancient poet: Bukowski like Catullus had also frequently lost money to ladies of the night who filched his wallet "from the sleeping drunken pants sick in the corner."

A later poem published in the posthumous *The Continual Condition* "what have I seen." returns to Catullus:

> I like your way, Catullus, talking plainly about the
> whore who claims you owe her money, or about
> the guy who smiled too much—who cleaned
> his teeth with horse piss, or about how the young poets
> come with their blameless tame verse, or about
> how this or that guy married a slut.[17]

This opening refers to four separate poems, 41, 39, 16, 58 and 78A, thus demonstrating Bukowski's familiarity with the whole of Catullus' *oeuvre*: "the/whore who claims you owe her money" is Catullus 41: "Ameana puella defututa/tota milia me decem poposcit" ["Ameana, that fucked-out little scrubber,/just had the nerve to ask me for ten thousand" [18] ;"the guy who smiled too much—who cleaned his teeth with horse piss" is Catullus 39: "Egnatius, quod candidos habet dentes,/renidet usque quaque....nunc Celtiber <es>: Celtiberia in terra,/quod quisque minxit, hoc sibi solet mane/dentem atque russam defricare gingiuam" ["Because Egnatius has those damn white teeth, he flashes them everywhere...But/actually you're a Spaniard, and on Spanish terrain/everyone hoards his night piss, which next morning/he uses to scrub off his teeth, and his sore red gums"[19]; "the young poets/come with their blameless tame verse" is Catullus 16: "nam castum esse decet pium poetam/ipsum, uersiculos nihil necesse est; qui tum denique habent salem ac leporem, si sunt molliculi ac parum pudici" ["Squeaky-clean, that's what every proper poet's/*person* should be, but not his bloody squiblets,/which, in the last resort, lack salt and flavor/if *not* 'unmanly' and rather less than decent"[20] ; "how this or that guy married a slut" is Catullus 59 "Bononiensis Rufa Rufulum fellat,/uxor Meneni" [Rufa, Bologna lady, sucks dear Rufus' cock—Menenius' wife" Green, 106/107, as well as Catullus 78A: "Gallus homo est stultus, nec se videt esse maritum,/qui patruus patrui monstret adulterium" ["A stupid fellow, Gallus; he can't see he's a married/uncle parading avuncular cuckoldry."[21] This should put to rest the idea that Bukowski was an uneducated primitive naïf: he clearly knew and loved his Catullus.

Another poem from *Targets*, 1960 turns from ancient Latin literature to an illustration of the influence of Asian poetry on Bukowski. "The Japanese Wife" features a husband whose wife has died (he humorously contrasts Japanese with American women at the beginning of the poem) and following her death there is "nothing but little Japanese prints on the wall,/all those tiny people sitting by red rivers/with flying green birds,/and I took them down and put them face down/in a drawer with my shirts,/and it was the first time I realized/that she was dead, even though I buried her;/and some day I'll take them all out again,/all the tan-faced little people/sitting happily by their bridges and huts/and mountains—/but not right now,/not just yet."[22] Bukowski frequently spoke of his admiration for Li Po and Tu Fu, and it seems likely he also knew the famous haiku by Taniguchi Buson: "An autumn chill goes through me/stepping on my dead wife's comb/on the bedroom floor." So too in Bukowski's poem a widower suddenly is compelled to confront his grief when he sees his dead wife's prints on the wall. Bukowski's virtuosity in absorbing and "recomposing" the themes of great writers he admired is clear in many poems from this phase of his career. Indeed, what is astonishing about this early period is the fecundity of Bukowski's creativity and how many imaginative, striking lines erupted from his imagination. He was inspired not only by other writers, but also composers. Several poems from the period allude to composers such as Hugo Wolf and Borodin; Chopin appears in "I fought them from the moment I saw light from the womb" from *Sun*, 1961:

> like Chopin drunk, clutching his Pollack soil,
> while all around him
> the whores were selling their bodies
> like beautiful things the bees like
> like beautiful things that bloom. [23]

This intense, rich, condensed incantatory lyricism combined with the genius for metaphor and simile we noted earlier—"the whores were selling their bodies/like beautiful things the bees like/like beautiful things that bloom"—demonstrates that Bukowski had begun to find his own true literary "voice."

Bukowski often struggled with the logistics of writing his poems and stories in the exposed circumstances of living above or below others in the cheap rooming houses and apartments he inhabited. He describes the complaints of neighbors about the sound of his typewriter, as in the uncollected poem "10:30 P.M." published in *Sun* #1, 1961:

> even Shakespeare's gone, and I'm no Shakespeare,
> and I guess that's what hurts too: to know you are limited
> forever,
> the sea coming in only so far
> and then rolling back,
> the hands the lips the eyes
> the bodies and sounds of bodies,
> knowing you at last as nothing
> and leaving as nothing
> while greater men hit little white balls
> upon green lawns and notate averages
> while in a shack off the East River

some man like a quiet prawn
gives us

        paint upon canvas
that would make these very walls scream,
and I look at razors caught with bits of hair,
caught from my dumb yet living skull,
and now they knock upon my door:
please, it's 10:30, we want to sleep, sleep sleep,
the typewriter,
and I carry it from the table

        to its hole against the wall
        (like a dead dog run over in the street)
        and I sit in my rented chair
        and the whole night comes over me like a gracious vomit
and death is nothing.[24]

It is striking here how in the expression of doubt, failure and limitation, Bukowski makes his lines sing so that in the telling of his failure, he achieves success: this becomes one of his major strengths as a writer. And as Kierkegaard wrote: "a poet is an unhappy being whose heart is torn by secret sufferings, but whose lips are so strangely formed that when the sighs and the cries escape them, they sound like beautiful music." The contrast between the smug golfers with their "little white balls" and the poor artist creating sublime art which "would make these very walls scream" is again the plight of Bukowski's *Kunstler* characters. He himself is at the bottom of the social hierarchy, noticing his razor blades "caught with bits of hair" and sitting in his "rented chair"—and while he attempts to create beauty, the neighbors intervene with their complaints, cutting him off (presumably) from his efforts to rise into ecstasy. Yet he succeeds—in the composing of this very poem—in defeating his seemingly intractable opponents. The ambiguous ending—"and death is nothing"—could be read as the proof that he has achieved a momentary immortality in the writing of the poem. Yet it also echoes the earlier use of "nothing"—"knowing you at last as nothing/and leaving as nothing," so that the poem finally balances right at the fulcrum of creation and non-creation. Bukowski was always anchored in the realities of the body: he never flew free of Earth into abstract systems. His life and work are anchored in his body: as the poem hymns: "the hands," "the lips," "the eyes," "the bodies and sounds of bodies," "my dumb yet living skull." So too Bukowski's scarred face, his bodily pains, evacuating, the pleasure of scratching his hemorrhoids, flatulence, vomiting. The body is bodied forth in all its horrible glory: the limitations and humiliations of the body are transformed into an affirmation in the very description of them. He makes his life work the story of his defeats and in the mastery of his telling transforms his suffering into creative affirmation, like Samuel Beckett: I can't go on, I can't go on, I'll go on.

One of the works he submitted to Sheri Martinelli's *Anagogic and Paideumic Review*, which appeared in 1961— "poem for my little dog who also growls quite well"—demonstrates Bukowski's tender sense of humor. It is a touching song to his canine who does not know about Dostoyevsky, Hemingway or Dylan Thomas but is a companionable tutelary spirit, a sweet *doppelganger*: "friend dog, I walk you now,/you and I, alone,/pattering up the leave-torn sidewalks,/and although you haven't read Kafka,/and until you do—/no woman will share /our bone"[25] When he was living with Jane, he had a dog which he described as "half- wolf, half-collie, but gentle, gentle," which was killed by an automobile when he had left it with her after they separated.[26] Canines often appear in Bukowski's drawings—on the wall in a picture frames, on the ground as mute observers of the passing scene—as well as in his writings. In this he was likely following one of his admired authors, James Thurber, who frequently drew and wrote about man's best friend. One brief poem "I Saw A Tramp Last Night" collected in *The Continual Condition* (2009) compares the poet himself to a raggedy dog strolling along, roughed up by life: "the way the old dog walked/with dotted, tired fur/down nobody's alley/being nobody's dog..."[27] Late in life, as Bukowski's life became calmer, he seemed to identify more frequently with the calm poise and *sang froid* of his cats rather than the dog's shaggy existence.

Bukowski composed a number of poems about artists—writers, painters and composers—during this period. They are part of his extended *kunstler-roman:* his desire to describe and celebrate the joys and sorrows of the artist's life. A somber treatment of this theme occurs in "ants crawl my drunken arms" which appeared in 1961 in *Literary ArtPress*: "O ants crawl my drunken arms/and they let Van Gogh sit in a cornfield/and take Life out of the world with a/shotgun." Rimbaud, Pound, Crane are invoked as other martyrs to art as the poet continues drinking: "and the ants crawl into my mouth/and down my throat,/I wash them down with wine/and pull up the shades/and they are on the screen/and on the streets/climbing church towers/and into tire casings/looking for something else to eat."[28] The lines move from the casual act of the poet swallowing ants as they move in surreal fashion from his throat to screen, to church towers, to tire casings, describing a kind of alcoholic *delirium tremens* in which phantasmagoric images emerge and collapse in a grotesque drunken parade. Bukowski often portrayed the life of the artist in both serious and comic styles— rather like Mozart who was fond of repeating one melodic theme in both major and minor keys—so too Bukowski explores the comic and tragic sides of the same romantic literary trope: the poet as spiritual outlaw.

"the sunday artist," originally published in *Targets*, 1961 anticipates the surreal onrush and prophetic roll of Bob Dylan's lyrics, with striking, insistent anaphora: "I have met Montaigne and Phidias/in the flames of my wastebasket,/I have met barbarians on the streets/their heads rocking with rodents;/I have seen wicked infants in blue tubs/wanting stems as beautiful as flowers,/and I have seen the barfly sick/over his last dead penny" :

cadillacs have crawled my walls like roaches
goldfish whirl my bowl, hand-tamed tigers;
yes, I have been painting these Sundays—
the grey mill, the new rebel; it's terrible really:
I must ram my fist through cleanser and chlorine,
through Andernach and apples and acid,
but, then, I really should tell you that I have a
woman around mixing waffle flour and singing,
and the paint sticks to my plan like candy.[29]

As with Dylan (both Bob and Thomas), what it all means matters less than allowing oneself to revel in the pleasure of the sound and rhythm of the music. Bukowski's symbolic menagerie is expanded here beyond the ants of the previous poem to include rodents, roaches, goldfish. And in a rare nod to his birthplace in Germany, Bukowski surprisingly invokes the ancient town of Andernach in a poem about "the Sunday artist" as might a painter who draws himself into his painting in a small cameo frame.

A wonderful brief comic uncollected poem," Fast Pace," typical of Bukowski's brilliance at fusing surrealism with rapid humor was published in *Brand "X"* in 1962:

I came in awful tired with a finger sliced off and frost
on my feet and the lightning coming down the wallpaper;
they hung three men in the streets, and the mayor was drunk

on candy, and they sunk the friggin' fleet and the vultures
were smoking Havana cigars; ok, I see where some bathing
beauty sliced her left wrist an' they found her in a
comatose
state in her bedroom—probably pining her heart out for
me, but I've got to move out of town: I thought I was a
no-sweat kid, a rock, but I just found a
  grey hair above my

left ear.[30]

Bukowski's "dramatic monologues" such as this often seem to be a kind of weird "found poetry" in which he simply transcribes an overheard speech or takes a core of actual speech and then improvises, as we have seen, as in the early poem "Voice in a New York Subway." They are just close enough to reality to seem authentic, yet refracted through his surreal imagination so they are also surrealistically comic.

"What Seems to be the Trouble, Gentlemen?," first published in the British periodical *Satis*, no. 5, 1962 also moves in typical Bukowski fashion from one absurd incident to the next and begins: "the service was bad/and the bellboy kept bringing in towels/at the wrong moment./drunk, I finally clubbed him along/the side of the head./he was a little man and he fell/like an October leaf, /quite done,/and when the fuzz came up/I had the sofa in front of the door/and the chain on,/the 2nd movement of Brahms First Symphony/and had my hand halfway up the ass/of a broad old enough to be my grandmother..."[31] The combination of cartoon-like absurd violence, cultural allusion (Brahms First Symphony) and outrageous sexuality will prove to be a formula Bukowski would use to great effect in his fiction as well. And the throwaway lines at the end—as the narrator has been clubbed over the head by the police and awakes chained to his bed the next morning in prison—"and I knew I'd be late for work,/which worried me immensely"—strikes the exact note of blasé reaction to the results of their rebellions which typifies his anti-heroes: a few years later his anti-hero extraordinaire—Hank Chinaski—would emerge in full glory in Bukowski's poems, stories and novels.

In "To a lady who believes me dead" from *The Outsider*, 1962 we encounter another Bukowskian canine: "I have a small dog that walks the sidewalks/like an idiot/looking back over his round shoulders/wondering if I still exist/I have a radio that burns my curtains with music/I have nights that come down without my seeing and/at once it is dark,/but I have mornings too,/and sunlight's good enough for birds, spiders/or/any new hero/old shoe/and my dog/my dog/our shapes fill the sidewalks with shadows..."[32] Again the lyric impulse moves through measured anaphora: "I have a small dog"; "I have a radio"; "I have nights"; "I have mornings." Bukowski achieves a mastery of mood and sound, with a lovely and startling image such as the radio "that burns my curtains with music," or a few lines after the above quoted lines a surprising historical reference "idiot dog/greater than/ the armies of Alaric."

One of his finest poems of this period, "the singular self" from *Epos*, 1963 portrays a solitary male character, sleepless, who has driven to the ocean. He walks down the sea-cliffs where he notices lovers on the beach "turning to stare/at the madness/of a singular self;/shamed, I move on through them/to climb a row of wet boulders that/break the sea-stroke/into sheaths of white;/the moonlight is wet/on the bald stone/and now that I'm there/I don't want to be there."[33] The merging of the lovers seeing him with the obviously sexual imagery of the scene—"wet boulders," "sea-stroke," "sheaths of white," "bald stone"—is sensitively achieved. There is an admirable concentration in "to climb a row of wet boulders that/break the sea-stroke/into sheaths of white" in which "b," "t," and "s" alliterate while the rhythm follows the cadences of the breaking waves. He then says "it is a bad place to die," and we suddenly realize he may be contemplating suicide since the next lines reveal "but better a yellow room/with known walls and dusty/lampshades..."[34] Again we return to the enclosing "walls" which become a central image in Bukowski's psychological topography of the "singular self."

"Part of an Ordinary Day of an Inordinate Man," an uncollected poem which appeared in *The Emerson Review*, 1963 has a coiled power: "the walls know me and/come toward me like a lover./hello, I say. hello."[35] Walls occur repeatedly Bukowski's work as a metaphor for being trapped—*Grip the Walls* is the title of one of his *Wormwood* collections—and are an essential part of the symbolic landscape of his poetic world: walls, landlady, music, alcohol. The poem is a collection of dissociated events and objects encountered by the narrator as he goes to "get my beer for dinner." A long sequence episodes are set one after another. First he encounters "a man with a trash barrel," moving to "the ladies walk by" to "fish in the market. a large fish/without a head," to "a large man in a well-waxed red car/really wants to run me over," to "a small fat boy/shoots a cap pistol up toward my window," to "the cars go by," to "a man goes by on a bicycle/It is Jesus Christ but he does not/recognize me." The poem is a bravura performance and one thinks of the Beatles' song "A Day in the Life" of a few years later: "Woke up. Got out of bed. Dragged a comb across my head. Somebody spoke and I fell into a dream. How many holes does it take to fill the Albert Hall?" As we have seen above with Bob Dylan, the worlds of popular music and modern poetry began to intersect in the 1960s as both poets and musicians began to expand into the avant-garde realms of surrealism, existentialism and absurdist philosophy.

Another poem "Fragile!" published in *Sciamachy* in 1964, also illustrates a new openness and flexibility in Bukowski's narrative poems:

> I tried all night to sleep
> but I couldn't sleep
> and I began drinking
> around 5:30
> and reading about Delius
> and Stravinsky...[36]

The speaker (Sam) hears people in his building rising and getting ready for the day. The phone rings; it is a lady who asks where he has been and he gets "rid of her/and pulled up the shades/and put my clothes on,/and I went down to the coffeeshop/and they were all sitting there/with bacon and eggs./I had a coffee and went on in." He goes to his job, empties the ladies' bathroom and the boss comes in and questions whether Sam has put the "fragile" labels on some packages (hence the poem's title). Sam takes a break, smokes a cigarette when

> One of the secretaries came back
> Rotating her can,
> Pounding her spikes
> On the cement floor.

She gives him an ironic smile, which says "I don't have to do much work,/but you do./then she walked away wobbling, /wobbling meat." And the poem ends with Sam "waiting/waiting for 5:30." The poem is significant because it has reduced the subject matter to a bare minimum: a sleepless night, followed by morning and work and waiting for the day to end, composed in verse which comes as close to prose as possible, and also using a rapid narrative style which Bukowski will perfect in his prose writing in the following years. There is a Homeric concentration on each action described in simple verbs, taken in sequential due course:

"and I went down to the coffeeshop," "they were all sitting there," "I had a coffee," "and went on in."

Thus we have seen the remarkable range of Bukowski's poetic creativity during the years 1946-1964. As the Sixties progressed, his approach and style would again shift as the influence of the Beats and Hippies began to make themselves felt in the American counterculture: his poetry and prose began to reflect the new *Zeitgeist*. I hope to have demonstrated in this essay that Bukowski—through both his natural literary talent as well as the impact of his early traumata, mid-life health crisis and ceaseless attentive reading of world literature (Catullus, Li Po, Tu Fu, Celine, Artaud, Dostoyevsky, Gorky, Turgenev, Saroyan, Fante, Hemingway among many others)—transformed himself into a great writer. His early period demonstrates how through hard work, constant productivity and persistent experimentation he succeeded in contacting what the ancient Greeks called the *daimon*: his inner source of creative power and genius.

NOTES

1.   Charles Bukowski, "ice for eagles," *Dust*, Vol. 1, no. 3, 1964,p. 75; *The Days Run Away Like Wild Horses Over the Hills*, (New York, 1969), p. 30.

2.   Robert Frost, "The Figure a Poem Makes: An Introduction," *The Robert Frost Reader: Poetry and Prose*, ed. Edward C. Lathem and Lawrence Thompson (New York, 2002), p. 440.

3.   John Story, *Cultural Theory and Popular Culture: An Introduction* (Harlow, 2001), p. 76.

4.   "Voice in a New York Subway," *Matrix*, Vol. 9, no. ¾, 1946

5.   "The Look," *Matrix*, 1951

6.   Gloria Anzaldua, *Borderlands/La Frontera: The New Mestiza* (San Francisco, 1999), Second Edition, p. 60.

7.   Piers Vitebsky, *Shamanism* (Norman, 2001), p. 139

8.   Bukowski, "Introduction," Douglas Blazek, *Skull Juices* (1970), n.p.

9.   "You Smoke a Cigarette," *Quixote* 12, Winter, 1956.

10.   "Layover," *Naked Ear*, no. 9, 1956

11.   Hart Crane, "Chaplinesque," *White Buildings* (New York, 1972), p. 17

12.   "Treason," *The Beloit Poetry Journal*, Winter, 1957-58. Another rare poem with an historical allusion is "Ivan the Terrible," *Ante*, vol.1, no. 4, 1965.

13.   Aristotle, *The Poetics* (Cambridge, 1965), pp. 88-91, 1459A

14.   "Some Notes of Dr. Klarstein," *Hearse*, February, 1958

15.   "To the Whore Who Took My Poems," , *Quagga*, Vol. 1, no. 3, 1960; Peter Green, *The Poems of Catullus: A Bilingual Edition* (Berkeley, 2005), p. 89

16.   Catullus/Green, Ibid.

17.   "what have I seen," *The Continual Condition* (New York, 2009), p. 110

18.   Catullus/Green, pp. 88/89

19.   Ibid., 86/87

20.   Ibid., 62/63

21.   Ibid., 106/107; 186/87

22.   "The Japanese Wife," *Targets*, September, 1960

23.   "I've Fought Them From the Moment I Saw Light From the Womb," *Sun*, no. 1, 1961

24.   "10:30 PM," Ibid.

25.   "Poem for my Little Dog Who Also Growls Quite Well," *Anagogic and Paideumic Review* no. 5, January, 1961, collected in *Beerspit Night and Cursing: The Correspondence of Charles Bukowski and Sheri Martinell 1960-1967,* ed. Steven Moore (Santa Rosa, 2001), p. 362

26.   Bukowski, *Screams from the Balcony: Selected Letters 1960-1970,*ed. Seamus Cooney (Santa Rosa, 1993), p. 247; a photo of (most likely) this dog appears in Howard Sounes, *Bukowski in Pictures* (Edinburgh, 2000), p. 2

27.   "I Saw a Tramp Last Night," *The Continual Condition* (New York, 2009), p. 113

28.   "Ants crawl my drunken arms," *Literary Artpress*, Vol. 2, no. 2, 1961

29.   "The Sunday Artist," *Targets* 5, April 1961

30.   "Fast Pace," *BRAND "X,"* No. 1, January 1962

31.   "What Seems to be the Trouble, Gentlemen?," *Satis* no. 5, Spring-Summer, 1962

32.   "To a Lady Who Believes Me Dead," *The Outsider*, Vol. 1, no. 2, Summer 1962

33.   "The Singular Self," *Epos*, vol. 14, no. 4, Summer 1963

34.   Ibid.

35.   "Part of an Ordinary Day of an Inordinate Man," *The Emerson Review*, Vol. 1, No. 1, Winter 1963

36.   "Fragile," *Sciamachy* 6, 1964

HENRY DENANDER

Bullshit

Charles Bukowski once wrote,
in a poem of his,
that you're not a real poet if you
have to go back to your poem
and change it;

you should be able just to
lay down the line.

Maybe that was one of
Bukowski's bullshit lines?

Maybe that was a poem
he should've gone back
and changed.

Originally published in
Bring Down the Sun (Art Bureau, 2005)

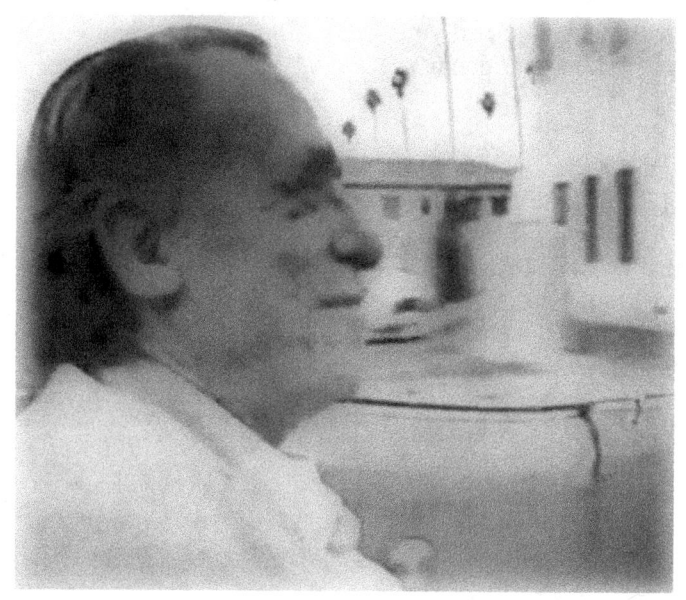

ERIK WOLTERSDORF

It Was Never Easy

I mean, this writing
of poems.

I think now of the
old man, Bukowski,
who knew how to do it;

and I sit here like a fool,
smoking cigarettes, staring
at a blank screen
on this computer;

it is the same
as an empty sheet of paper
scrolled into a typewriter;

I mean, these two things
are irrevocably equal:
the blank screen and
the empty page.

technology changes,
certainly,
but the occurrences
stay the same;

except that
this blank screen
is so white—it is blinding.

and I think of Bukowski,
who chiseled his simple line
into paper, cigar in mouth,
grinning,

up there in that room with
his Buddha statue and
his ashtray.

he made it all seem
so feasible, so easy;

but the great ones
have always done this.

Bukowski: writing poems
by the thousand;

Bukowski, like Babe Ruth in
the batters-box,
knocking the mud from
his spikes,

then watching
the impossible flight of the fastball
and effortlessly
intersecting its trajectory
with the sweet-spot of his lumber;

crushing the ball
once again,

over light towers, past
the flags and the
battlements
of the great stadium;

creating awe, and
a sense of wonder
to bewilder
the watchers...

but it has never
been easy,

this writing of poems.

and tonight as I type and
then revise
these feeble lines,

I imagine
the barking of sea lions
on some oily beach
near San Pedro;

yet the old man is
no longer there,

and his once young,
pretty widow is
herself
now wreathed with age;

perhaps living with
his apparition,
in that house with
a balcony
overlooking the harbor—

a house which will
one day receive pilgrims
who are not yet living.

and I think of all those
blank pages
that he fed into his typer,

to be scrawled
with such a splendid gathering
of words upon paper,

words which would ripple
that very paper
right through its center
and out to its edges,

like an excellent flight of ducks
landing upon the lake
and drifting.

it was all so lovely,

the old man, his poems,

his pages; he left us
more than enough.

he made it all look
so easy;

but it was never easy—
it was genius,
sublime and resplendent;

and yet, here I struggle,
as the meek inherit
nothing.

but it is hell.

MARVIN MALONE

Wormwood Review and Charles Bukowski
(written in mid-1980s)

This editor tries to avoid literary criticism and speculations about the private lives of the poets published in *Wormwood*. However, a bit of history might be interesting to those who follow the little magazine scene. Since the very first, *Wormwood* has had a policy of not publishing the writings of the editor's intimate friends. On the other hand, manuscripts are not secured in a purely random manner via the U. S. mail. The arrival of Charles Bukowski in our pages was the product of a sequence of inter-related discoveries, associations, and affiliations.

In 1948, I discovered the *New Directions* annuals, which led me to read all of the authors sponsored by James Laughlin—including Henry Miller and Céline. About the same time, I came across *The Little Magazine: A History and a Bibliography* as written by Hoffman, Allen, and Ulrich (Princeton University Press, 1946). The book launched a personal enthusiasm for the little magazine as a publishing institution that has not yet dimmed.

At that time, the only publishers unafraid of the "unpublishable" Henry Miller were James Laughlin, Bern Porter, and Judson Crews. In the process of collecting and reading Henry Miller, in collecting and reading little mags, and in moving to Albuquerque, New Mexico, I would eventually meet Judson Crews in Taos, New Mexico.

A poet and a one-man publisher of astonishing books and little mags (Motive and Este Es presses), Crews had just published Bukowski's "Layover" in his current mag titled *Naked Ear*. Even though *Naked Ear* was very modest in size and format, it is now regarded as a little magazine classic. Crews has always had a good ear for the authentic and was then picking up and publishing many new poets who were (like Henry Miller) considered too far out for the established literary quarterlies of that day. Bukowski's debut was in issue 9 (1957), and he shared the pages with people as diverse as Mike McClure and Larry Eigner (new poets) and Norman Macleod (an establishment outsider). Crews, generous and proselytizing, gave me copies of *Existaria* #7 (published by Carl Larsen in Hermosa Beach, California) and *Hearse* #2 (published by E. V. Griffith in Eureka, California). *Existaria* contained three good Bukowski poems and *Hearse* (subtitled A Vehicle Used to Convey the Dead) contained one. Crews terminated *Naked Ear* at about that time, indicating to me that *Hearse* was its "spiritual successor." I placed subscriptions for both *Existaria* and *Hearse* and began a limited correspondence with Larsen and Griffith. Griffith launched a series of chapbooks with number one being Carl Larsen's *Arrows of Longing* and number five being Bukowski's first book, *Flower, Fist and Bestial Wail* (1960).

Moving to Connecticut in 1960, I became involved with the *Wormwood Review*—defunct after two issues. Resuscitation seemed possible. At about the same time, Larsen moved to New York City to seek the big-time literary scene. Being a literary neighbor of sorts, he was approached for manuscripts to relaunch *Wormwood*. Larsen was then producing a mag called *rongWrong* (one of the first mags of the so-called mimeo-graph revolution), and Bukowski was scheduled for the second issue. At that time, Larsen and Bukowski were friendly rivals and frequent corre-spondents, so it was easy for me to get Bukowski's address and send him complimentary copies of *Wormwood* (probably issues 5 and 6) without comment. Poems were received for consideration—also without com-ment. In issue 7 (October 20, 1962), Bukowski made his debut with "Thank God for Alleys." Appropriately, that issue (printed offset from paper plates) also featured Carl Larsen and Judson Crews.

Many other editors have written me for Bukowski's address and have received it— notably d.a. levy and Douglas Blazek, who went on to pub-lish some of Bukowski's most sought-after books. This rather casual process (based on literary enthusiasms) is typical of the best of the little mag scene and keeps literature alive and current. I should point out that I have never met Bukowski. I met Crews once, Griffith once, Bern Porter once, and Larsen twice. Our associations have been primarily through our publications and secondarily through correspondence. Certainly there is some mutual respect there, but it would be very difficult to say that we constitute a group of personal friends. One common denominator is that we all operate independent of the present literary establishment, and this seems important to us. I do not believe a magazine filled with one's per-sonal friends can be taken seriously as literature, and I do not believe a magazine filled with establishment figures can be contemporary in a meaningful way.

Wormwood was given the right of first refusal on the poems not used for the two Bukowski books produced in 1963 and 1965 by Loujon Press, owned by Lou and Jon Webb, who started out by publishing the famous little mag *The Outsider*. Since that time, *Wormwood* has always had a thick sheaf of unpublished Bukowski poems. Virtually every issue (chapbook issues excepted) contains two to four Bukowski poems that seem to fit the general mood of the issue. *Wormwood* has published four special sections (chapbooks within the magazine) featuring Bukowski: *Grip the Walls* (issue 16, 1964), *Night's Work* (issue 24, 1966), *55 Beds in the Same Direction* (issue 53, 1974), and *Good-Bye to Hollywood* (issue 81-82, 1981). In addition, issue 71 was wholly devoted to *Bukowski's Legs, Hips and Behind* (1978) and issue 95 to *Horses Don't Bet on People and Neither Do I* (1984). Twenty-four copies of issues 16 and 24 were numbered and signed by Bukowski and are probably the most elusive items for collectors. Issue 24 also printed the first bibliography of his work (assembled by this editor). Forty copies of issue 53, sixty copies of issue 71, and 50 copies of issue 81-82 were numbered and signed. In 1969, Bukowski was awarded the Wormwood Award for "the most overlooked book of worth in a calendar year" for his first book of prose, *Notes of a Dirty Old Man*, which was published by Essex House, a "dirty book" publisher. Four years later, it would be republished by City Lights Books.

The following quotes appeared in letters written by Charles Bukowski to Marvin Malone over their long association.

"Crazy guys like you keep crazy guys like me goin...I know that the bad poems will come back and that you are man enough to know them." (1965)

"Wormwood appears to be consistently and eternally #1 of the literary mags, and it's going to be a sad day for all of us when you hang up the gloves." (1968)

"I have never had any magazine treat me like dear old Wormie...I'm lucky. And I'm lucky that Wormie has been around. I sometimes think of you. Then I think, it's lucky we have never met. It's lucky we have a professional distance. It's lucky you do what you do and I do what I do and we do it without politics and personal relationships. It's lucky, Malone, lucky, we have been a splendid pair. I salute your guts and your way." (1978)

"You are the quiet worker of magic...I believe your comments on some of the rejects are right there—After the stuff comes back from you, I go through it again, agree that most of it isn't so good but usually find a few to send elsewhere." (1982)

"You are one of the quietest most invisible editor-publishers about. You do your fucking work without self-fanfare. And as I've said before, the day you lay it down, that day is going to be a sad sad bad bad horrible, sad and horrible bad day and time and year for many including this Chinaski...You have scored a wonderful fight. Indeed." (1985)

ANGGO GENORGA

For the Record

Charles Bukowski
made poetry simple.
he shoved metaphor
out of his way and
never look back;
something the academics
will never understand.

RD ARMSTRONG

For Chinaski

I could never get it up for anyone like I did
for Chinaski
Oh, I tried the other boys (some of the old-schoolers were interesting)
but I didn't think the odds of survival in the nineties,
pretty boy, soundbyte, mini-mall, computer-enhanced,
MTV landscaped, SPOKEN word world,
would be too good, for the boys of yesteryear.
But Chinaski...
Now there was a man!
Chinaski was the voice, the Walter Winchell of the damaged, the
drunken,
and the loner...
Chinaski took sloth and made it sound virtuous
he took debauchery and turned it into a democratic right
he made the DTs sound like a rite of passage
and he cooed to us, he lulled us into bed
willing and able, wanting to be raped.
Chinaski
He worked the crowd like Elmer Gantry
he didn't have to pick your pocket while he mesmerized you with tales of
madness;
you paid willingly!
You bought that lakefront property in Arizona—
you bought the myth...
Step right up!
Three for a dollar!
Chinaski was the whore with a heart of gold
He could blow away your troubles and mercifully let you sleep it off between
clean sheets...
Chinaski
Even the name sounded good, tough and clean
He was the x-rated Indiana Jones, bullwhipping his way thru skid row
rescuing madwomen from nazi power junkies of corporate America
and their ass-licking toadies: "40 hour week" and "overtime."
He always kicked ass and even got some along the way, as he fought for
the next pint,
the next long-shot winner...
Chinaski
he was the long shot that finally paid off

the horse that snuck out of the pack on the last turn
and beat the odds-on favorite by a nose.
And what a nose!
In his last days, as everything shrank, only the nose remained
feeding on the dying embers of his face, the nose loomed…
Chinaski
After cheating at so many things,
after cheating the hell outta life,
with only so many ways to cheat death,
only so many cards,
his hand played out, finally
Chinaski folded (someone else will cash in his chips…)

Chinaski

A name, a nose, a voice
Women
Hot Water Music
Ham On Rye
Post Office
Factotum
Love is a Dog from Hell
You get so Alone
War All the Time
Mockingbird
The Days Run Away
Earth Poems
Screams
Living on Luck
Betting on the Muse

The body of work lives on, the memory of the man lives on
But the body of Chinaski is gone,
vanished
And we…
We move on, excitement junkies waiting for the next turn-on
But I doubt I'll ever get it up again like I did for him
For Chinaski!

Portrait by David Barker
Originally published in
Charles Bukowski Spit in My Face
by David Barker (1982)

S.A. GRIFFIN

The Next Bukowski

sits anonymously before his keyboard
stinking of life and language
dead lifting the intoxicating helix
of the poem

lit by the hot eyes of the sun
he cannot hide spinning silently
inside of his own remarkable chaos

he holds up the corner liquor with a Cheshire charm
like a monkey jacking off for kids at the zoo

people point and whisper
   he is the one
   the ugly one, the crazy one, the genius,
   the brawler, the drunk

hungry shadows crush the
loitering landscape

the poet stumbles drunk past wounded alleys
seeking a soft spot under some fugitive moon
where he can surrender for the night

he takes one last tug off the bottle
then curls up inside of what remains
to sleep off the tired centuries hung over from war
religion and other forms of
civilized madness

anxious horses approach the gate
freeze for one tense second
scratching a fertile wound into the
resilient earth

dreams breed hope

the inexorable call of train song
punctuates the hours

night retreats into day

the old maker wakes and laughs at the sky
as once again the poem sings and the words
come home to meet the page

Part Four
The Artist

Portrait by Lautir

http://stores.ebay.com/LAUTIRS-ART-AND-PAINTINGS-A-GO-GO

LINDA KING

Loving and Hating Bukowski

(Excerpt from Chapter 6)

When I arrived at his house, he was drawing. It looked as if he had picked up some the beer cans.

"One of these drawings will be an added bonus with each hardback of my new book, *Post Office*."

I looked through a stack of paintings done with bright oil sticks. "These are great. You're so good with color."

"John Martin took a chance on me and got me out of the post office. It was killing me. I owe him."

I couldn't imagine him working in the post office. It didn't fit his image. I was fascinated by how he painted so fast, making bold strokes. The pictures were alive with color.

"I can sculpture, but color is hard for me."

"Tell me about yourself."

"I'm divorced. I've got two kids. I'm not working. My father left me a little money, and I'm living on that right now."

"Tell me about the madwoman in your poem."

"I spent a couple of weeks in the madhouse. I've been writing a book about it. The novel is called *Mad Ouija*. It started on the Ouija board."

We began telling stories about our pasts. The night seemed to fall like a soft mist around us. He drew more pictures and he asked more and more questions. He seemed to have no fear or unusual reactions, as most people did, to my having been considered insane.

"There was a voice that came through me," I said. "I called it the voice of God, but they locked me up and shocked the byebeejesus hell out of me."

"Show me, I want to hear this voice."

"No, I don't think you want to hear it." I laughed. "My family was very happy to have me shut it up. I'd have shut up, too, if they beat me with clubs. Of course nobody else thought it was God at all."

"And what do you think now?"

"I don't know. It was part me, my voice that I hadn't claimed. I still like to think sometimes it was the voice of God. I could never explain, even to myself. I saw a light I saw coming down three different times."

"Let me hear the voice."

I agreed to try. I reached back into myself and the same deep booming voice, which had been quiet since my breakdown, came out quite suddenly.

"CHARLES BUKOWSKI, YOU WILL STOP THIS FOOLISH DRINKING AND GET ON WITH YOUR WORK!"

I was embarrassed. I hadn't expected that. I told him I didn't really know what the voice was going to say in advance, like my own voice. I had put that voice away after shock treatment, years ago, and it caused no small alarm that it had come back so easily.

"I think I've had too much to drink. I'm going home," I said.

He calmed me by describing a vision he had when he was young and alone in San Francisco sleeping on a park bench.

"I looked up and two angels were above me talking. One angel said, 'He has so much talent.' The other one said, 'But look how frightened he is.' Then they disappeared."

On this visit, he didn't come on to me. He just kept painting and seemed careful not to scare me away. When I left and drove through Griffith Park back to Burbank, the sun was coming up over the mountains. Only then did I realize that we'd talked all night, time had gone by so fast.

Originally published in
Loving and Hating Bukowski
(Kiss Kill Press, 2012)

ABEL DEBRITTO

Atomic Scribblings from a Maniac Age:
the Artwork of Charles Bukowski

By 1966, Charles Bukowski's work was featured in so many little magazines that he was soon to be hailed as a "spiritual leader" of the so-called mimeograph revolution that was taking place across the United States. His poetry was unabashedly promoted in hundreds of alternative periodicals, which eventually earned him the indisputable honor of being the most published author of the decade. Shortly before the "mimeo" revolution reached its peak, Bukowski began to work on an unusual project titled *Atomic Scribblings from a Maniac Age*. While Bukowski had illustrated some of his previous publications, such as *Longshot Pomes for Broke Players*, *Atomic Scribblings* was to be the first book where his artwork would be predominantly showcased, with a few interspersed poems, thus turning the volume into a *rara avis* in the Bukowski canon.

However, despite Bukowski's intense, passionate involvement in the project, it was finally aborted when the publisher, Wayne Philpot, vanished with Bukowski's drawings in 1966. Philpot, who had printed Bukowski's poetry in his little magazine *Border* in January 1965, was probably stunned by the quality of the drawings and doodles Bukowski selflessly decorated his lengthy letters with. Philpot requested Bukowski several drawings and, one of them, titled "Sunday Afternoon In Heaven," graced the front cover of *Border* #2 in April 1965. Bukowski's illustrations had such a vivid impact on Philpot that in April of that year he prompted Bukowski to tackle the book of drawings and poems: "I have a proposition that may...or may not...interest you...Border Press...would like to bring out a limited edition of Buk's drawings (black & white) with only a few poems along w/them (4 or 5)." Bukowski gladly complied by sending dozens of drawings to Philpot during the ensuing months.

Bukowski was corresponding with several authors and editors at the time, and he discussed the ongoing project with them. As he confided to Canadian poet Al Purdy in June 1965, he had already begun "a book of poems and drawings, mostly drawings, untitled and undone so far, but that I will work up in a couple of months for Border Press." Bukowski so enthused about the notion of having his drawings published in book form that he even showed them to Henry Miller in August 1965. Two months later, he declared to Purdy that he was still working on *Atomic Scribblings*. In another undated letter from Philpot to Bukowski, probably from late 1965, he listed the fifteen drawings he had accepted so far for the book: "Easel of a Fanatic with Indigestion," "The Death of Karl Marx," and "Portrait of a Dog Elected to a Senatorial Seat" were the titles of some of the drawings to be published in *Atomic Scribblings*.

Promotional flyers, order forms and adverts were issued in late 1965. However, in a common, yet infuriating practice among small press and little magazine editors, the project came to nothing without a single explanatory note. Bukowski, who had undergone similar experiences, such as a joint William Corrington/Charles Bukowski chapbook cancelled halfway by Marcus Smith in 1962, suspected that Philpot's artistic enterprise would not be completed, and he remarked as much to Douglas Blazek in July 1966, who had advertised *Atomic Scribblings* in *Olé* earlier that year: "Please do not run any more ads...this guy does not respond to inquiry and evidently isn't going to publish the thing, yet he's hooking all the $3.50's [retail price] that come in and make me look like a crook." Almost six months later, in November 1966, Bukowski confirmed his suspicions to Marvin Malone, and in November 1967 he summed up the episode to Allen De Loach, editor of *Intrepid*, where his work would appear in several issues in the late 60s and early 70s: "I sat up night and day for 3 weeks, drunk, naked, laughing to myself, awakening in the morning...covered with India ink...I gave him a title...*Atomic Scribblings Upon a Farting World* and mailed the batch to him. I saw ads for the book here and there. I wrote Wayne. No response." For some unfathomable reason, Bukowski concluded, Philpot burned all the drawings.

However, not all those sketches were destroyed because eleven of them eventually surfaced in 1971 in the second issue of *Harrison Street Review*, a little magazine edited by John Arnoldy and Lawrence Alton. According to both editors, the drawings were "part of a series in the fifties that were to have been published under the title *Photo of a Dogs Heart*. Drawings lent by Wayne Philpot." Inaccuracies and change of title notwithstanding, in June 1971 Bukowski confirmed to Arnoldy that Philpot had disappeared with his illustrations without further notice: "On Philpot the story is sad...he dropped out of contact after I'd drawn him up 2 or 3 hundred drawings." When asked about Philpot and his lending the drawings to the magazine, Arnoldy's reply did not cast light on a rather unusual chain of events: "He said his name was Wayne Philpot and he had a cache of drawings by Charles Bukowski that he wanted to donate to *Harrison Street Review*. We thanked him...we never saw him again or learned how he had come into possession of the drawings." At any rate, even if two or three hundred illustrations had been destroyed or lost, Bukowski was elated to see them in print. Bukowski had always believed that his drawings and Thurberesque doodles were as valid an art form as any, and the fact that he attended art classes in late 1956 and early 1957 at Los Angeles City College corroborates his passion for painting. Despite the five-year delay, it is undeniable that Bukowski was delighted to learn that some of the *Atomic Scribblings* drawings had been finally made available to the public.

Fig. 1. "Elevator," one of the many drawings intended for *Atomic Scribblings from a Maniac Age*, eventually published in *Harrison Street Review* in 1971.

Editors and publishers alike acknowledged Bukowski's art by printing his drawings in their publications. As early as 1946-47, Whit Burnett, the legendary editor of the prestigious *Story* magazine, urged him on several occasions to submit more sketches for consideration. In April 1947, Bukowski explained to Burnett that he did not have "any other pen sketches, without stories, right now. *Matrix* took the only one

I did that way." Indeed, *Matrix* had reproduced a somewhat uncommon Bukowski drawing to illustrate his short-story "The Reason Behind Reason," published in the summer of 1946 issue. Even though Burnett did not recall having published him in *Story*, much to Bukowski's chagrin, he was especially fond of his sketches, and in March 1952 he mentioned them in glowing terms: "It was pleasant to hear from you again, and particularly to see your wonderful drawings." Since all the short stories from the mid to late 40s were hand-printed, Bukowski illustrated them lavishly in order to highlight them, as he noted in 1953 to Caresse Crosby, *Portfolio* editor. While he claimed that he had destroyed all the rejected short stories from that period, he occasionally requested some of them to be returned since he was prouder of the drawings than of the stories themselves. In November 1948, he asked Burnett to send back the short-story "A Kind, Understanding Face" because the drawings "came out especially well."

Bukowski's letters were embellished with drawings as well, and the center sections and front covers of the Black Sparrow Press volumes of selected correspondence evidence their relevance. In some singular cases, as in a 1946 letter to Crosby, the illustrations became stories in themselves, where Bukowski used words as mere captions. It was an art form that he successfully cultivated in the 1970s, when he conceived several cartoon strips for underground newspapers. The drawings from the 1946 letter to Crosby bear a striking resemblance to the comic strips featured in *Los Angeles Free Press* almost three decades later. Cartoons had always been yet another outlet for Bukowski's prolific output, and not only in letter form. He submitted a group of them to a mainstream magazine in the mid-to-late-1950s, most probably when he was taking art classes at Los Angeles City College with Fry. As he explained to William Corrington in an unpublished April 1962 letter:

> Fry once egged me on to make a bunch of cartoons with captions, the joke bit, and I stayed up all night, drinking and making these cartoons, laughing at my own madness …I mailed [them] to either the *New Yorker* or *Esquire*…I wrote about my 45 cartoons and they never came back. 'No such item rec. from you,' wrote back some editor… [Then] I came across one of my largest no-caption drawings (I mean, the idea of it, it was not my drawing) upon the front cover of the *New Yorker*, then, I knew I'd had it.

Years later, when he was feverishly corresponding with Sheri Martinelli in the very early sixties, she published his first cartoon strip ever in the *Anagogic & Paideumic Review* #6 (Sept. 1961). The untitled series was made up of nine drawings with relatively long, humorous captions, the last of which showed Ezra Pound and Aldous Huxley embroiled in a heated discussion.

Critics realized that editors appreciated Bukowski's art since they regularly published his drawings and doodles in their magazines and chapbooks. As early as 1970, bibliographer Sanford Dorbin remarked that Bukowski's *Poems and Drawings* "included three of his drawings. Since then a number of his books as well as some of his newspaper and magazine appearances have featured his own art work." Indeed, besides the unusual illustration printed in *Matrix* in 1946 and the cartoon strip reproduced in the *Anagogic & Paideumic Review* in 1961, Bukowski's drawings appeared on the front cover and throughout his second chapbook, *Longshot Pomes for Broke Players* (1961), in *It Catches My Heart in Its Hands* (1963), where they illustrated poems such as "Old Man, Dead in a Room" or "The Tragedy of the Leaves," on the front cover of *Border* #2 (1965), in several *Open City* issues (1967-69), including a captionless cartoon titled "The Horseplayer" (1967), and in the first issue of *Open City*'s literary insert, *Renaissance* (1968), featuring a series of illustrations dedicated to his daughter Marina.

His artwork was similarly showcased in underground newspapers, little magazines and small press publications in the ensuing decades. The most remarkable case was *Los Angeles Free Press*, where his fiction and poetry were championed in over 200 issues, most of them displaying his illustrations as well as several comic strips titled "The Adventures of Clarence Hiram Sweetmeat" that Black Sparrow Press and Paget Press subsequently issued as *Dear Mr. Bukowski* (1979) and *The Day It Snowed in L.A.* (1986). Bukowski seemed to effortlessly produce so many "Clarence Hiram" cartoons that in the early 1980s, when he was no longer contributing to the *Los Angeles Free Press*, he suggested to the *High Times* editors, who were publishing Bukowski's short-stories on a monthly basis, that he could revive those cartoons for their magazine, but the project never crystallized. The "littles," however, did promote his art, which appeared in the main pages of literally hundreds of issues and even on the front cover of alternative publications such as *The Sunset Palms Hotel* (1974), *The Moment* (1990) or the *New Censorship* (1991), to name a few.

Likewise, booksellers used Bukowski's drawings to illustrate their catalogues, hence increasing their value. Jeffrey Weinberg recalls that Bukowski was "cooperative, friendly and humble" and selflessly sent him a poem and several drawings for *Under the Influence*, a Bukowski-only catalogue released in 1984. Three years later, in spite of the success brought about by the movie *Barfly*, Bukowski was generous enough to give away his artwork to Nick Drumbolis, a bookseller in Canada: "I decided to produce a list of my Bukowski holdings for collectors, inviting Hank to contribute a cover drawing. He doodled up four submissions—of which I used two." Editors and publishers alike valued Bukowski's art throughout his career by printing his unmistakable drawings and doodles or, as in the case of Black Sparrow Press or Loujon Press, by selling limited editions of his books with unique paintings that turned them into highly priced collectibles over time.

Fig. 2. One of the drawings that Drumbolis used in his Bukowski-only catalog in 1987.

Indeed, John Martin, Bukowski's longtime publisher and editor at Black Sparrow Press, realized from the very onset of their "unholy alliance" that Bukowski's art was financially profitable: ninety original drawings by Bukowski were tipped-in in the limited edition of their first lengthy literary venture, *At Terror Street and Agony Way* (1968), which was soon to become a much coveted possession by collectors. Shortly before *The Days Run Away Like Wild Horses Over the Hills* was released in late 1969, Martin asked Bukowski to produce fifty illustrations for the signed, numbered edition, hardbound in boards, of the first comprehensive bibliography of his work, *A Bibliography of Charles Bukowski* (1969). Although painting was apparently the easiest art form for Bukowski, as recounted in the short story "East Hollywood: The New Paris," he occasionally complained about the fact that Martin commissioned him dozens of illustrations for each new book, as if they were strictly compulsory. Moreover, he was acutely aware of Martin's ulterior motives: "I threw 30 paintings in the garbage and Martin just about killed me...He claims I threw away 2 or 3 grand. Now, Sanford, you know I didn't throw away 2 or 3 grand, I threw away some paintings that didn't look good to me," he explained to his bibliographer in April 1970—the next day he sent a similar letter to poet and friend Harold Norse, mocking Martin's financial concerns. Even though Martin's businesslike vision of his art, where paintings equated with easy money, seemed to disappoint Bukowski, he continued to duly create hundreds of illustrations and drawings for Black Sparrow Press up until his death in 1994. Painting was, ultimately, a compulsion tantamount to writing, a most incurable disease he adamantly refused to fight against.

A similar version of this essay first appeared in
Fine Books & Collections,
February 2011

Part Five
Collecting

ROSS RUNFOLA

cleaned out

I live in respectable chaos in my house.
the respectable chaos has grown to be my best friend,
after my collection of Charles Bukowski.

women come and go in the house but the chaos and Bukowski
are as dependable as the sun coming up every morning
until Mary moves in and decides to tame the wild beast in me and my
house.

Mary's first project is scrubbing, disinfecting and lobotomizing
the bathroom until I am reluctant to puncture the pristine
look of the newly created bathroom-museum
by using a toilet.

the kitchen is soon fit for everything but eating since Mary constantly
complains
that I am prone to leave peanut butter prints and a beer
bottle or six in the kitchen.
I now retreat to my office to eat and drink alone.

I draw the line when Mary preaches my Bukowski room
is a waste of space and my Bukowski books are a
waste of money better spent on a new roof.

I reluctantly agree on a new roof and picking up after myself
to keep what's left of the uncomfortable peace between us.

when it rains, the new roof leaks, causing the ceilings to collapse.
the first room I run into is not the bedroom to check on Mary's safety
but the Bukowski room to check on my true love, my Bukowski
collection.

Mary, being a clean house lover and not a lover of Bukowski, is
inflamed when I clumsily say:
"The Bukowski collection is the most important thing in my life."

Mary starts screaming, "What about me! What about me! All you do is
read Bukowski, collect Bukowski and write vulgar poetry like
Bukowski.

I've had it. It's either me or Bukowski. Make your choice."

I do not hesitate a millisecond.
Bukowski is better company and is not demanding like Mary.
And Bukowski never lectures me
about the secret of loading the dishwasher properly.
        I choose life.

        I choose Bukowski.

HENRY DENANDER

a record and a letter

It was 1982 and I was sitting in my office
trying to balance the books of the company
I worked for.

They call
me from the record store: "Hey,
your Bukowski record has arrived!"

I had forgotten about this, ordered
the record over a year ago.

I picked it up; the store was in the centre
of Stockholm. The record looked really good
Bukowski wearing his jacket the wrong way.
On Takoma.

(Two years later when I was working for
this big Swedish Record company
distributing the Takoma label I could say: "Hmm,
Takoma, I know about them, they
have some good stuff…")

From the record store I drove the small car
to my flat on the south side of town. Over the bridges.
Cold but no snow on the streets.
Always rain.

When I opened the door
with the Buk record in my hand
there was this letter on
the floor, sender Bukowski, San Pedro.

I remember
I wrote Buk after reading
Factotum, six months ago.

Bukowski wrote that he was happy that
his books worked for me.

These things
made me
feel honored in some
strange way.

Originally published in *Chiron Review* (2000)

HENRY DENANDER

Charles Bukowski Never Came to Sweden

Some time in the spring of 2000, I bought a signed copy of Charles Bukowski's *Post Office* on eBay.

I had been reading Charles Bukowski since 1978 and after a few years I had started to collect the beautiful hardcover first editions from Black Sparrow Press. I usually bought the signed deluxe editions, which included a Bukowski print, and I bought my books directly from Black Sparrow Press in California.

I didn't have a good copy of *Post Office,* and therefore I bid for the signed hardcover copy on eBay. Maybe I was rushed or just too eager, but if I'd read the description carefully I would've noticed that it wasn't a first edition. And when I received the book there was not just the Bukowski signature there but a long dedication as well. This was not mentioned on eBay but I kept the book anyway, there were two small drawings by Bukowski, and since I lived in Sweden I liked the inscription:

"To Ben Pleasants, see you in Sweden in 1980. Then we'll wait for 1984. Charles Bukowski."

I found out Pleasants was a writer and I got hold of one of his poetry books from a secondhand book dealer. It was *Airmail From Oblivion*, written in 1975, with a foreword by Steve Richmond. The book I bought was signed by Ben Pleasants and inscribed to some neighbors.

I managed to get in contact with Pleasants through the publisher Al Berlinski, who apparently was going to publish a book by him. I emailed Pleasants and asked him about the Charles Bukowski inscription in *Post Office* and I also asked him the story of the actual book and how it could have ended up here with me, had he sold it or had it been stolen?

In September Ben Pleasants replied. He was really surprised I had that book, although he didn't comment on how he'd lost it. He wrote that he'd fallen in love with a Swedish girl when he had visited Sweden and that's what Buk had joked about. Ben Pleasants wrote that he had sent me "a book of poetry published in the seventies that deals with a beautiful woman I met and fell in love with in Sweden. That's why Bukowski wrote what he wrote about Sweden, though he did make fun of winning the Nobel Prize."

A week later, I received the book from Pleasants, which turned out to be the same *Airmail From Oblivion* that I had bought earlier. But this one had a nice long inscription to me, with details about the two poems that described his love affair here in Sweden and the real name of the woman mentioned in the poems.

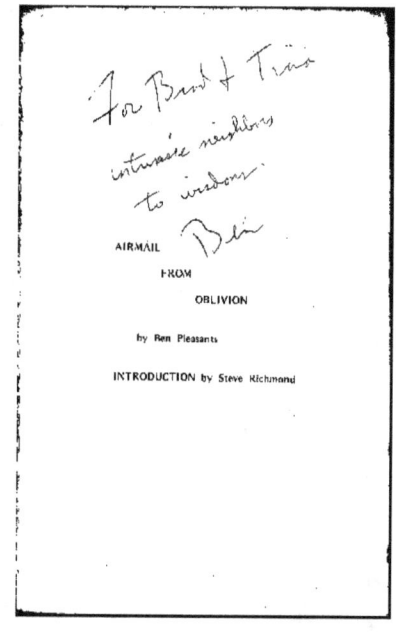

The inscription ended "Thanks for your letter from Stockholm. Hope to see you some day in Sweden."

I had just read *Bukowski in Pictures* by Howard Sounes with photos of Bukowski's Carlton Way neighbors Brad & Tina and I realized that Tina must be the girl called Gina in Jim Christy's infamous *The Buk Book*. The book included a lot of nude photos of her, in some of them she was sitting naked in Bukowski's knee, him looking overjoyed.

And when I had a look again at the inscription in the first Ben Pleasants book I bought, I realized it said "For Brad & Tina, intensive neighbors. To wisdom Ben."

I wrote Ben about this and he replied in November:

"Yes, that is amazing! I never lived on Carlton Way, but I was doing my taped interviews of Bukowski at that time and we both worked at the *Free Press*. I did know his two neighbors and yes the pictures are of Tina. Thanks again for the revelations."

I like coincidences and, who knows, maybe this is just the beginning of the story.

Originally published in *Beat Scene* (2010)

HENRY DENANDER

The SASE

On eBay I bought a self-addressed and
stamped envelope that the poet Charles Bukowski
sent to *Chiron Review* in the 80s.

This is the system, you send poems to a
magazine or a publisher and if they like them
they will use the SASE to reply to you.

More likely they will not use your poems and
return them in the SASE with a brief standard note
telling so.

Many poets have written about how they received
their first rejection letter or how they have their
drawers full of rejection slips.

Even Bukowski got rejection slips. In the early days.

I have framed the Bukowski envelope and
it looks nice on my wall.

It's a nice conversation piece; when someone asks
about it I tell them the story of how it works and also,
sort of by the way,
I tell them that *Chiron Review* is
actually the magazine where I had my
first poem published.

And I don't mention any of my
rejection letters.

Originally published in *Chiron Review* (2002)

D.A. PRATT

Encountering Bukowski—Some Canadian Notes

In *The World of Sex*, Henry Miller divided his readers into two groups, based on what he thought they preferred about his writing. With a somewhat different schema in mind, I believe that Charles Bukowski's readers can also be divided into two groups. The first would include those who have experienced him directly, either personally or through his writing as it appeared regularly while he was still alive and actively creating it. The second includes the rest of us. I'm in the latter group since I first encountered Bukowski much later than I would have liked.

While mulling over this thought recently, I realized why I came to encounter Bukowski as late as I did—I live in Regina, Saskatchewan, Canada, which is far, far away from the world of Bukowski in so many ways. In the era of the Internet and hand-held devices that are increasingly ubiquitous, this may sound strange. However, years ago and for far too many years, Regina did not have a bookstore that was imaginative enough to stock Bukowski's books. I'm sure I would have been attracted instantly to the Black Sparrow Press editions of his writing had they been there—I can say this because this is exactly what happened when I finally saw one. The lack of clues from the shelves of bookstores also meant that I failed to see any of Bukowski's books at the Regina Public Library (they are there now, of course).

Regina now has Canada's version of a "big book store" and it routinely stocks various Ecco Press editions of Bukowski's books, simply as a matter of "the business of selling books." A City Lights edition also appears from time to time. Frankly, twenty-first century book-buying readers in communities like mine now have a much better chance of encountering Bukowski than I did when I was younger—and "enquiring minds" can also access the Internet too, to learn something more about both him and his writing. Nevertheless, twenty-first century access to Bukowski's works is not what it was for those who encountered him more directly, when he was appearing in "small press" publications that were not readily available to many readers.

⌘

My own first encounter with Bukowski is amusingly unique (yes, I'm going to use the word 'unique'). In November 1994, Buzzword Books opened on 13th Avenue in Regina, not far from where I was working at the time. This small bookstore (its space was not much bigger than my dining room) was eclectic, to use the word, since the proprietor took the general approach of stocking books that he wanted to sell, which was refreshingly different than the "books as product" approach.

One day, I saw two books on the shelves of Buzzword Books, virtually side by side, with the same title—naturally, this oddity jumped out at me! One was a fairly large hardcover from Columbia University Press, while the other was a paperback that had a more interesting "feel" to it—the latter was a copy of the Black Sparrow Press paperback edition of *Women* and anyone familiar with the BSP will immediately understand this comment. The hardcover was a translation of the novel by Philippe Sollers originally entitled *Femmes*. I ended up buying and enjoying both books but I opted to purchase the Bukowski book first. Amazingly, in spite of being a reader and avid book-buyer since the later 1960s, when reading D.H. Lawrence's *Lady Chatterley's Lover* "changed everything" for me, this was indeed my first encounter with Charles Bukowski's writing.

I now have a fairly extensive Bukowski collection and it is has a prominent place in my accumulation of books: his poetry, his prose (novels and his shorter prose efforts), his letters and various biographies, as well as a multitude of memoirs by those who have chosen to write them. I turn to his writing with some regularity, although "his stuff" has to compete with what is in the rest of my personal library.

⌘

My introduction to Bukowski's life was also amusingly unique, if I may be so bold to say. When one thinks about it, we meet people through a random series of vignettes, usually through what they choose to tell us about themselves in conversation, and not via a straight-line narrative going from birth to death. With this in mind, I opted to read my first Bukowski biography by starting at one point in time (I chose the chapters describing the period during which he wrote *Women*) and then drawing lots to determine the reading order for the other chapters. Frankly, I was fortunate in choosing *Locked in the Arms of a Crazy Life* by Howard Sounes to do this—few biographies are written in a way that will allow this approach. I have since read other Bukowski biographies but the Sounes biography remains one of my favourite books.

⌘

I've recently begun reading Bukowski's "selected letters", as edited by Seamus Cooney in three volumes published by Black Sparrow Press (by the way, I miss the BSP). Early in the first volume, I was reminded that Bukowski indeed had a "Canadian connection", in case anyone is actually wondering. Parenthetically, he did a reading in Vancouver, British Columbia a long time ago but that fleeting moment in time isn't it. Here is how Bukowski introduced this "Canadian connection" in 1964, within a letter to Douglas Blazek:

> "[…] the best living poet I know of is Al Purdy, 185 Wellington St., Belleville, Ontario, Canada. You might [write him] and tell him of *Ole*, hide nothing, tell him it's only mimeo but talk a little bit about what you think (my suggestion) & ask him if he might send something rejected dejected or otherwise. It will be good. whatever it is. I have read his collection *Poems for All the Annettes* and I turned the pages one by one reading in a state of pisspoorpissgreatstun within myself at what he was doing. he writes like chopping down trees; he writes about those bees that are stinging the inside of his head. he lays the words down as if they were real instead of angelcake."

The language in this partial quotation demonstrates that Bukowski's letters, clearly written without any sort of publication in mind, represent a pleasure worth pursuing. Al Purdy wrote a favorable review of *It Catches My Heart in Its Hands* and forwarded a copy to Bukowski. His letters suggest that the publication of this book in 1963 was an emotional high point for Bukowski and I can imagine that receiving Purdy's review would have added to the overall experience of seeing this book come into being. The two writers began an extended correspondence, which was ultimately published by Paget Press in 1983—the book is one of the uncommon items in Bukowski's bibliography. Sadly, they did not meet face-to-face and they ultimately quarreled over Purdy's inclusion of Bukowski's letters to him in a sale of his papers.

After Bukowski's death, Al Purdy wrote a poem entitled "Lament for Bukowski." In case readers have not seen it, here is the first stanza:

It isn't only the Great Bards
who "perne in a gyre"
believe in "the dark gods"
and court the Muse
wearing condoms:
it's also a guy
in his undershirt scoffing

a hot dog and 6-pack
in a crummy LA bedroom
betting a $350 horse
losing on a hundred dollar whore
and watching "the golden men
who push the buttons
of our burning universe"
and writing it all down

⌘

In 2013, we are approaching the twentieth anniversary of the death of Charles Bukowski. As the twenty-first century progresses, Bukowski's readership is going to enter into a period of renewal. The oldest generation of his readers will give way to a new generation who will not experience what I have called "direct contact" with the man—the new generation will not have met him, drunk beer with him or read any of his best-known publications as they were being published. Bukowski's new readers will "meet" him in ways that will be completely different than the ways his earliest readers encountered him.

I have written elsewhere about the effort to which I went to give a book of Bukowski's poetry to a young woman in Regina—rather than pick up an Ecco Press edition at Regina's "big book store", I opted to order an old copy of the Black Sparrow Press edition of *Love Is a Dog from Hell: Poems 1974-1977*. (By the way, not surprisingly, Regina's used bookstores rarely see older Bukowski books—therefore I had to go online.) I wanted her to experience the feel of reading Bukowski in this way. This reflects my on-going concern about how new readers will first encounter Bukowski, since I believe that there is now a wrong way to enter his myriad of writing—wrong because it would be unfair both to the new reader and to the writer himself. More on this in a moment.

Bukowski's work can be sub-divided into poetry and prose. I first "met" Bukowski as a prose writer but I suspect most of my North American contemporaries probably first "met" him as a poet. While obviously different, both types of "first encounter" are perfectly fine. However, there is a different way to subdivide Bukowski's writing: by fairly distinct periods and one of the periods, in my eyes, is actually the wrong place to start reading Bukowski.

Frankly, I believe that it is not difficult to see four periods in Bukowski's writing. In the proverbial nutshell, they are: first, his earliest period, which includes his work and publications prior to the end of the

1960s (most of these publications are getting both hard to find and expensive); second, the period of his prime, in my opinion, which includes his work in the 1970s; third, the period from 1981 until his death; and, finally, the period of his posthumous publications, the list of which seems far more extensive for Bukowski than most other writers.

In my eyes, new readers ought not encounter Bukowski for the first time through any of the posthumous collections of his poetry. While these books are not devoid of "interesting stuff," they are not the best way to start reading the man's poems. I've dutifully purchased each one of them for my collection but, frankly, I find them dryly presented—in complete contrast to two posthumous volumes of prose that David Stephen Calonne has edited for City Lights. The Ecco Press editions of the books of poetry from the second and third periods I've identified would be completely appropriate, of course, and the Ecco Press editions of his novels would work just as well too, as would the City Lights editions of his writing. However, it strikes me that much of Bukowski's early work, as it first appeared, is now virtually out of reach for new readers—have you checked the online prices for some of his earliest books lately? In addition, not all of his early work has been reprinted—for example, here's a question: how would a new reader manage to read all the poems in *It Catches My Heart in Its Hands*, let alone experience the "feel" of the original book from 1963?

As the twenty-first century progresses, I do wonder who will "encounter" Bukowski and adopt him as a "favourite poet." For many of the older generation of his most avid enthusiasts, such a thought may seem strange—but we're in a different world now, one increasingly dominated by what comes into people's lives via handheld devices. I think it is unclear what part poetry is going to play in this different world, especially as Bukowski wrote it. A changed world is indeed upon us and I, for one, hope that Bukowski's writing remains a part of it.

INTERMISSION
GREEK CHORUS

HEADS No. 4—C. Bukowski
by Christopher R. Adams
www.corvidopolis.com

MICHAEL LIMNIOS

Excerpts from Interviews
Posted at Michalis Limnios BLUES @ Greece

DAVID STEPHEN CALONNE

What motto of Charles Bukowski you would like to stay forever?

Many of Charles Bukowski's aphorisms and quotations are wonderful: I don't know where to begin. But I've always liked the following from *Factotum*: "Frankly, I was horrified by life; by what a man had to do simply in order to eat, sleep and keep himself clothed. So I stayed in bed and drank. When you drank the world was still out there, but for the moment it didn't have you by the throat."

JOAN JOBE SMITH

What motto of Hank you would like to stay forever?

"The world has shaped me and I have shaped what I can."

JON MONDAY

Why did you think that Charles Bukowski continues to generate such a devoted following?

Like many of the original and unique true musicians I loved and worked with, Bukowski was a true artist, who found his voice early and matured in his work. It was very telling that the Huntington Library brought his archive and papers into their permanent exhibit of top American authors, alongside of Mark Twain, Christopher Isherwood, Jack London, etc. It would be like John Fahey being considered the likes of Beethoven, Bach, etc. Bukowski speaks to people's hearts and feelings—with no bullshit hit and a clear but dark expression of what's real.

DAN FANTE

Why did you think that Charles Bukowski continues to generate such a devoted following?

Bukowski speaks of his condition and the human condition with a genuine voice. When a good writer writes from his balls and his passion, people hear him and they listen.

GERALD LOCKLIN

What's the legacy of Bukowski nowadays? If he was between us, what do you think he would tell us?

He already told us on his tombstone: "Don't try." I guess he meant for us to let things come naturally, as they will if they are meant to. I think he also meant for us not to try to piss on his ashes—or a curse will descend upon us.

HARVEY KUBERNIK

Which memory from Charles Bukowski makes you smile? How you would spend a day with him?

Reading his regular column in the *Los Angeles Free Press*. I didn't know at the time as a teenager Charles Bukowski attended local Los Angeles High school. I did spend a long afternoon and very long evening with him with producer Denny Bruce when we did a live reading album with Bukowski that I helped release on disc. If I had another day with him, I would ask about his writing process. Did he spend a lot of time editing his poems and columns before publication?

NEELI CHERKOVSKI

Which memory from Charles Bukowski makes you smile? What advice Bukowski has given to you?

Hank met my partner Jesse, and he took me aside, whispering, "I'm so glad you met somebody. I hope you guys are staying the night." I must have gotten a sardonic view of life partially from Bukowski. He didn't mean to be a teacher, but he was. There's a twenty-five-year age split between us. I loved hearing his stories of growing up in Depression-era Los Angeles of the 1930s—a gone world. He had a terrific sense of humor, and he loved to poke fun at standard ways of thinking. There is a surface anti-intellectualism in him, but much of that was a pose. He's always say, "Get in the arena. Keep the poems coming. Don't stop." That was solid advice from someone who worked on his writing all the time he could. Sitting down at a typewriter was like going to a job at a factory as far as he was concerned, but nicer. "If you're not enjoying yourself while writing, then something is wrong," he often said.

A.D. WINANS
Which memory from Charles Bukowski makes you smile?
At a reading in San Francisco in the seventies, Bukowski thanked the crowd that was whistling and yelling for an encore. Especially loud was a young man in the back of the auditorium who kept shouting, "More. More." Bukowski flashed the young man an impish smile and asked the kid how much he had paid to get into the reading. The kid took the bait. Three dollars," the kid said. "And you're a $3 audience," Bukowski shot back, much to the delight of the crowd.

Originally published at http://blues.gr/profile/MichalisLimnios

PART SIX

SPIRITS

Portrait by Alvaro Pozo
www.alvaropozo.com

HENRY DENANDER

Hollywood (in The Hospital Library)

I had a really painful problem with a kidney
stone and was put in the intensive care at a big
hospital in Stockholm.

After two days the pain was better and the
painkillers put me in a better mood. Late at
night when I was desperate for a new book to
read I found three shelves of library books at
the far end of the corridor.

There were a lot of adventure novels, romance
books and religious stuff but at last I found
two books that were acceptable. But when I
returned to my room I realized one of them
was really a religious drama and the other one
was the basis for a film I'd seen.

Today I was moved to a department where
they specialize in problems with kidneys and
those parts of our bodily functions.

I had a cup of coffee in the day room and saw
new shelves of books. This was a different
selection, more crime stories and other good
stuff. Suddenly I see *Hollywood* by Charles
Bukowski and I see his face on the cover.

A book by Bukowski in the hospital library, I
couldn't believe it.

Perhaps it's not so strange; people who love
Bukowski also love to drink beer and
if they drink too much they will have
problems with their kidneys and
they will end up here

in this department.

This is how they thought when
they ordered this book
for the library.

I am sure.

Originally published in *Bukowski Review*

ED GALING

bukowski

the guy sittin next
to me in philly
down around tenth
and race,
in sloppy joes bar,
was downin em
one after the other.
i usually stopped
in this tenderloin
godforsaken part
of town whenever i
felt down and out;
when the fuckin
poems i was writin
came back with rejection
slips;
hell, i was only twenty
four years old, alone
and single,
and it was around 1958
when nobody had any
money to talk about,
and the only way you
could ease the pain
of livin in this world
was to drink until you
didn't feel the misery,
and sloppy joes was one
helluva place,
you know what i mean?
real dark, a small radio up
in the corner playing
some baseball game, and
all the best drunks in
the world sittin at the
bar, just gulpin it
down.
  and when i slid into
the barstool this guy

with a pockmarked face
and big nose was nursing
his drink, like it was
some kind of remedy
for what ailed him and
then he would gulp it down
real fast, like a pro
always does, and it made
me laugh a little, cause
i am the kind of drunk who
sips the booze slow,
know what i mean?
anyways, after a while
this ugly guy sneaks a
peek over at me, and
nods his head, so i
guess i am gonna say
something, and i say
howyadoin, buddy?

      he shakes his head,
and says, fuckin booze…
trying to chase the damn
world away, just got laid
off in this fuckin factory
i was workin in

      well, i said in return,
i know what you mean, i just
got laid off my own job,
that makes two of us

      fuckin job was no good
anyway, this guy says,
lookin at me with some interest,
always some goddamned boss
telling me what to do, or some
half-assed manager telling me to
work faster.

      i know what you mean, buddy,
i agree, i got the same damn
trouble, can i buy you one?
yeah, sure, he says, with a
grin, i like jack daniels with a
chaser.

      you got it, i reply, waving

to the bartender who was listenin
in, the bartender nods and grabs
the bottle, and puts the drink in
front of this guy who i just met

he picks up the drink and hoists
it towards me and smacks his lips, and
says, here's lookin at you, buddy, thanks.

the drink does down fast, and he
gives a small hiccup, and then he says
my name's Bukowski, what's yours?

i tell him my name, and we
shake.

i got a new job, he says, i
am gonna work in a post office, know
what i mean, sortin the mail, and all
that...but i don't wanta work there
too long...

good luck, i say, and wave the
bartender for another drink, and he
pours it,

and then i say, ever write poetry?
this time he looks at me and kinda
moves away from me, then he
says in a kind of harsh voice,
listen, keep away from writin
poetry, it's worse that this cheap
booze you and me are drinkin...

yeah, i do write a bit, sit up
in my room banging away on the typewriter,
sending em out to different places...
they keep comin back, the sons of bitches,
but i keep writin em

know what you mean, i say, it's
tough writin poems...

the trouble is, says this guy
bukowski, is that there are so many
poor drunks like me and you in this world,
and nobody can speak up for em...but
i am gonna keep writin em, until someone
listens...

well, i get up off the stool and
say, nice to have met you, bukowski,
you got a funny name, are you Russian?

then he replies, i am german, but
don't let that bother you one bit...
live alone and like it that way...
write my poems, sometimes get laid and
fucked, and that's what i do...and sometimes
i get my ass kicked in by other drunks...
last week i got the shit beat out of me
when i left this place...four guys beat up
on me...left me lyin there in my own piss...
but it don't bother me...
i give em back what they give me...
keep writin, he says, and someday when
you read my shit somewhere you will say
you met me in this shitass bar...remember
the name bukowski...charles bukowski...
i left this guy sitting there at the
bar when i left, and forgot all about him,
until about thirty years later, when i
picked up a book called YOU GET SO ALONE
SOMETIMES THAT IT JUST MAKES SENSE,
and the author was charles Bukowski...
this is the way it was many years
ago when i was pushin the pen, tryin to
be a poet, and met up with the best damn
poet in the whole damn world, bless his soul.

Originally published in *big hammer*

S.A. GRIFFIN

Bukowski to the Curb

it was like
falling thru a
hole

a glowing halo of
rich ruby red light
reached out to us from
the open door and
asked us in

this place was a
Miami of red vinyl and corrugated steel
full of holes like starlight
on leave from
a strange piece of 1947

the leading motif of some
hybrid punk
anxiety
working its way into the beer

"Is this place a bar?"

I decided that
stupid was the
best
way
in

the happy drunk on the end responds,
"I dunno, whaddya think?"

Rafael says,
"Cool." shrugs his shoulders
and we are both
stupid together

a square looking guy
enters behind the bar

"Got any beer?" I inquire
"I dunno, if we did have some
 beer,
 I mean, what would you want?"

"Whatever man."

he produces a couple of Buds

they are a dollar a pop and I give the guy an
extra buck
just to keep the place floating

and fuck it

outside on the street
at the
Bukowski memorial
where we had been
minutes ago
they are still
calling out

     Beeeeowwwwskiiiiiiiii
               Beeeeeooooowwwwwwwski this

  and   Beeeeeeeooooooowwwwwwsssssskiiiiii that

  and beeee ow ski
       bee owww ski
        be ow skeeeeee

they don't even know who the fuck they are talking about
but hey
that's what's going on and what in the hell
let them go on in their stum-bum tumbling dumbness

I am really starting to
feel the light here

some guys come in and get pissed off and
leave because
they didn't want their bags searched

one bartender says,
"Fuck it man,
 I don't know them and
 they don't know me."

"This is downtown fucking L.A.," says the
 second bartender,
"you don't know what in the hell they got in them bags."

more beer
this place is jukin'

soon there is a juicy fat joint going around
and we are pounding the air with smoke
and we are shaking hands and
laughing

more beers

more laughter

one of the bartenders starts to speak of
Charles Bukowski
and it is agreed that he
changed the way you see the
colored lights go
when you read the way his
poetry has
legs on it that walk you into his
best room of fear and love
and the way that the typewriter and the bottle
dance the dance

we dance the beer
and the smoke
we dance the anger and the
pitiful hatred outside
wilting under the
generous embrace of yet another earthquake

one more round and they are
closing the door

the beer tumbles down my throat
like a small brook

I think of possible heavens

as we redesign the landscape
with whatever things we know
and
catch the 3 bus into
Hollywood

this is how we
found
Bukowski

Previously published in *Numbskull, Sutra,* and *Das Ist Alles,* and *Blue Satellite*

Portrait by Jocelyne Desforges

BART PLANTENGA

CO-WRITTEN WITH BLACK SIFICHI IN PARIS
VIA OLD-FASHIONED MAIL

Contemplating Charles Bukowski

A lot of questions were rolling around in Bukowski's head as he entered the Palomino Bar & Grill. The guy next to him ordered up another Salty Dog. Bukowski got a beer. Bukowski thought maybe he'd like to kiss a woman named "Babine." A French woman'd be perfect, he figured. Dyed apricot hair, a collar around her neck. In fact, it just HAD to happen because Bukowski had recently learned the power of the will. The responsibility of Dreams!

He ordered another beer & listened to the jukebox. The new juke, he was sure, had been installed to mock him & maybe force him to find a new hole to get soused in. The songs were just too happy—like Valentines from a planet he'd never been to. The gold brocade, the sombreros & lacquered maracas were meant to attract a new clientele. A clientele bereft of soul who needed dining dioramas like some needed dialysis machines.

The situation: It was sadder than a glass of flat beer. It was sadder than an unworn hat. It was sadder than a NO SMOKING section. It was sadder than a dog tied up in a hot sun. It was sadder than burying his mother. It was sadder than no money. It was sadder than rejection. It was sadder than the cardboard I'M HUNGRY signs. Charles, with lights flashing in his eyes, was alone again. No kiss. No friends. No money.

"Fuck this," he thought. "Life's hard, but fuck this. I'm gonna get pissed tonite & then get myself kissed. Roll the dice. & read the race sheets tomorrow. Blow fifty bucks. So what if I got nothin' now. That don't mean I won't have $50 tomorrow. That don't mean 'Valentine Kiss' can't come in at 43 to 1. $50 times 43. Now that'd be OK."

Charles started to sob. It was just too much. These speeches he made to himself in order to fortify some fledgling spirit were getting thinner & thinner. Face it. Even dogs were ignoring him because he smelled of nothing good. He didn't even smell like a different dog. He smelled of dust, of dead pollen, of washed-out cigarette butts. He smelled like a finished fire. Like nothing to even piss on. He smelled invisible, absolutely invisible.

He seemed to have so many problems. "Life creates you, steps on your face & then spits you out. What else is there?" Bukowski asked himself.

He walked along in a dream. In history. Not a history that he invented or had ever commanded. A history that just happened. The giant kiss had all but affixed itself to his pickled brain. He thought being a good kisser might eventually open doors into sumptuous homes, better restaurants, drinks in fancy bars. Be a Playboy. But what was he gonna do? He really didn't have a clue. Later he got some work filling a truck. For money. He thought they'd agreed on $50. He got $35.

The wad of dough lay thick inside his becrusted slacks. $1000 bucks could certainly sing his tune. But what tune? He rode a taxi back from the Santa Monica Track with a big smokestack Havana stogie puffing from his kisser. He imagined this was Howard Hughes must've felt in the early days. & Bukowski imagined his first museum: THE CHARLES BUKOWSKI BEER MUSEUM. In Hollywood he bought a silver tie clip with a thorough-bred on it. A thousand bucks just because you entrust your money—all of it—to a horse that darts around some hardcake track. The absurdity of betting, however, didn't in the slightest dent his sense of triumph.

Originally performed at Finnegan's Wake in Paris, France, and published by *Massacre* (London 1993), Beet (New York, 1995), *Light Trauma* (New Jersey, 1996), and *In Other Words: Merida* (Online, Mexico, 2012).

JEFFREY GRAESSLEY

A Life-Long Lover

Charles Bukowski discovered drinking
in his childhood days; a love he never
let falter, cooing bottles through evenings
watched, where another stalking leopard
walked, and only the old love remained
to rest his head upon, like an altar
he brought himself to pray at, while the flames
of Los Angeles scorched the water
dry. he threw punches in bar back alleys
for entertainment, got his ass handed
to him often. countless scars like valleys
from pulled steel up his arms, disenchanted
 with the world from the start, he gave his pain
 to words, line breaks, and the wine in his veins

SHERIL ANTONIO

Barfly

"You have to die a few times before you can really live."

Charles Bukowski[1]

I will be looking closely at the film *Barfly*[2] (directed by Barbet Schroeder) to discover its screenwriter Charles Bukowski. This analysis is an opportunity to attempt to unravel his way of seeing the world. I begin knowing only that Bukowski was a poet and writer and that this story is semi-autobiographical. Having just completed a fourteen-week semester encouraging two hundred and fifty students to understand, among many other things, how to discover an artist's way of seeing via close examination of his/her work, I must now commit myself to that same task. To visualize this process in class I use a clip from Akira Kurosawa's film *Dreams* 1990[3] that tackles a similar idea in a section entitled "Crows," which is about a literal and figurative journey through Vincent Van Gogh's body of work.

I also use quotes to help students understand my thinking about a topic and the one that appeals to me here is from E. L. Doctorow:

> Fiction is a mega-discipline that employs reportage, confession, history, myth, legend, superstition, science, religion, philosophy and the intuitive knowledge that resides in the combination of words. It excludes no data; everything is acceptable and equally appropriate, from the laws of physics to the mutterings of poor and mad people in the street.[4]

The idea is to answer the question: how can we gain insight into an artist's world? Below is the gist of how I envision and render the process. The spectator looks at art to discover the artist to find out something about how that artist sees and experiences the world.

Spectator – looks at →ART – to find the → Artist – to see how he/she sees → THE WORLD

Henry Chinaski (Mickey Rourke) is our main character and first impressions tell me he is not anchored in a reality I know or understand.

He is an outsider and much like Van Gogh seems to be another tortured soul. Along with my students, I too go immediately to past familiar experiences hoping to understand this character and the world he occupies or in many ways creates in this story. Thus, The Golden Horn bar, the first space we enter, has an atmosphere similar to the bar in Eugene O'Neill's play *The Iceman Cometh*.[5] Meeting and getting familiar with Henry in the first few scenes, I can imagine him an ancestor of the main character in the popular film *Fight Club* 1999.[6] Henry, like The Narrator (Edward Norton) in *Fight Club*, is obviously not enticed by "normal" life or its trappings and appears to be self-destructive. As we drill deeper into *Barfly's* story, it becomes clear that Henry has self-selected to be an outsider. The question then is why?

The film opens with a gritty nighttime tour of a selection of bars somewhere in the seedier part of Los Angeles, California. We enter one establishment, The Golden Horn, with a deliberate camera moving downwards from a section of its neon sign that reminds me of the opening in *Citizen Kane* 1941.[7] Like the upward movement in *Kane*, we are headed somewhere: inside a room, inside a world, and inside a man's life. Soon after entering the bar we leave immediately out a back door to meet Henry in the midst of a fight with Eddie (Frank Stallone). When we shift in the next scene to daytime, nothing looks better. We are offered the continuation of a mood, one I have defined as daytime noir, where the mutterings of an aged prostitute inside the bar, a passing man's stained jacket and pawnshop outside reinforce the texture of the life that adorns Henry's existence. As we follow our main character, he studies an angry barking dog in a car, taking in the creature's rage and calling what he sees—"beautiful." As we begin our relationship with Henry, another bartender offers an analysis of his life saying that—"he refuses to join the rat race, he drinks and waits." What he is waiting for, if anything, becomes a key question as we follow him through a range of options and choices.

Following Henry home to his grimy hovel with a well brewed patina of squalor and the ironic ambiance of Mozart and Mahler playing on the radio, we hear the first words of his creative life—"some people never go crazy, what truly horrible lives they must live." Watching closely, we find out about his circumstances and discover something about life in the margins. He pursues this role of other with a vengeance and when he can no longer, it seems, succeed at being what we may call self-destructive, he engages the help of his nemesis a bartender at The

Golden Horn, Eddie. Fights are clearly a refrain and metaphor in this visual narrative. We begin with a fight, the plot is punctuated with them, and we close with one. Henry eventually informs us that Eddie is the personification of his demons saying—"he symbolizes everything that disgusts me!"

Henry steals food to live, either from a fellow bar mate or unsuspecting neighbor, and refuses money even when fairly earned from a fight saying—"hey what do you think I am? A bum?" The only time we see him wash himself is when he is badly bloodied and this takes place at a leaking fire hydrant or with a bottle of alcohol. While his appearance is mostly awful throughout, we still see him comb his hair with some regularity, telling us he has not completely given up on his appearance. Henry invites these fights with Eddie either as a way of being physically, as opposed to emotionally, battered or as a means of invigoration. After one such fight he accepts a few dollars to buy drinks at a bar across the street since Eddie refuses him service at The Golden Horn.

After ordering his beer, Henry becomes intrigued with Wanda Wilcox (Faye Dunaway) when told—"she's crazy." This is of course no surprise as by now we are getting to know and strangely, understand him. The romance begins to blossom as he asks—"what do you do?" to which she responds—"I drink." After buying a few drinks Henry announces "no money, no job, back to normal" and indeed we are beginning to understand what normal is for him. Wanda invites him to her place after stopping to mooch alcohol and cigarettes from a "patron" then asks—"why is your face so beat up?" to which he asks—"you don't mind, do you?" Her response surprised me—"no, it looks beautiful." This immediately returns me to the scene where Henry looked at the angry dog saying—"beautiful" and believe it or not this fifty-three-year-old Black woman is now hearing verses from Lady Gaga's song *Bad Romance*[8] in her head:

I want your ugly
I want your disease
I want your everything
As long as it's free

I want your loving
And I want your revenge
You and me could write a bad romance
As they get settled at Wanda's place she demands—"just one thing, I

don't ever wanna fall in love." "Don't worry" he retorts—"nobody's every loved me yet" and this touches me. Finally I too am smitten, but without abandoning my repulsion for his way of life. What has shifted is that I am beginning to understand his deep psychic appreciation for life's filth and the other side of the American Dream. I am also asking myself, in what I call the "distinction versus identification" battle embedded in our attempt to identify with or distinguish from the character, what allows us "normal" folks the privilege or discipline or training to wash off our psychic filth? Wanda's walls are almost as dirty as his but she has a semblance of what some of us call home, even hints of decor but still in the grimy impoverished style of the film.

After trying to eat stolen corn that is too green, Wanda gets frustrated saying—"nothing ever works right in this life." It is here that we begin to see the difference between the two characters, she is still trying and he for the most part has given up on the things so many of us pursue every day. Since Wanda has now lost her patron, Henry does something unexpected, he tries to get a job to care for her. Through this act we witness his desire for attachment and continue to discover more and more about Henry as he quotes Tolstoy, goes to the aid of an abused woman and almost sings this phrase every time he is asked if he hates people or cops—"no, but I feel better when they're not around." We are now beginning to notice the parts of Bukowski residing in Wanda, ergo Henry's attraction to her, particularly in her declarations like—"I'll do anything to get booze" and "we're all in some kind of hell, but in a madhouse you know it."

Stitched into this story are two "normal" looking people, consequently "outsiders" to this neighborhood and way of life. They are pursuing Henry and clearly have an interest in his writing. Their intentions elude us until we find out that he actually submitted a story for publication, which caught the attention of the owner of the magazine, Tully Sorenson (Alice Krige), who wants to meet and pay him for the piece. Plot wise, she is also there it turns out to give him a shot at what most of call the good life. Shortly after this informative exchange they drive to her home in the wealthier part of Los Angeles where she offers Henry her guesthouse to pursue his work saying—"you can write in peace there." Henry makes his intentions known by saying—"nobody who is worth a damn can write in peace." "I don't feel right here," he says—"I feel like I can't breathe." They spend some time together, drinking of course, and as expected he refuses his shot at the American Dream lamenting that "nobody suffers like the poor." Henry returns to Wanda and his familiar way of life with his earnings but Tully returns once again to try to claim his genius. Wanda ignites a physical fight with her over Henry and just before leaving the bar, the defeated Tully realizes something important and says to Henry—"I know you need this, good luck."

As noted before fights are important in this film, representing the visualization of Henry's struggle for survival. We leave the bar and our story backing out the same door and returning to the streets seen in the opening. It is now clear that Bukowski has created a main character whose art is not just writing, but authoring the life of an outsider. We leave *Barfly* with some understanding that both men, Bukowski and Henry, occupy the strange space of the white male other, albeit with the privilege of self-selecting to be other. We have, I believe, witnessed the life of a tortured soul, evidenced in Bukowski's own words—"If you're losing your soul and you know it, then you've still got a soul left to lose."[9]

I have never penned a poem and am not sure this counts as one but in taking notes as I watched the film over and over again and thought deeply about Charles Bukowski's characters and writing, these words stuck with me throughout and I have put them together in this way:

Ode to Buk

Living freely, freely living.
Days have the order you give them.
Time was someone else's currency.
Knowing only intellectually the protest you lived,
I admire the bravery of moments that repel me.
No anger in your words nor pain in your face,
I watched, wanting to condemn, wanting to look away.
So it's my legacy to refrain from judging you.

NOTES

1. Goodreads Quotes.
   http://www.goodreads.com/author/quotes/13275.Charles_Bukowski

2. *Barfly*, DVD, directed by Barbet Schroeder (Los Angeles, CA: Golan-Globus & Zoetrope Studios, 1987).
   http://www.imdb.com/title/tt0092618/?ref_=sr_1

3. *Dreams*, DVD, directed by Akira Kurosawa (Los Angeles, CA: Warner Bros., 1990). http://www.imdb.com/title/tt0100998/

4. ¹E.L. Doctorow, "Address to the Students of the Tisch School for the Arts, New York University, September 14, 2001" in Artistic Citizenship ed. Mary Schmidt Campbell and Randy Martin (New York: Routledge, 2006), 55.

5. Encyclopedia Britannica.
   http://www.britannica.com/EBchecked/topic/281364/The-Iceman-Cometh

6. *Fight Club*, DVD, directed by David Fincher (Los Angeles, CA: Fox 2000 Pictures, 1999).

7. *Citizen Kane*, DVD, directed by Orson Welles (Los Angeles, CA: RKO Radio Pictures 1941). http://www.imdb.com/title/tt0033467/?ref_=sr_2

8. Lady Gaga, Official Site.
   http://www.ladygaga.com/lyrics/default.aspx?tid=18497744

9. Goodreads Quotes.
   http://www.goodreads.com/author/quotes/13275.Charles_Bukowski

Raymond King Shurtz

The Great Drunken Poet

I'm standing in front
of the house on Edgewater Terrace,
high on speed,
yelling at the ghost of a poet,
watching him vomit in the front yard ivy.

The chaos is breaking out amongst
the meat puppet muses
in the house I call home—
I'm rushing towards that
gorgeous poetic image
the whole world is waiting for.

I walk in the house,
past John Bennett,
past my Aunt Linda,
past my mother,
past half the worthless
drunken word shepherds in L.A.

past the drunken actors,
past the stoned painters,
past the posers in gauze shirts,
finally past Bukowski himself,
trying to hold court from a blackout.

He lets out a howl when he sees me,
"Where ya' goin', kid?"

"Up to my room, Hank, where you going, NASA?"
He stares at me for a moment,
trying to determine if my statement is in fun or folly.
I don't give him a chance,
I'm off to my room,
and out on the roof to smoke a joint.

The gray dome of L.A. looms above my head,
I'm in seventeen-year-old angst,
cursing all poets,

cursing all writers,
cursing all sons and daughters of writers.

I yell at the smog
its blocking my way to the stars,
I yell at the moon
because it hasn't a face,
I yell at God because
he left town
after the earthquake of 1971.

I hear the voices of my Aunt Linda and mother,
laughing at the wit of the great drunken poet,
like shills charming up the great joke—
as the room burns up like a brush fire!
As the room burns up,
I hear the devil beckoning me to suicide—
I hear the great emptiness of the silver lake—
the roar of all the young souls lost on rooftops.
I smoke another joint,
now I'm beginning to hallucinate,
the voices downstairs are comical now,
the poets are all Saturday morning cartoons,
I walk down to see the show.

I go to the fridge to get a beer.
The great drunken poet greets me,
as my hand reaches for the writing fuel,
He says to me, "Have a Schlitz, kid,
just don't tell your mother I gave it to you."

I want to say, "Thank you great drunken poet, thank you
for giving me what great poets in training need!"
But I don't,
I don't say anything,
I laugh at the great drunken poet's wit,
like everyone else does,
ashamed of us all.

I go up on the roof to smoke yet another joint,

suddenly, I'm sobbing.
I'm shaking,

160

I'm frantically looking around me,
I'm looking...

I'm looking for the way down from the speed,
I'm looking for the way back to God,
the way back to my lost childhood,
the way to death,
the way through the smog,
the way to my high school graduation,
the way to satisfy this great emptiness,
the way to paradise,
the way to find some courage,

the way to find some fucking courage!

Then I'm screaming,
there is no sound in my screams
my silent scream—
I'm screaming up
seventeen,
I'm screaming up
youth,
I'm screaming up
my guts and my blood,
I'm screaming up poets.

Silence.

Sobs.
I'm sobbing up the silent screams,
I'm sobbing up great possibilities,
I'm sobbing up great thoughts
I'm sobbing up demons
I'm sobbing up God
until I am empty.

I'm looking for the way out,
I'm looking for the way in,
I'm looking for just one fucking answer,
I'm looking for the way,

far from great drunken poets.

Originally published in *Dark Party Review* (Sept. 14, 2007)

Rodger Jacobs

Bukowski and the Movie Star

It was ten o'clock on a Tuesday morning. Bukowski wrestled with a looming deadline and an insatiable thirst. The thirst had to be satisfied before the blank sheet of paper could be addressed. He loitered outside the Lock and Load Lounge on Hollywood Boulevard, drawing hard on a hand-rolled cigarette and studying the busy car wash across the street. All the pretty people, the vital and productive citizens, rushing to meaningless jobs but really rushing to the grave, making their cars pretty and shiny for their journey to Valhalla.

A brand-new 1978 Jaguar XJ6 was rolling off the belt, a handful of hard-working Mexicans giving the bright chromium and steel a once-over with chamois cloths. The new-model Jaguar was easy on the eye, as far as land yachts go, but Bukowski could never surrender his Volkswagen Beetle for a shiny new Jag. The Beetle represented the apex of German automotive technology, the one thing that Hitler got right: a car affordable enough for the average working man.

Bukowski polished off his cigarette and swiveled through the doors of the Lock and Load Lounge. He settled onto a barstool, ordered a draft beer from the surly bartender who looked like he got kicked in the teeth the minute he rolled out of bed that morning, and considered the face of the stranger occupying the stool next to him: jet-black hair, well-built, late-fifties perhaps, the hearty Midwestern good looks of a marquee idol, though the youthful gloss was fading and the trembling hand that held the martini glass was betraying something more than a mere case of nerves.

"Anyone ever tell you that you look like that movie actor?" Bukowski dropped half of the beer from the frosted stein down his parched throat. "Gig Young?"

The man slowly turned to face Bukowski, drunken eyes swimming in their sockets like panic-stricken fish. "I am Gig Young. Motherfucker. I am Gig Young."

"Horseshit. What're you doing in the Lock and Load Lounge?"

"Not many bars in town will have me," he slurred. "Not the good ones, anyways. I've been 86'd from the Polo Lounge, Trader Vic's, the bar at the Marmont, the Beverly Wilshire…"

Bukowski scrutinized the man's craggy features and determined right away that he was indeed gazing upon the handsome supporting player who stared down at him from the silver screen and sometimes on the TV in old reruns of *The Twilight Zone* and *Alfred Hitchcock Presents*. Gig-Fucking-Young. Who gives a shit? Bukowski returned to his beer.

Before he could down the last swallow, the actor's vodka-laced breath was assaulting Bukowski's flaring nostrils. "I won an Oscar in 1969, you know, worst goddamn thing that ever happened to me. Best Supporting Actor. The kiss of death, end of the line. When I walked up to that stage to collect that fucking hunk of junk, I thought 'Here we go, now they're finally gonna create a Gig Young movie,' you know, a vehicle I could star in instead of just being fancy wallpaper in the background but it doesn't happen that way. There's a whole goddamn curse along with the Academy Awards. You win one and suddenly the phone stops ringing; everyone assumes—they fucking assume—that your price went up or that you got an attitude all of a sudden and are difficult to work with or...I don't know. The so-called accolades of your peers are the lowering of your coffin into the grave. My career was over the minute they called me up on that stage."

Actors, Bukowski knew, particularly movie actors, are an insufferable lot, prone to drama and histrionics, even more so when they're drunk; he avoided eye contact with the man and threw his words into his empty beer stein instead. "I heard differently about you. You had one hand on the throttle and the other hand on the bottle."

"Hey!" The actor laughed and tossed his hands in the air, nearly falling off the stool in the process. "One hand on the throttle, one hand on the bottle. You're a goddamn poet!"

Bukowski rolled another slim cigarette in his calloused fingers. "Actually, I am."

The actor's eyes narrowed to small slits. "Who the hell are you?"

Bukowski hiked his shoulders. "I'm an average guy. Nothin' special. Writer. Poet. Dying in a steaming pile of shit, just like you."

"Here's to steaming piles of shit!" The fading movie star hoisted his martini glass, polished off the lukewarm remains and signaled the mean-faced bartender. "Two more, barkeep!" He licked his dry lips and returned his attention to Bukowski. "Now, what's this garbage that you've heard about me and how the hell would you know anything anyway?"

"I know a few monkeys in the movie business; it's a residual effect of life in L.A. You got shit-canned from *Blazing Saddles* because you were having DTs on the set."

"Well…that's true," the actor softly confessed. "My first wife, Sheila, she died of cancer one year after we were married. Did you know that, Mister Smart Ass?"

"And my father beat me damn near every day when I was a kid. So what? No one needs excuses to climb into the bottle. Life gets complicated and fucked up the second you pop out of the womb."

With a scowl, the bartender deposited a fresh beer in front of Bukowski and a dry martini refill for the inebriated movie star.

"You're a philosopher too," the actor mumbled, as if talking in his sleep. "I got fired from *Charlie's Angels* last year. I was gonna be the voice of Charlie. Too goddamn drunk to record my lines so they brought in John Forsythe. I mean, I had things going on at the time so, yeah, I was hitting the sauce a little. Jesus. Give a guy a break, huh?"

They sat in silence for several moments, the steady hum of traffic on Hollywood Boulevard flooding through the open door and filling the void with white noise. The actor completed his work on the martini and rose, staggering, swaying precariously like a suspension bridge in the wind.

"Someone pour me into a cab," he muttered, floundering toward the door and the harsh white sunlight that was filtered through billions of particles of airborne automobile exhaust.

Bukowski never saw Gig Young again, not in life and certainly not in the movies.

Six months later, on a crisp October afternoon with a hint of a Santa Ana wind in the air, Bukowski perched himself on the very same barstool in the Lock and Load Lounge. He ordered a Michelob and unfolded the front page of the *L.A. Times*. The story in the right-hand panel just below the banner and above the fold immediately caught his eye:

The dateline was October 19, New York City. Actor Gig Young, the wire service reported, shot and killed German actress Kim Schmidt, his bride of three weeks, and then turned the gun on himself in their New York City apartment. The direct cause of the murder-suicide, authorities stated, remained unclear. Young was almost sixty-five; his bride was twenty-one. An NYPD spokesman said that an Oscar statuette was found between the bodies of Young and his wife.

Bukowski downed the Michelob in one long swallow and turned to the *Daily Racing Form*. It was a good day for a drive out to Santa Anita.

Originally published in *Mr. Bukowski's Wild Ride* (2008)

HARRY CALHOUN

An insomniac thinks of Bukowski

fear of not falling asleep
fear of dreams
without local anaesthetic

a not-so-mythical Prometheus
with doses of alcohol
perpetually eating the liver

as Bukowski said
"Try not to think of the liver,
and maybe the liver will not
think of you."

And Bukowski's end was leukemia
so the alcohol vulture
was cheated of its eternal meal

Originally published in *The Legendary*

SUZUKI LIMBU

Intoxication

my friday nights are
reserved for one
but my bed, for two—
pour me a glass of your
finest poetry and
i'll down it
like you down
your whisky
hard,
with the bitter etching
on the back of your
throat;
i swallow your
words,
raw.

DAVID S. POINTER

The Superhero Zone

Alcoholics? I mean
Tarzan of the Apes
can get brewskiitis
and morph fast into
Barzan of the Grapes,
gutter bound and gone
as Superman swigs
and gurgles, into
Looperman while
Charles Bukowski
becomes a best
selling author, icon
and underground
liquor disposing
legend influencing
countless middle
class writers to
leave their social
class seeking bottom
dog status zipcoding
past burning projects

WILLIAM BARKER

Drinking with Bukowski

A man hunches
in the drizzle,
three thousand
miles from home,
among pale inscriptions,
spurious order and greenery.

He pours beer from a brown bottle
onto the grass in deference;

As the golden suds soak the soil
he takes a long sip in celebration
of the man buried beneath his feet.

He touches the cold stone
in silent appreciation, pours
and sips again, draining the bottle.

Echoes of spirit and voice
storm, memories of legendary
words form;

For this singular moment
life and death
are only of the mind.

PART SEVEN
THE TRACK

Portrait by David Barker
Originally published in
The Form Appears: Bukowski Watercolors by David Barker
(Bottle of Smoke Press, 2009)

MARK TERRILL

The Art of Victory

A hot, smoggy day in LA.
Bukowski wheels out of the lot
at the Hollywood Park racetrack,
past rows of cars shimmering
in the brassy California sun.

Bukowski is ninety bucks ahead today.
He roars out onto the freeway,
slips over into the fast lane,
turns up the Mahler symphony,
lights a big black cigar.

For the time being, he is
beyond poetry, beyond women,
beyond the post office, back-rent,
and that long war of attrition
we all know as Existence.

He grins sublimely, focused on the
hard, glittering diamond of Fortune,
like a Zen monk tuning in
to the true meaning of life,
which is essentially the same thing.

ADRIAN MANNING

Poem written at the Charles Bukowski exhibition

I take a backward glance,
catch myself off guard,
and for a moment,
a brief second in time,
you stand before me
in the shirt, trousers and shoes
you used to wear and
that now hang in this
mock closet.
you whisper
"I gotta get out of here, kid,
even in death they won't leave
me alone"
I am wrong but I think I see
your hands reaching for the keys
to the old volks,
now under glass,
on the wallet with a couple
of dollars
and some loose change in it
and the race track card
from Santa Anita
that you have scribbled on
and that tells me
the outside horse
has already run in
ahead of the crowd
and is waiting
at the gate for the rest
to follow.

Written after attending an exhibition of Bukowski work and
memorabilia in London, 1996.
Previously published in *Lummox Journal* (2000)

"Bukowski Bets the Horses"
Drawing by Michael O'Brien

SUZUKI LIMBU

Hank

hank,
i would've liked
thursday nights best—
coming home from the races
muttering about
"*that damned horse*"
you lost out on,
slump down on the worn out
(and the only) armchair we'd own
because you'd spend the rest
on booze and eggs.
i know you like 'em
hardboiled with
old scotch and me
in the morning.

HENRY DENANDER

At the racetrack

On eBay I bought four whisky glasses from
Santa Anita Park; this was Charles Bukowski's
favorite race track and he spent a lot of time there.

I've never betted on the horses myself but there was
a race track close to our summer house in Sweden
and I went there when I was a kid.

I never really liked to watch the horses run but
I came to see my uncle Allan who was a
regular at the track. I liked him a lot and he
always gave me money for ice cream,
so even without betting I came out ahead.

And now, 45 years later, here I am
with my large Santa Anita whisky tumbler
with the engraved horses and jockeys,
a couple of ice cubes and a large splash
of Glenlivet whisky.

Maybe I'm slowly
beginning to understand
the art of horseracing
after all.

Originally published in *Last Call:
The Bukowski Legacy Continues*
(Lummox Press, 2011)

PART EIGHT
WOMEN

"Georgia & Hank"
Painting by Jocelyne Desforges
after a photograph ©Joan Gannij

Pamela "Cupcakes" Wood

Charles Bukowski's Scarlet

Chapter 2

We were standing in front of two rows of plain, box-like, beige bungalows facing each other—three on the left side and one on the right. There was a small courtyard in between with a sidewalk down the middle leading to a two-story building at the back of the lot, consisting of four units—one on top and the other facing the street. The front bungalow on the right was set back much further from the curb than the others—that's where Bukowski lived. There were a total of eight units in the bread-and-butter complex.

As we approached his bungalow, there was a galley-type porch with an old davenport taking up most of the space. I had to lean over it to ring the doorbell.

On the top half of his front door was a small window covered with ratty looking Venetian blinds. The blinds parted, and I saw an eyeball staring out at us.

"Who is it?" a voice growled.

"It's us," I said. "Pam and Georgia—the birthday girls."

The door opened a crack. "Are you alone?" he asked, looking beyond us.

"It's just us chick-a-dees," Georgia said.

Convinced we were alone, he opened the door and invited us in. He was fairly tall and fairly old, with a large head and ravaged face. After one glance, I averted my eyes. I didn't want to hurt his feelings by staring at his scarred, pockmarked skin. Wow, I thought, this guy has had a rough life. It looked like a roadmap to hell imprinted on his face.

Bukowski made a slight turn, and I could see a knife behind his back. I didn't feel threatened. I understood right away that the knife was for his own protection in case we were there to roll him. Considering the neighborhood, it didn't surprise me at all. Georgia and I glanced at each other, but said nothing about it.

His eyes moved from my face, to my chest, to my empty hands.

"You've got the cleavage, but you don't got the six-pack," he said.

"Sorry," I said. "I tried, but I didn't want to get the kid fired."

Georgia held out her hand. She had on three-inch platforms, so she was close to Bukowski's height—about six feet all. She looked him straight in the eyes.

"I'm Georgia," she said, extending her hand.

"Call me Hank," he replied in that same tired, Snagglepuss drawl.

The phrase "Exit stage left" flashed through my mind. I quickly shook the silly thought and introduced myself.

"I'm Pam, but my friends call me Cupcakes—Cupcakes O'Brien."

It was a pet name given to me by my last boyfriend—a creative-thinking screenplay writer—and it never failed to elicit the desired response.

Bukowski half smirked and half smiled, then glanced again at my chest and nodded.

"Have a seat, ladies," he said, gesturing toward the sofa.

Georgia flopped down and lit a cigarette. She gazed around the room with an awestruck look on her face—as if she were in the Sistine Chapel. She was sitting in her hero's apartment.

I took a seat next to her on the sofa. I tried to see the place through Georgia's eyes, but the charm escaped me. It was the most rundown-looking dump I'd ever seen. An old sofa with a faded red blanket thrown over it; across from the sofa sat an overstuffed, worn-out, mustard and brown striped chair with blotchy stains; in between was a round coffee table which was too big for the room and covered with debris, including overflowing ashtrays and empty beer bottles; the rug was stained and covered in lint—dust was everywhere, and newspapers were strewn about. To my right was the entrance to the kitchen. The wall connecting the two was partially painted in a chocolate brown. It looked as though someone got too tired to finish the job. To my left was the entrance to the bedroom. From what I could see of both, they looked just as bad. The entire place was approximately five hundred square feet and a hundred miles from bohemian. It was just plain seedy.

"Would you ladies like something to drink?" he asked.

"Do you have any champagne?" I said.

"Jeezus," he said with a hint of a lisp. "What do you think this is—a nightclub?"

"We don't care," Georgia said, shooting death rays at me with her eyes, "whatever you have, man."

He shuffled into the kitchen and we heard him yell, "Hey, ladies, you're in luck."

He came back into the living room holding a bottle of champagne and three jelly glasses.

"I forgot I had this," he said, "must be left over from my last lovely."

While he opened the bottle, I took my first good look at him. He was wearing a white T-shirt that was two sizes too small, so that a bit of his beer belly peeked out. He had on baggy blue jeans that came up well above his ankles. He wore old black socks with no shoes. His thick, wavy, salt and pepper hair was on the long side, slicked back with water or maybe Brylcreem ("A little dab'll do ya!")—apparently, the only thing he'd done to get ready for our visit.

On his ravaged face was a large, bulbous nose. He had a funny mouth that made him look a little like a Muppet, covered by a well-trimmed beard. From what I could see of his eyes, which were always at half-mast, they appeared to be a beautiful, pale greenish-blue. Aside from a slight beer gut, he had a strong-looking physique. He looked to be in very good shape for a man his age.

He poured champagne, and we clinked our glasses together.

"Happy birthday, Georgia," Bukowski said.

"It's not my birthday anymore," she said. "It was on the ninth. What is today—November eleventh?"

"This was a day I always looked forward to when I worked for the post office," Bukowski said. "Veterans Day—it's a holiday."

Georgia laughed. "I read the book, *Post Office*," she said. "Did all that shit really happen to you?"

"Unfortunately, yes," he said.

Georgia asked Bukowski some more questions about his writing. I was afraid he would ask me about one of his books or columns—and find out I knew almost noting about his work.

While they talked, I ambled over to the kitchen, which was right off the living room. A 1950s-style kitchen table with chrome legs and Formica top was pushed up against the wall. Sitting on the table was an old, black, manual typewriter, with a transistor radio beside it. One small, armless, chrome chair with a vinyl seat was pushed underneath the table in front of the old Royal. On the left side of the table sat a two-foot trash can full of empty beer bottles and wadded papers.

I must have been really deep in thought, because the next thing I knew Bukowski was standing by the open refrigerator retrieving some beers. He looked around the room and grinned.

"Not what you expected, huh?"

"I don't know how you can write in here," I said. "It doesn't look very comfortable."

"You thought maybe I'd have a cozy writing den with a blazing fire?"

"Something between that and this," I told him.

He handed me a beer, but I held up my still-full glass of champagne.

"Better drink up," he said, "before your friend and I finish it all."

He turned his weary eyes on me and seemed to see right into me. From the look on his face, it didn't appear as if he liked what he saw.

I was confused. I couldn't remember the last time a man hadn't been immediately attracted to me. And this one actually seemed to *dislike* me. He acted guarded and aloof toward me. It was a shock to my self-image.

We walked back into the living room. He sat in his striped throne and I sat on the sofa next to Georgia. She was looking at herself in the big silver mirror she kept in her oversized purse. Knowing Georgia, she'd probably opened her purse to get some pills, and had then become distracted and started gazing at herself. When she saw us watching her, she grabbed an eyebrow pencil and began to touch up her eyebrows. Bukowski and I stared at her as though she was an artist painting an interesting piece of sculpture.

Her legs were now splayed out on the couch. Her skirt was hiked up, with her garters in full view. I would soon learn that he was a leg man par excellence. Never before, or since, have I met a man who adored women's legs the way Bukowski did. He just went gaga over them. Someone once told me that "leg men" were often momma's boys when they were young, deriving great comfort and security from holding onto their mother's calves. Georgia's legs were long and skinny and her nylons were bagging around her knees. The effect was more sluttish than sexy. But Bukowski didn't seem to mind.

Georgia looked up and noticed Bukowski watching her. Since she was a fan of his writing, she probably knew how he felt about women's legs. That may be why she was all spread out like that on the couch, or she was too stoned to care.

"I hate pantyhose," she said. "The motherfucker who invented those should be strung up by the balls—probably some female-loathing homo."

"Couldn't agree with you more," he said.

Georgia continued penciling her eyebrows as she continued her rant, "With those fucking pantyhose, your twat can't breathe, so you end up with a vat of buttermilk in your crotch."

Bukowski laughed, throwing his head back. I could see the gaps on both sides of his mouth where he was missing teeth.

"Pam wears pantyhose," Georgia said, putting away her mirror and eyebrow pencil.

Even though Georgia and I were friends, I never completely trusted her. Every time she had the chance, she slung a barb or two my way. I guess she figured I could take it. I admired Georgia's acerbic, irreverent wit, but sometimes the barbs stung, though I never let on. I assumed she was envious of all the attention I got from the opposite sex. Though right now, she was the one getting most of it.

"I have to wear them at work," I explained. "It's part of my uniform."

"Uniform?" Bukowski said. "Don't tell me you work at the post office."

Georgia let out a horsy laugh, complete with a couple of snorts.

I tried to think of a witty retort, but figured anything I said would fall flat with these two.

"I'm a waitress at the Alpine Inn on Hollywood Boulevard," I said, hoping to close the subject.

"She wears a girdle," Georgia said.

"A dirndl," I corrected.

"I was born in the land of dirndls," Bukowski said, "though I don't remember much about."

"Maybe you should come over to the Alpine Inn," I said, "and refresh your memory. You can wear your lederhosen."

Georgia curled her lip at me. It was as if we were both vying for Bukowski's attention. I wasn't really interested in him, and didn't think she was either—at least not in a romantic way. But I figured this was her night, so I was fine with giving her the limelight.

Georgia tugged again at her black stockings. Her skirt was hiked up exposing the garters. She was now attempting to tighten her nylons.

"Need some help with that?" Bukowski asked, as he stood up and headed for the sofa.

He sat down between us. I decided to move to the floor. Georgia flopped her legs over Bukowski's and he began to gently smooth out her stockings.

"That tickles," she said, laughing.

I smiled. I had definitely given Georgia the best birthday of her life.

More drinks followed. Now we were all lying on the floor, with Bukowski in between, and he was playfully stroking Georgia's legs and mine. Somehow his right foot ended up in Georgia's purse, which was also on the floor. He rolled it over and her pill bottles spilled onto the carpet.

"What are you holding, woman? Looks like you robbed a drug-store." He sat up and grabbed a couple of bottles, shaking them like maracas.

"You name it, Baby—I've got it, " she said. "Want some?"

"Sure, why not?" he said in that cool, slow drawl.

I would later learn that he would try anything once. He never really listened to anyone's advice, never had any preconceived judgments, and had to figure out everything for himself. He had a high tolerance for trial and error. But when it came to pills or any kind of drug, Bukowski usually ended up sick and sorry for the experiment.

He swallowed a pill and said, "Okay, girls—let's celebrate!"

I was surprised at how much his mood had changed. He'd shifted from the wary, defensive sad man with the knife behind his back to the fun guy who was ready for anything. We were all in pretty good spirits by now.

Bukowski was now back in his striped chair. Georgia was sprawled out on the couch and I stayed on the floor, seated beside him. He pointed to Georgia and said, "You've got the soul." Then he looked down at me and said, "You've got the looks."

He took a long pull on his beer and his eyes rolled toward the ceil-ing, as if he were deep in thought.

"I'd like to combine the two of you into one person," he told us. "The looks and the soul. I would then have the perfect woman."

I glanced at Georgia, wondering if she was as insulted as I was. It was a bizarre, backhanded compliment and/or insult.

"Hey, Baby, beauty's only sin deep," Georgia quipped.

"Yah, yah, yah," I sang, hoping to lighten the sting.

I began putting the pill bottles back in Georgia's purse. She had given Bukowski a Dexi.

"You're not going to get any sleep tonight, Mr. Bukowski," I said.

"Why?" Are we going to have a threesome?"

I looked over at Georgia for some help, but she was beginning to pass out from the booze and downers.

Pleasantly buzzed and feeling rather playful, I said, "You want me—it'll cost ya."

"How much?"

"Oh…at least a hundred," I teased.

"Okay," he said.

Worried that he thought I was serious, I laughed and said, "Hey, I was just kidding."

"Well, what will it cost?" he asked.

By this time, his ravaged face was beginning to look less intimidating. He was gruff on the outside, but underneath it he had a vulnerability that I found appealing. I wasn't sure if it was the booze taking over, but I began to find him strangely sexy, in a rugged sort of way.

I looked into his eyes, and with a "come hither" look, flashed him a coy smile.

"Oh, no, Cupcakes," he said, "I don't think I can ever pay that price again."

I took a dramatic puff on my cigarette and slowly blew out the smoke.

Then I said in my best Lauren Bacall, "Sure you can."

He studied me with his head tilted to one side, then said, "You're dangerous, Red."

We both broke out in laughter. His guard was coming down, and I felt relieved. It had been a while since any man had held out so long against the redheaded charm.

"I like your earrings," he said, pointing to the big gold hoops I was wearing.

"You want them?" I said, starting to take one off.

"They look a lot better on you," he said.

We continued with our silly banter and laughed and drank some more. I was having a good time with him. He didn't act as if all of this was just a prelude to a bedroom romp.

After a while, Georgia woke up. It was close to five a.m.

As we were standing at his door ready to leave, Bukowski said, "Thanks, girls. Come back any time."

As we started down the courtyard sidewalk, I could hear a typewriter clicking away inside Bukowski's bungalow.

"Now that's a fucking writer," Georgia said, as she piled into the Camaro.

I dropped Georgia off at her apartment in Hollywood, where she lived on welfare with her boyfriend Bill and her two little girls. Then I drove to my rented guesthouse about ten minutes away in Los Feliz. My daughter was spending the night with my mom.

Since it was Veterans Day, they both had the day off. I would pick her up that afternoon.

When I crawled into bed, I thought about what an interesting night it had been, never imaging that I'd see the old man again.

"What a trip," I said to myself before I fell asleep.

Excerpted from *Charles Bukowski's Scarlet*
by Pamela "Cupcakes" Wood (Sun Dog Press, 2010),
USED BY PERMISSION

Portrait by Jeff Morgan

Pamela "Cupcakes" Wood

For Hank ~

After all these years
I still feel tremendous guilt about your bluebird
I swear I thought the cage door was secure
Before I let the cat in

RENE DIEDRICH

Bukowski Was an Asshole

Bukowski was an asshole
That's one of the reasons I love him.
If I'd known him I would have hated him too.
Sure. He played it up sometimes.
He was a barfly.

I love the film clips. B&W
he's driving the beat-up old bug.
The windshield is smashed in.
The dashboard is taped together.
A door hangs by a hinge, but
Bukowski coaxes the engine to purr
And they drive along hollywood near vine.
Hank and the guy with a giant camera.
That dirty old man was his close up.
He is wearing a grin.
Smoking and drunk.
And he starts getting philosophical.

What I love is how he didn't rehearse.
It came…
It rolled…
Baby it was beautiful.
Sometimes I don't agree
with a word he says
Others, I recognize
Well, it's all bullshit.
In later clips,
there 's color now—
1984 looks primordial yet dull
Orwell got the date wrong
Big Brother arrived late
Bukowski is gone.

I want to join him.
A bottle of blackberry alone,
I watch the last footage caught.
Bukowski is still pretty shitfaced.
His legs are still strong.

He's like a hundred years old!
But he is majestic.
He roars, bares his teeth,
kicks his wife.
Tiny as she is
I know she provoked him.
Maybe he deserved it too.
Because he is being an asshole.
It's an ugly moment.
A marriage.
It's what you remember after it ends.

Bukowski was an asshole.
Yet I turn to his words.
They're still alive, and
I guess it's been a very long time
I have gone to him for courage
Which I need
To face more of this.
Endurance, he says.
And I struggle on.

A blond I know says
Bukowski gave her permission.
To write life, which is raw.
And ugly for girls.
Even worse for women.
But we ride it out
In a beater, a bike, a BMW…
What else can one do?
We don't hope for the best.
We will only be disappointed.
After all
In our way and, if nothing else,
We are the daughters of Bukowski.
He taught us about life.
He told us stories before bed.
He said: tell yours true
You are you
Sorry, kid.
That's how it tumbles.

They say he sold out.
Because he didn't die alone,
in a cheap room
Face down in a puddle of vomit.
As usual,
they're wrong.
He rose.
And that counts
When you are poor
and scarred
When you are a
Nobody
or less
I know.

Sure.
Bukowski was an asshole.
But if he were here
I'd stroke what was left of his hair
And kiss that big head
Because he pulled angels to earth
So he could write poems for girls
He'll never know he had

Originally published in *Gutter Eloquence*

ANN MENEBROKER

Interview by Fred Voss
September 2000

FRED VOSS: *You met Charles Bukowski in the early 1960s when he'd just been "discovered" by* The Outsider *magazine and the two of you were just starting out as serious poets. How did Bukowski affect your writing? Your life?*

ANN MENEBROKER: I'd been getting some things published starting in 1957. But I was publishing under a different name: Ann R. Bauman. That's who I was when Bukowski and I began our correspondence. That's the name he wrote in his books and mailed to me: *Crucifix in a Death Hand, It Catches Its Heart in My Hand*—Works of Bukowski's beautifully published by Lujon Press in New Orleans. Bukowski was writing to me from there when he went to help these good people with his books.

He and I were being published in some of the same mags. He had already begun to make a name among the poets and editors with his work. He was different—the way things are when someone is touched with uncommon talent and separated from the crowd. Combining his letters with the poetry I saw in the littles I thought he was one of the most fascinating poets on the scene. And we added phone calls to that. I was moved through my admiration of the strength of his work to become what I hoped was more authentic in my poetry.

In the end, we write the way we can write and think the way we want to think and no crowd or single person is going to make a hell of a lot of difference. But what he did was release the "bug up my ass." He made me feel like a wilder sort of person.

The actor from the 1950s, Sterling Hayden, once wrote: "In the worship of security we fling ourselves beneath the wheels of routine—and before we know it our lives are gone." Bukowski, I believe, was terrified of this kind of living—The Suburbia of the Heart. Something in his earlier years made him angry at daily living, jobs, survival, buying a new couch, celebrating holidays, all of it. Bukowski's poetry was Bukowski's judgment of the world and his place in it.

FV: *Do you think Bukowski's writing persona was a fake?*

AM: No. I've read a lot of his prose and poetry, which I know you have, too, Fred. *Everything he ever was* is in them. It's enlarged, perhaps, and painted with more literary colors, but, all in all, Charles "Hank" Bukowski was authentic. He never lost his roots, his need to remind us how he felt about the suburban dreams and hopes, the luckless guy or gal who he felt compassion for, the absurdity of how life can be wasted. He caught love and gentleness in his writing, as well as the harsher side. And he saw humor, dark humor, in just about everything.

Excerpted from
Charles Bukowski Epic Glottis: His Art & His Women (& me)
by Joan Jobe Smith, with additional material by Fred Voss
(Silver Birch Press, 2012)

RODGER JACOBS

Bukowski and the Red Socks

One morning in May of 1992 when the sinus-burning scent of smoke from the Molotov-cocktail-induced fires of the Rodney King riots still clung like a vise over East Hollywood, Bukowski awoke fitfully in his gray-striped soiled mattress, hung over and with a head throbbing like a kettle drum beaten by a cretin with no sense of rhythm, as usual, and with only a very vague recollection of events from the evening previous, also as usual.

He groped for the pack of Winstons on the nightstand and regarded the slats of sun trying to sneak passage through the green venetian blinds with what could be described as disregard at best. The Bic lighter was secreted in the hip pocket of the sweat pants that he slept in nightly. He lit the cigarette, rose with an exaggerated groan, and considered his thin-ankled feet dangling over the bed; red knit socks adorned both of his feet.

"What the hell...?" He pulled on the cigarette, long and hard until his lungs expanded, and considered the bright red socks; he didn't own a pair of red socks, just white cotton socks, the kind his mom bought him for gym class in high school. Woolworth's in Santa Monica. Five bucks for a pack of ten.

Bukowski reclined on the bed again and tried to recall how red socks might have wound up binding his feet. He remembered through a vague haze—maybe a better picture would emerge after a bowl of Fruit Loops—a meeting at Musso and Frank in Hollywood the night before with a journalist from a French lit mag. FRANCINE? FRANCES? He had told her that his daily writing routine could never commence until he first moved his bowels in the morning.

"Why is that?" she had asked, lined eyebrows rising provocatively. She was intriguing, that was for sure, and she had just that right naïve quality that Bukowski found enticing.

"Because only then can I get the SHIT out of my system and write the TRUTH."

She had devoured the answer feverishly, flashing that ridiculous grin that journalists flash when they think they're getting an inside scoop, scribbling furiously in her notebook, an apostle writing down the messiah's words as they flowed from his mouth like honey—albeit a tainted and total bullshit kind of honey—and that had pleased him immensely.

But it still did not explain how he ended up with two red socks on his feet.

Originally published in *Mr. Bukowski's Wild Ride* (2008).

KAREN FINLEY

An Affair to Remember

"Charles, I'm pregnant," I said while sitting on the edge of the bed unwrapping my baguette from the café.

He didn't turn around but continued doing the crossword puzzle in the *National Enquirer*. "What was Geena Davis's first role on television?" he muttered.

I stared at him again and wondered if I should repeat the news, cry, or become even more emotionally distanced than him.

"The show was *Buffalo Bill*," I said blinking.

"That doesn't help me. That's the show title. I want the character's name…" Charles put the pencil down but sill didn't look up. "Go to Mexico. I know a doctor there."

"Chuck, abortion has been legal for over a decade. Besides, we're in St. Barths and nothing happens between Christmas and New Year's. We're supposed to be on vacation," I reminded him.

Bukowski was sometimes disoriented from his years of drinking, but that wasn't the issue here. The issue was Brautigan.

"You went to Mexico when you got pregnant with Richard," he said hissing. I could see the spittle spray on the newsprint image of Mary Tyler Moore.

I sprayed back. "Yes, and that was when abortion was illegal! You can't let him go, can you? Besides, he's dead! He's dead! I was only a kid."

"Yeah, Frida Kahlo was a kid when she met Diego Rivera and SHE NEVER LET HIM GO! Her entire life's work was about having babies, not having babies, Diego Diego. Diego is present in Frida's work. Richard Brautigan is in your work. It never leaves a woman," he theorized.

"I don't think Richard has influenced my work," I said because it was my turn.

"You both write bad poetry."

"You're wrong, Chuck."

He turned toward me now for I called him CHUCK. Calling the great, brilliant writer CHUCK always got his goat. No one called Charles Bukowski "CHUCK." Not even Sean Penn. And for greater impact I called him CHUCKEE when one of his many wives called to let them know I was in charge. "CHUCKEE! Linda is on the phone. FrancEyE is on the phone."

I know what you are thinking. You think I'm a bitch. But I had to call him CHUCK and deflate him a bit for I couldn't depend on the BRAUTIGAN ISSUE to get his attention that was reserved for special occasions.

Take Note: THE BRAUTIGAN ISSUE
Trout Fishing in America, The Abortion. Oh, that Richard Brautigan.
I met Richard Brautigan at Enrico's café on Broadway and Kearny down the street from the City Lights Bookstore in San Francisco in 1971. It was 1:30 a.m. and I had just ended my shift as a cocktail waitress at the infamous strip club The Condor. Enrico the owner of the bistro wanted me for I was underage and looked it. HE promised to set me up in my own apartment. HE never had me but would rub my knee while I ate my club sandwich and drank my hot cocoa. HE would always give the taxi driver ten dollars to take me home.

Enrico introduced me to Richard Brautigan in mid-January, and it surprised Enrico when I told the table that I had written a term paper on him the year before as a sophomore in high school. That is when Enrico stopped wanting me, for the turn-on was that I knew nothing and now that I revealed myself I would have to pay for my own damn sandwich. I knew Brautigan's poetry by heart, and when I spoke Richard became enamored. Richard was drunk, despondent, depressed, and disillusioned, but I was a devoted fan.

So that is how I met Richard Brautigan. I later met Kathy Acker as my teacher at the San Francisco Art Institute, who introduced me to Gregory Corso, who introduced me to Bukowski at Brautigan's funeral.

The Brautigan issue for Bukowski was that I became pregnant with Richard and had an emotionally high-charged, dramatic illegal abortion in Mexico. A conflict and intimacy that Charles grew envious and jealous of as his feelings for me deepened. The fact that I actually read Brautigan and never read Bukowski made matters worse. So now you know. I had an affair with Bukowski and never read any of his goddamn books. I loved him for the man and not for the writer and it tortured him.

Charles had returned to his daily crossword habit and I watched him spell Geena Davis's name in twelve down and I tried again.
"CHUCK, we need to talk…"
"Karen, what's Jim Rockford's father played by?"
"Noah Beery."
"Is that with an E or an A?"

"Chuck, you are a goddamn Polock."

Charles put the pencil down and this time he glared at me with that man testosterone look like he's stronger than me, smarter than me, bigger than me, own the whole goddamn world more than me. At that moment, I realized Bukowski was in my work, in a reactionary way. Hell, if I was ever going to let him know.

He looked at me with his eyes bugging out with the pupils dilated so big they lost all meaning and color. He could do this at will. This look was just as important as his craft with the word. And he kept reminding me of this. "A writer is as important as their reputation." He believed this so sincerely that he sometimes isolated so he wouldn't appear too happy or content. I tried to remember this while looking into his eyes as he said sternly, "If you have that baby, I'll change my identity and leave the country."

"I turned over to give him back some of his own medicine and said, "Who do you think you are? Jack Kerouac? Jack wouldn't have to say it. He was man enough to just do it."

Oh, this made Charles mad. And he was trying hard not to show it. So I turned the screw more.

"Why don't you have a vasectomy or become a faggot like Burroughs?"

Many homes have rules that are just left unsaid—no ball playing in the house, no hat wearing at dinner—but in this house it was no reference to Burroughs. I used the word faggot before he could because every other word out of his mouth was faggot. I think it was more generational than actual homophobia but I never let him get away with it.

My morning sickness had worn off so I unwrapped the egg salad baguette. I didn't even get it in my mouth.

"You're eating egg salad? Do you now what that cholesterol will do for you? Mayonnaise! On white. Karen, this is awful for you."

"What do you want me to eat? Ham on Rye?" I answered with no expression. "Charles, it's Christmas. It's Christmas. Yes, I'm eating egg salad. I'm in St. Barths. We're on a French Island. They couldn't wrap the salade niçoise. So what? No one tells me what to eat. I feel like I'm in *Pygmalion*. I don't think I want to be in this relationship anymore."

"OK. OK. I'm a noodge. But you are going to end our six-month affair over a sandwich," he explained.

"Charles, it's more than that. You are so controlling. Cleaning up after me. Refolding my clothes. Restacking the dishes. Reclosing the lids after I do on the Chinese takeout containers. And last night you woke me up at a quarter to four to ask me why I wasn't as successful as Laurie Anderson! Karen, Karen why can't you be like Laurie? It was fucking Christmas Eve."

"Karen, and what did you answer?"

"'Cause I don't play the stinking electric violin," I chuckled.

"Well, Lou Reed probably wakes up Laurie and asks her why she can't be like Karen Finley, take off her clothes, and stick a yam up her ass."

I had to laugh at that but I had thrown my egg salad sandwich away and it was hard to stay in character. I was an emotional wreck. I wanted the baby. I wanted this repulsive, neurotic, drunken slob genius's baby.

He stood up and said, "Let's get Peg and go for a ride."

Charles had a dog at that time named Peg. The dog had only three legs but could run like any other dog, perhaps even better. I would hold the dog in a little knapsack as we rode on the motorcycle going through the traffic in St. Johns. We let Peg go off on his own through the tourists begging back in his own turf. He loved that little three-legged thing. I don't know what this had to do with the story but I felt I should tell you that Charles was an animal lover.

Charles also believed in plastic surgery. And before he died he was seriously considering a facelift. Charles loved to make fun of me being a feminist. And one night while we were still in St. Barths listening to Mozart—I think *The Magic Flute* was on—I commented on our hostess's beauty, and he reminded me that she had had a facelift, maybe two. We both agreed that she was beautiful to begin with but I knew he was looking for an argument. And we did have one. We fought over the aesthetics of fake breasts. Our argument was always the same that I felt beauty was an imperfection and he always felt that was insincere intellectual rubbish. That he had seen both pleasing natural breasts and ugly natural breasts and pleasing fake breasts and ugly fake breasts. And that he had had sex with women with fake breasts and liked it. It went on and on till we reached the topic of nursing and the La Leche League. He ended the argument with accusing me of being so politically correct all the time and that I was so conventional and that I was a conventional beauty and that if I went into a shop no one thought I was a shoplifter but when he entered a store they wanted him out.

I answered with, "They want you out of their store 'cause you smell like the bottom of a beer cooler." He laughed. He was endearing.

I only saw Charles get angry in public once and that was when he wanted his bottle of Perrier on the table with his dinner and the waiter would have nothing of it. The waiter was new at Elaine's and for some reason the waiter liked to keep the Perrier off the table and do the refilling himself, like champagne. The waiter probably thought he'd get a bigger tip. But Bukowski was on the wagon and liked his water on the table like his scotch. What was funny was that Charles was stone sober but he grabbed the waiter by the neck and gave him what his reputation was built on.

On the last day on St. Barths, we somehow got locked in the villa. The inside lock broke and all the windows had hurricane shutters. It was simple and complicated. We had to call the United States to get the phone number of our hosts so they could send the servants to let us out. But Charles became obstinate in his machismo. Issues about his father. Things I learned later that I was insensitive to, should have been more empathetic to, were being triggered. And I just lay in bed laughing like I was on an episode of the *Dick Van Dyke Show,* and I rolled in laughter with tears streaming down my face. Charles continued to refuse to call for help and the more he refused the more I laughed. I couldn't help it. He just refused to call for help.

"I'm Charles Bukowski, and I'm not calling to have some servant open a door for me. No one opens a door for Charles Bukowski. I've opened every one of my own doors." I'd never seen him so sincere in protecting his reputation at all costs, by any means necessary. That was when things fell apart for us. We enjoyed life differently.

But there is on thing I regret in not telling Mr. Bukowski. I never wanted Brautigan's baby, but I wanted his baby.

Previously published in *Drinking with Bukowski: Recollections of the Poet Laureate of Skid Row* (Thunder's Mouth Press, 2000)

FRANCEYE

Interview by Fred Voss
September 2000

FRED VOSS: *Which poets or writers have amazed you or influenced you as an artist the most?*

FRANCEYE: When people ask me who my favorite poet is I always say Sharon Olds and Charles Bukowski. As far as I am concerned, neither one of them ever wrote a bad line. Both of them write in free verse, but it is not the form that I adore, it is the willingness to hew to their own personal truth at whatever cost to bourgeois ideas of taste or manners.

FV: *I understand you've been a poet since your early years. How did your relationship with Charles Bukowski, during or after, affect your writing?*

FE: Reading Bukowski confirmed for me some idea of what really matters in poetry that I had been groping toward with some trepidation; I suppose you could say that his writing gave me permission to try to write the way I had always believed one should. I don't think that my personal relationship with him affected my writing; it affected me in other ways.

FV: *Which of Bukowski's poems is your favorite?*

FE: If I'm reading Bukowski, my favorite is whichever poem I am reading right now. Most recently that was "Escape," from the posthumous collection *Betting on the Muse.* Probably my all-time favorite is "Poem for Personnel Managers" from *The Days Run Away Like Wild Horses Over the Hills.* This is a long prosy poem that many people don't like, but I go back to it again and again, and it is the one I always recommend to people who know Bukowski only from his prose. Another that stays with me always like a mantra is "the priest and the matador" from *It Catches My Heart in Its Hands.*

Excerpted from
Charles Bukowski Epic Glottis: His Art & His Women (& me)
by Joan Jobe Smith, with additional material by Fred Voss
(Silver Birch Press, 2012)

LINDA KING

Loving and Hating Bukowski
Chapter 5

I arrived at his place on DeLongpre around two in the afternoon. He didn't answer the door. I turned to leave. He peeked through the blinds.

"Morona!" he said.

"I've come to take pictures for the sculpture."

"Pictures?" He seemed to have forgotten.

"For the sculpture, remember? I wrote you a letter. I talked to you on the phone."

"Hold on a minute." I could hear him through the screen door puking in the bathroom.

"Shall I come back when you feel better?" I yelled.

"No, No. I'll be all right. I'll be fine in a few minutes. Come on in."

I entered and looked at the drawings scattered about on the coffee table. There were beer cans, papers, paints, and clutter everywhere. I had an orange and threw it up and down nervously. He finally came out dressed in an old bathrobe.

"It is Morona. I remember you."

I held out my hand. "I was here with Peter. I'm also an actress. My playwright sister wrote me a part in her new play called *Queen of the Morons*. That's my name in the play. My sister believes I'm the moron of the family. My four sisters used to tease me and make me cry telling me Mama ran out of brains for number five."

"I see. Can I get you a beer?"

"Sure."

He got us each a beer.

"I'm going to put on my pants. Don't leave."

When he returned, I looked at his head. His face was red and swollen from drinking. His stomach was also swollen. Had I been wrong to start this project? I was embarrassed. I kept throwing and catching the orange.

"How do you want me?"

"Maybe I should come back in a couple of days. I don't want you looking your worst in these pictures."

"No. Go ahead. It's all the same." He gagged on his beer.

"I can start the sculpture right away."

"Can we start after the Christmas holiday and the sick season is out of the way? Then the world gets back to its natural game of murder."

I got my Polaroid camera out. "Stand over against this white wall. I think that would be the best." I started taking pictures. "I need pictures from every angle. I can get the head started before you come. I'd like to do this sculpture at my place. Is that going to be a problem?"

"No. I like to get out of this rat hole now and then."

I finished my beer and drew a little map of how he would get to my place. "I'll call you after the holidays. I have two kids. I'm going to be busy, too, shopping for Christmas."

"Would you like another beer?"

"No, but I'd like to use your bathroom." The pictures were as good as I was going to get today. Daylight didn't help his looks.

That night I wrote poetry.

Dirty

His bathroom was a collage
collected months of old razor blades
and razor paper in artistic disarray
glued with grime and dirt
settled and undisturbed on
the washbowl, bathtub and toilet
a rubber duck in the corner
a pumice stone
strange poetry book and magazines
a red enema bag hung
from the crooked shower pipe
an enema bag? He must be constipated
The razor and toothbrush were used
and the tub and toilet
told by the pathways
on the dirty floor

> This guy must be something
> to be so oblivious to dirt
> It's wonderful!
> When a woman keeps her place
> like this they call her a pig
> her house the pig pen

And there is my friend Helga
"Oh, Linda, what a mess
How can you live in it?
You're the messiest chick I know."

"It takes courage, Helga.
You couldn't do it.
I raise my feet high.
It keeps the curve of my leg beautiful."

"Your husband could have saved
your marriage," she said, "if he'd
had sense enough to hire a maid
and let you write and sculpture."

"No, Helga, what I need
is a dirty man."

I sat and I shat and I thought
Can this be the dirty man for me?
He writes dirty stories and dirty books
He's got a dirty mind and a dirty house.
Too good to be true
There must be a catch somewhere.

I flushed the toilet
and went back out to see
     Linda King 12/70

He probably wants some woman to clean his house. Not this Liberated Billie. I ended my marriage by refusing to cook breakfast one morning for my hardworking husband. He thought that was grounds to separate and never come back, not mentioning our separate lives under one roof. A more reasonable man might have said, "Okay, dear, let's go out for breakfast."

Originally published in *Loving and Hating Bukowski* (2012)

LINDA KING

Who loved?

I loved your meanness
I loved your sarcasm
I loved your wit
I loved your punishment
I loved your sharp comments
I loved the weight of you
I loved your hands
I loved your slow deep voice
I loved you sleeping beside me
I loved your confidence
I loved how you loved yourself
I loved your poetry
I loved writing with you
Acting with you,
Painting with you
I loved the horses
I loved your kisses
Your kisses
Your kisses
I loved, I loved
I was the one who loved

Originally published in *Bukowski Undigested* (2012)

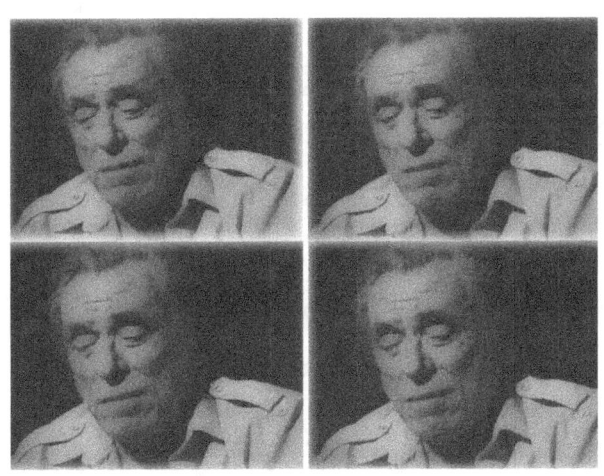

TIM YOUD

Women by Charles Bukowski, three hundred and four pages retyped on a single sheet by artist Tim Youd, using and Olympia SG1. The artist creates the diptych by taping two sheets of paper together and repeatedly running them through the typewriter. The top sheet receives the ink and the bottom sheet the indentation, creating a counterbalanced positive and negative image. The piece was made in Youd's Hollywood studio in February 2013, taking approximately fifty hours of typing to complete.

PART NINE
READINGS

Portrait by Vanessa Wilken

Joan Gannij

Bukowski Reading, 1974

All the femlib propaganda
Hasn't prepared me for this poetic encounter
I sit with emotions in check
Hoping to appear mysterious
In my close proximity
Afraid of being too solicitous,
yet tempted to open
continuous bottles of beer,
rescue his discarded poems from the floor
Hell, I just showed up to listen,
Take a few pictures, check him out
I wasn't ready for the barrio hecklers
Whisky bottle props, disjointed obscenities,
their childish taunts
a rhythm of urban angst
When he chose not to react
He sealed the bargain
The crowd was restless, almost disappointed
When no blood was shed
He remarked later that
some people might figure that he brought them along
for adversity
But after they walked off with his beer
any speculation died off
about that.

Originally published in *Twelve Poems*, 1976

RICHARD MODIANO

Drive All the Horses at Once

One Saturday afternoon in the autumn of 1967, I was visiting the Dialog Bookshop on Fulton Avenue in Van Nuys California. The bookshop was across the street from the campus of Valley Junior College (now called San Fernando Valley Community College) and students browsed the shelves afternoon and evening (it stayed open until nine o'clock on Friday and Saturday.) I was a sixteen-year-old high school student, and the Dialog was the store to visit for underground newspapers, obscure literary magazines as well as political and pacifist magazines.

The store had a bulletin board where notices of local anti-war rallies, informal study groups, rock concerts, be-ins and love-ins, and poetry readings were posted. I saw a flyer for a Sunday afternoon reading in Echo Park with a list of poets scheduled to read, among them Charles Bukowski. I followed his column "Notes of a Dirty Old Man" that was published weekly in *Open City*, a Los Angeles-based underground weekly (the column appeared in the *Los Angeles Free Press* after *Open City* folded). I also read some of his broadsides in situ, since I couldn't afford to buy them.

Two high school friends who also dug poetry knew about the reading, and one of them had a car so we drove to the Echo Park reading a week later. The reading was held a private residence and the host was the poet John Thomas. In fact, it was his house where the reading was held. I didn't know who John Thomas was and I'd never seen Bukowski, and in the small living room Thomas seemed to take up most of the space. Meantime, sitting on the floor with his back to the wall was a man who was sipping Brew 102 from a can, a partially finished six-pack between his legs (Brew 102 was a local Los Angeles beer that sold for seventy-five cents a six-pack.) To his right was a reel-to-reel Webcor tape recorder.

John Thomas read some fine work and was followed by another poet whose name I don't remember and then an exotic-looking woman with red hair. Finally Thomas said, "Our next reader is Charles Bukowski." The man sitting on the floor pressed the start button and we listened to four prerecorded poems while Bukowski continued to sip his beer. Even then Bukowski didn't like reading in public. I don't remember what poems he read but I do remember liking them a lot and thinking that I too could write poetry if only I knew how.

After the reading, I went up to Bukowski and kneeled next to him and asked, "Mr. Bukowski, what do you have to know to be a good poet?"

He answered, "Kid, you have to know how to drive all the horses at once."

MARJORIE GILBERT

The Night Bukowski Read His Poems

His reputation preceded him
Campus police guarded the doors
The written word can be dangerous you know
Bukowski was going to read his poems
The only request from Charles
Bring plenty of beer
Everything would flow
What a show!
From the stairwell he stood
Never looking up
Beer can in one hand, poem in the other
The pockmarked face
Showed the ravages of the life he had known
And the seeds he had sown
He read matter-of-factly
Laughter permeated the air
He didn't care!
He sipped his beer between sentences
As he finished the page he tossed it on the floor
Several pages were scattered about
The words lay in repose
He was loaded and so were we
But in a different way
Raunchy verse from a man who had lived in flop houses
With winos, prostitutes, drug addicts, and other unsavory souls
Images of a life we would never know
This nether world revealed to us by a man who lived his prose.

Originally published in
the *Los Angeles Times*
February 14, 2013

PAUL NEBENZAHL

Charles Bukowski

Friends were assigned to pick up Charles Bukowski
At O'Hare a signature piss on the right front tire of the Volvo
Hank marked his ground like a dog a
Special Chinaski attack dog always the legs
His own legs he so admired
How sturdy they were when he was fucking
Or being shit scared of fucking that's the other whole half
Of Charlie the raw castration drunk that he was
He was his own nasty Nazi scientist

Reading the stories used to be a favorite pastime
My brother-in-law the rock drummer in Minnesota
Had them all; all Bukowski all the time
The Christmas pj's and the fire
The kids playing the drums in the living room
The family games and the drinking
And then the reading of Bukowski late at night
When all were prone pine I read them

Honestly if I was looking for a stroke book
These would not be them
It was moth-flame all bathroom tile green
The books virtual puke boxes
The lazy drunk the fucking
The bums the beer the post office
Fucking Southern California
The mindless mind drum worse than Vonnegut's *Sirens Of Titan*

It was all that I could do to stomach myself
Imagine stomaching Charlie's bile
The stories of the college tours
The German odyssey of grime and bad poetry
The leather caps
The thieving and marauding not only
Of the victim of the day his fucking enemy/partner
But the ample robbing of books nonpublished casts
The line bloody long of an editor's toil told

SCOTT WANNBERG

White House Poetry Gig

Charles Bukowski
reads at the White House,
the 1st lady faints,
"Hope it was something I said,"
Bukowski comments,
as two secret service guys
escort him off the grounds,
"Tell the little lady
if she's ever in Hollywood
to give me a ring."

"You're going to have to fill in the gap,"
the Coordinator of Poetry for the White House
yells at the president
who's downing a 5th of Wild Turkey 101 proof,

"Who should I get?"

"Rod McKuen wouldn't offend
anybody
important...

Rod McKuen
just gave a reading
at the nuclear submarine base in Portsmouth...
I don't think he'd want
to spread himself
too thin.

Hell, ain't there a big book of poets?
Something like a phone book?
Look in the yellow pages
under poet
get the cheapest one."

The president,
by now too drunk to care,
falls asleep.
The Coordinator,

himself a very frustrated rhymer,
rolls up his sleeves,
spits into his palms,
rubs them anxiously,
walks up to the microphone
with a strange
twisted
grin.

JOHN DORSEY

doctor bukowski's monster

in the sunlight of madness
bukowski's monster
has been turned into
the shadow of a young james dean

the meaning gets lost
caught up in the moment
where stanzas get tattooed
into the golden forearms
of nelson algren's overmedicated grandchildren
searching for cool
with a broken flashlight
beamed toward karma

there is a junky born
every minute

read the label
shoot dice
ask questions later
ask the dust for its last dime
spit words at the sun
an eternal hot walker
wait for the photo finish
become a split second god
in another man's miracle

a house on fire
we came here to watch the words burn
golden like shelley's sperm
like cassius clay's draft card
like the embers of johnny cash's
last folsom cigarette

like the senseless dying of the light
we were built to rage against

like freedom fighters
searching for a match

in the rain

Originally published in *Sodomy Is a City in New Jersey*
(American Mettle Books, 2010) and
Last Call: The Bukowski Legacy Continues
(Lummox Press, 2011)

Part Ten
The Typer

©Joan Gannij

For information about purchasing fine quality prints of
Charles Bukowski portraits by Joan Gannij,
send an email to joangannij@gmail.com.

ADRIAN MANNING

the old master

I sit at my old typer, at a desk
in my room.
above me is a shelf full of books
by a writer called Bukowski.
I read the titles and think to myself
if I could only come up with one line
like one of those titles
I could really have something.
there are many books and magazines,
I have not counted them,
and there are possibly more poems in them
than an army of men could produce
and they are mostly very good and
if not very good they are good.
I wish the words were like bees
humming around my head in a storm
of vibrant movement. I could possibly
catch some of them and nail them down
with a Bukowski book.
he sits in a photo, on one shelf,
in his later years, the hard work behind him,
one arm resting on his chair, the other
raised to the temple of his head
and he looks thoroughly unimpressed.
he's telling me, work it boy, gotta keep going,
you're nowhere near yet.
I look up at the photo
and tell him you're right,
you son of a bitch,
you were always right.

Written at home upon gazing at my bookshelf!
Previously published in *Lummox Journal* (2000)

DIRK VELVET

breathing bukowski

he used the smallest words
he could find
to
tell his
tales

he knew that
the large ones
could get
stuck
going in

and

never
come
out

he knew
what we all
needed
to live

to
breathe

in
and
out

Bukowski - proof 9/9/83 David Barker

Portrait by David Barker
Originally published in
Charles Bukowski: A Bibliographic Price Guide
By David Barker
(David & Judy Barker Booksellers, 1983)

MICHAEL O'BRIEN

Verse 412—Anyone?

A poet said that
"some men never
die
and some men never
live."

ok

but then he said that

"we're all alive
tonight."

who?

by "we all,"
in the second poem,
Bukowski is not referring to "everybody."

no, he seems to be referring
to himself, and his
teachers,
and his typing
machine.

wildly waltzing
the lines
and the stories.

must have been quite a
show.

As they who never lived
stood stiffly by.

And some of they
who never die
still work to keep
our weary, misled spirits all
from fading into
nothingness.

DAVE ROSKOS

new typer

new typer, very old
& loud
antique
"underwood/forum"
must weigh 50 pounds
or more.
could probably write
some heavy shit
on this heavy typer.
feel like Bukowski
in 1958.
don't know about this
heavy beast of a machine
it's too slow
has no eraser tape
is so loud don't think
I'll be able to type
at night, which is
when I do most
of my typing.
not to sound ungrateful now,
cuz I'm not, & I do
appreciate the novelty
of its antique type,
may use it to typeset
an issue of *Ball Peen*.
the shittiest piece
of writing will look
like heart-hewn
literature on this
machine.
now here's a real writer
editors will think
when they open up a
manuscript typed on
this thing.
it's older than Coltrane
been around longer than
Dizzy & Bird; shit,

Bix Biederbeck coulda owned
this thing at one point
& he probably hocked it
for a quart of gin.
He's here now & he wants
it back. I offer him coffee
for lack of gin or even beer;
no alcohol in this house,
just a broke-down typer.

WILLIAM BARKER

A Scarecrow, Unlabeled

Bukowski at his typewriter,
a Royal or Underwood, dim room, smoke dancing around
the dust-encrusted bulb like wispy serpents. Phone off the hook,
the punch of keys, some frantic Morse code in the night only
writers see as symphonic. It's dead summer, an oscillating fan
and open window fight the Los Angeles humidity. Our poet is shirtless,
wearing only shorts, the stink of the city deep in his bones by now.
A wine glass, half-filled with Pinot Noir, sits next to a small red radio,
where Debussy ejaculates through the speaker. Nearby, a wastebasket
overflows with empty beer, wine and whiskey bottles. Outside, dogs bark,
couples quarrel, children play and police sirens screech—the sounds
of the universe. Things are happening.

An always volatile life
lived along the edges of nowhere has slowed to only a simmer now.
Our fellow is settling in, finding notoriety and chasing the muse
purposefully. Prolific barbarian hammering away at the delicate
bedrock of poetry until its surface resembles the mad moon or his own
countenance. The marrow of Earth bubbles with possibility, life. Feelings
of being a factotum slip to memory, lightening darkened eyes. People
are crowding, poetry readings selling out, women are noticing
and the literary world clamors like a pale bell with his name—Bukowski!
Our poet smiles more, finally feeling a sense of certainty; a mild comfort
he never takes for granted as his words finally begin to sustain him
and worries fade behind a pleasing ritual like the sun
behind dark mountains.

Detractors are many by now,
but there is no stopping a force of nature both sculpted in the warrens
and forged by white fire. It's laughable to our guy who pours it all into
the cauldron as more material for future expedition upon paper
and toasts the shit storm with a glass of Riesling! Hollywood, women, horses,
liquor, music, the literary world, life, death, sex, abuse, poverty…it's all inside with a
dash of deadpan, a pinch of wisdom, and two cups of grandfatherly insight.
The twentieth century's Whitman, in our lifetime. You can almost see him
still sitting there, leaning into the machine. If you listen closely you may
hear the keys thumping when you read the legacy he left us. The ember of hope,
however small, must be kept lit, as it will start the greatest fire anywhere, anytime.
Our hero is proof of that.

ADRIAN MANNING

What You Have Left Bukowski

when all that can be said
has been said
and all that will be done
is done
the beer and wine
have stopped flowing
the women
do not come around
or leave anymore
      and
the typer
has wrung out its final
      key
all that is left
are the words
words on the page
what you have left Bukowski
beyond everything else
reminding us
what bravery we have
still remaining
needs to be hammered
to the clean white sheet
with a heavy duty rhythm
to carry carry carry……..

Written after attending the Bukowski exhibition in London, 1996
Previously published in *Lummox Journal* (2000)

Part Eleven
Don't Try

©Joan Gannij

Paul Fericano

The Three Stooges Meet Charles Bukowski in Heaven

The day is like any other day in Paradise
where angels hang out on street corners in between gigs
smoking filtered cigarettes, drinking ginger ale
and swapping stories about the Son of Man.

Everyone has an eye fixed on Jesus.
He's on his knees in an alley shooting dice
with the Three Stooges
and the poor bastards are losing their shirts and their pants.

The Savior of the World is on fire.
In flowing red robe he rattles the bones in his hand,
brings them to his ear, shakes them like the Second Coming
and blows on them once for luck.

He arcs his fist before release and shouts:
"Come on mama, baby needs a new pair of shoes!"
then tosses them with the same force his father summoned
to create the Milky Way.

When he flashes that wide, resurrection smile
the one he showed the Romans right before they nailed him,
he scoops up his winnings with a wink and a nod
and everyone knows: The Lamb of God is on a roll.

The Stooges are victims of divine intervention.
They make the sign of the cross and Jesus smiles,
"I like you guys," he says, slapping their faces affectionately
and just like that, three morons become saints.

Leaning against a wall, drinking beer from a bottle
always cold, never empty, is Charles Bukowski.
He shifts his weight like a man itching to start something,
eyeing the action as if he's writing his last poem.

Jesus stands now and introduces them.
The Stooges pull back, unsure of what to expect from a guy
who once threw up on Norman Mailer and just last week
tried to look up the Virgin Mary's dress.

Bukowski hesitates, too. He watches their fingers closely,
remembering what it's like to almost lose an eye in a pie fight,
their mutual mistrust creating such heavenly tension
even the Holy Ghost is frightened. And that's when

Jesus stands on his head. It's a small miracle,
nothing great, like changing a commercial for Dodge trucks
into a made-for-TV movie, but it makes everyone laugh,
especially Jesus, who clearly isn't wearing underpants.

KAREN FINLEY

Charles Bukowski
Square Sun

What if we had a Square Sun
No globe
No circular circumference
To gaze
Blasting Anger
At elemental abstractions
Start giving a shit
Once in awhile
I hate illustrated poems

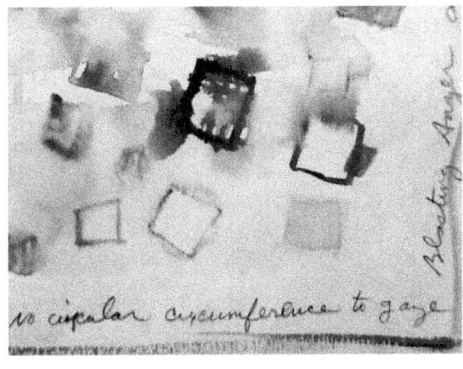

"Square Sun" (detail)
Painting by Karen Finley

HARRY CALHOUN

Bukowski, God and me

Bukowski's girl
reading the bible
outside his window
is now doubtless gone

and so is he
and soon I will be too
and if, as in his poem,
he is God,

and if I, creating this poem
am also God,
where will I be ever after?
Maybe Bukowski and I

can talk about it.

Originally published in *Momo Reader*

RD Armstrong

The Old Dog

When the day comes
when the final bell ends his last
round
when the needle scratches
the last groove
and the last exacta is run
then they can have him.

When the last cunt-induced
sleepless night is over
when the last drop of wine is drained
when the last hangover fades
then it won't matter where he's gone.

But until that time
let him raise a palsied paw
to the sky
and howl at the moon for all he's worth.
So what if the swaggering blowhard
has been replaced by a staggering old pup.

Leave him alone and he'll still amaze
us
with that
one
last
perfect
gesture.

ROSS RUNFOLA

Nothing Left to Write

Henry Chinaski is dead.
my world turned ass over when I heard the news.
rooming house man whose come will spread no more.
only death renders Buk incapable of erections, ejaculations,
exhibitions, and tales of ordinary madness.

heir of John Fante.
more bard of the barroom than barfly.
translator of Los Angeles skid row.
fucker of rhymes and visionary poetry
in favor of bleakness and truth.

major figure in European literary circles
horseplayer outside the winner's circle of American literati
until the average American he gives meaning to
tries to make him a cultural icon.

Bukowski refuses to let celebrity devour him like Ginsberg.
stale middle-American air
the sailboats of San Pedro
Madonna's Hollywood
do not make him soft.
living hard on the street made him fear life not death.
I pay homage to the great one by donating money
for a toilet stall inscription in the women's john at my college
"To the underground poet Charles Bukowski who discovered more
uses for toilets in American bars than Thomas Crapper could have
ever hoped for."

A fitting tribute to Buk, who even in death
can be near young snatch.
the college president says the inscription is unfit for the academic
world
as if his fear of the unholy is fit for any world.

Hell—Nixon got a twenty-one-gun salute.
why can't Hank rest in peace in the women's shitter?

ADRIAN MANNING

The grave

I drive the car in through the gates
and move up the driveway
until I find a place to park.

I show one of the grave tenders
the number I have and he directs
me further still.
I get out and leave the car in park.

There are no other people here.
It is a very quiet afternoon in San Pedro.
The sun is bright but not hot and the grass
looks very green and alive.

I look for the grave but have great difficulty finding it.
I remember a photograph I saw,
poets reading at the spot
and try to picture the image amid the trees.

I struggle and ask a middle-aged Hispanic guy.
Oh him, he says, I know where that one is.
I know I'm not the first to come.

He takes me there
and leaves me alone.
I look over at the harbour
and it all seems very peaceful,
far from what I imagined of the resting place
of one of the world's most famous
and brilliant hell raisers.

Written after visiting Bukowski's grave in San Pedro 2001
Previously published in *Laura Hird Showcase* (2004)

SUZANNE LUMMIS

Charles Bukowski, 1920-1994

A large gravelly head, deep-set eyes often hidden in shadow. This is either the head of some creature that staggered from its cave to tear Sinbad and his sailors limb from limb, or a profound and formidable visage that would look fine on Mount Rushmore alongside the other notables.

A face like that must give a man a sense of destiny. Los Angeles poet and fiction writer Charles Bukowski, who died of leukemia on March 9th [1994] at the age of seventy-three, managed to create a life worthy of his face. And he produced a voluminous body of work that documented that life in the underbelly of Los Angeles, tales of ribald exploits laced with self-deprecating humor. Prostitutes broke his heart. Beefy men beat him up in fights he usually started. And there were old men, too, in this urban landscape, generally "in four dollar rooms / looking for socks in dresser drawers / while standing in brown underwear…" (from "lack of almost everything").

Bukowski went by the alias Henry Chinaski in his fiction and by his own name in his poetry, but the boorish, half-endearing underdog persona never changed. It won him a folk hero status in the international literary underground.

Bukowski once wrote that style came from lack of pretension. Well, Bukowski had a little pretension, all that magnificent self-debasement, those public displays of excess. Yet he had a style anyway, a blunt, no-frills one, and it spawned a ton of imitators.

Wordsworth, Whitman, William Carlos Williams and The Beats in their respective generations moved poetry toward a more natural language. Bukowski moved it a little farther. He was never a university poets' poet but a populist voice, a Carl Sandburg for the down-and-out set. "I like desperate men, men with broken teeth and broken minds and broken ways," he wrote in his story, "Guts." "I also like vile women, drunk cursing bitches with loose stockings and sloppy mascara faces."

Unlike Sandburg, though, Bukowski never declared himself to be an ambassador of the people; that would have been too corny. He never declared himself to be anything except a hard drinker, a womanizer, a racetrack aficionado and above all—absolutely above all—a poet.

And one more thing: He declared himself to be Bukowski. His biographer Neeli Cherkovski recalls that Bukowski was fond of saying: "When I met Neeli he was sixteen and I was Bukowski."

When word of Bukowski's death got out, John Martin, Bukowski's editor at Black Sparrow Press in Santa Rosa, received calls from readers in Latin America, France, the Netherlands, all over, many of them crying. The owner of a coffee shop in Seattle called: "Someone's put a sign outside my place that says Charles Bukowski's dead. People are crying. Is it true?"

And here in Los Angeles, poets who liked him and those who didn't will remember for a long time where they were and what they were doing when they got the news.

On Saturday, March 26, drivers passing the 8300 block of Beverly Boulevard must have wondered briefly at the rows of folding chairs on the sidewalk and the standing-room-only crowd gazing through the window of Arundel Antiquarian Books. KCRW had set up a microphone so that the overflow crowd could hear the Bukowski memorial addresses taking place inside. Several speakers recounted a similar experience:

"I heard a poem on the radio and recognized it as Bukowski's, but it was an AM station. I thought, 'oh oh, this can't be good." (Bill Mohr)

"I was in Hawaii. I saw his name on the front page of the news with a photograph. I knew there was no Nobel Prize. I knew it was something dreadful." (Neeli Cherkovski)

Those who'd known him called him "Hank" or "Buk," and those who hadn't nevertheless felt as if they had. Though he'd been living rather reclusively in San Pedro with his wife and had not given a public reading for years, in literary L.A. his presence was keenly felt. He didn't hold out for prestigious publications; the most famous poet of the region published in everything, even homemade ventures, stapled, photocopied, lousy-looking things. As Charles Webb testified, one only had to ask and he'd send a bunch of poems with a note—"Take what you need…Buk"—and always a little doodle next to his name. Of course he could afford to; he turned out poems like one possessed or driven, as if that dog from hell noted in one of his titles was nipping at his heels.

There were anecdotes and laughter on this occasion, but Joan Jobe Smith altered the mood, suddenly putting down her book. "I don't want to read anything," she said quietly. "Charles Bukowski has left the building. Charles Bukowski has left L.A. Hail Bukowski."

"Hail Bukowski," said the audience.

But although he had been writing about and imagining his death for thirty years, it seemed impossible that Charles could leave L.A.

Bukowski was born in Germany on Aug. 16, 1920, and came to Los Angeles at age three. He had the kind of childhood that qualifies people to weep on all the afternoon talk shows. Brutal father, indifferent mother. In adolescence he broke out with terrible boils, which scarred his face and deepened his sense of isolation. (Much of that period is revealed in the novel *Ham On Rye*.) Until he began to make a living from his writing at around age 50, he worked every odd job known to man or woman, in a dog biscuit factory, a New York subway, women's dress factories and meat-packing plants, on a track gang laying train tracks across the country, two days as a janitor at the L.A. Times, and finally, a job that lasted for a while--at the Central Post Office. He commemorated that one in his first novel, *Post Office* (1971), a turning point for the writer who till then had only a tiny cult following as a poet.

Later he would write about those rough years honestly and sometimes humorously, but seldom with the raw vulnerability revealed in his more personal letters of the time. In September 1962, Bukowski was bleeding from a drinking-related malady and suicidally depressed over the conditions of his life. Jane, the woman he is said never to have forgotten, had recently died of alcoholism. "Blood again this morning. And do you know it's ugly? Not the bright red that floats at the top.... They drained it out of my love when she died. She used to wear my torn yellow bathrobe and walk about the room. Plop, plop, plop, she walked like a simple child. And I loved her. I loved her from Armenia to the top of the sun, and now the yellow robe hangs in my closet and she's rotting in a grave. So I sit here in my triangle; madness, death by hemorrhage, and suicide..."

He had little reason to believe at the time that thirty years down the line his collected letters, *Screams from the Balcony*, would sell ten thousand copies in two days. (The letter to Jon Webb quoted above appears not in that collection but in Webb's 1960s magazine, *The Outsider*.) He didn't imagine that someday a famous actor named Mickey Rourke would give a comic, affectionate portrayal of him in a film called *Barfly* and that Faye Dunaway would play Jane.

The unguarded emotion in the letter is stunning, coming from one who later would insist on being perceived as a crusty anti-romantic. And it seems to contradict the charge that he didn't like women.

"What are you going to say about Bukowski and women?" a woman called to ask me when she heard this article was in the works.

Some women have noted Bukowski's insensitive language—he liked to talk dirty—but this caller had a more serious complaint; she'd been shallowly characterized in one of his books. One must say this: He did not often draw his women characters with much depth or distinction. He did not often let his readers glimpse the Bukowski of Sept. 12, 1962. He was probably as leery of sentimentality as he was of self-pity. He did not always do much better by men.

He seems to have felt something, though, for the women he kept crawling back to after they'd struck him down and left him for dead. Henry Chinaski is beaten up by more women than any man in Western literature.

Of course, Charles Bukowski was politically incorrect before some thinly talented radio personality made it the rage. He sported the grunge look before a Seattle band set the fashion. He predated the new appreciation of older women; he declared women are the most desirable at the age when they're just starting to fall apart, which is good news for some of us. He continued to drink hard liquor straight from the bottle long after imported water had replaced martinis on the social scene, and only the influence of a woman he loved, then married, was able to slow him down. He was a writer who insisted on being out-of-step with his times.

"The most important thing to realize about him," said John Martin, "is that he didn't want to go with any trends or join groups. Charles Bukowski stood alone."

Something else is important to know about him. He said of his typewriter, as Scott Wannberg recalled at the memorial: "It all begins and ends here. In the moment." His "typer" he called it, and it was the love of his life.

Bukowski said: "The first thing writing must do is save your own ass." And so it did, for longer than he imagined it could. Writing, poetry: the mad dog nipping at his heels, and the wild horse running away over the hills.

Originally published in
the *Los Angeles Times*
April 10, 1994

AUSTIN MITCHELL

Things I Whisper on Bukowski's Grave

They said those who admire you and write
poetry are a disgrace, a cheap imitation
of style and faux hard luck. And so,
I read your books with love and wrote
some poems, trying to do the opposite
of all you did, while loving other poets too
and doing the same.
If they ever care (I doubt they will) who I read,
maybe I'll lie and say Frost, but I know

the road less traveled is full
of assholes.

Listen to my dull speech.
I can barely stand to think my own words
out loud. I'm just one more young man
who thought himself a poet,
come to knock on your death door.

You're spinning down there, I know,
like an empty bottle on a bare L.A. flophouse floor.

I want to tell you something.
My life is a surreal joke:

Last night very late, with not much money left
and only this one expensive beer,
I thought long and quite hard
about savoring every drop.
But instead I threw it back to the nose
until a cherry river burned
a gaping dimension on the inside
of my throat,
and it poured coldly
over the nape of my neck.

WILLIAM BARKER

The Death of Charles Bukowski

Nineteen years ago

our world
lost a mountain;

the skyline
hasn't
recovered.

JOAN JOBE SMITH

Eggs Over Easy

I was frying eggs over easy when
I heard Bukowski had died and
suddenly the yolks came alive,
grew to the size of heavyweight
Golden Gloves smashing my spatula
and jaw awhile the kitchen swelled
shut around me like a big, blackened
eye. Bukowski's obit was in the Thursday
newspaper, my favorite paper of the
week for the Food Section, the recipes
(this week sickening ones of what to
do with peanuts), the supermarket ads
(this week St. Pat's Day specials,
corned beef for 89 cents a pound,
cabbage for nine, rye $1.69 he'll
never eat again, if he ever did,
or the wine I later drink with my
husband who mourns more than me
as he listens to a Bukowski Live tape
and reads over and over the only letter
Hank ever wrote him. Hank never knew
was too busy to care, that his life
changed ours, that we'd come to know
his mojo poetry as well as the backs
of our hearts where manna and mortality
are stored. We'd wanted him to
live to be 400, after all, he was 200
at age 30, he was supposed to keep telling
it like it is forever, be our Poet Man,
nexus and code breaker of nether worlds.
But no one dies when you want
him or her to, death seldom an Ides
of March or hemlock time for which
you can set your alarm clock as, as he
was quoted in his obit: You carry in

one hand a bundle of darkness that
accumulates each day. The eggs
over easy were the coldest I ever ate,
a March ninth wind blowing in through
the window turning them to ice.

March 9, 1994

S.A. GRIFFIN

Blowtorch On A Pig

I made a pact with myself to never
write anything Bukowski again

then comes this via the Pony Express of my computer,
"Would you like to send unpublished poetry
or/and an essay on Charles Bukowski…"

I never met the man

never got loaded with him
talked shit about women
writing or the track

never laughed it up at one of his
infamous Hollywood shindigs

never pressed that flesh

more than once over the years
I'd walk into Baroque Books & Red would say,
"Kid, tomorrow at Musso's,
noon. Be there."

"Okay Red, see ya then."

I had nothing to offer but nerves
which of course always
got the better of me

did see him once in 1987
when Barbet Schroeder's *Bukowski Tapes*
debuted at EZTV in West Hollywood

Bukowski stood before us, cased the room,
"I don't smoke weed man. People who smoke
pot are just fucking idiots. They do nothing, they
read Zap comics & watch too much TV.
It slows you down man, takes the
edge off. It's a dull way to go."

with steady grace he raises the
green bottle in his fist & pulls on it,
"This," he slaps it, "is something," his face relaxing into a
generous grin that lights the room
& captures everything

he takes another tug,
"This shit makes the world
a better place."

Bukowski chuckles
a bluebird circles overhead

"Makes me feel like
the gods are smiling down on me,
like maybe I've got half a chance
coming out of the gate."

he fixes a sober gaze upon the audience
shifts his weight a bit like an old prizefighter,
"Okay, okay... I've talked enough.
Enjoy the movie."

& he & his beer
are gone

22 years later & a few miles west of Santa Anita
just past the long green money
& kept lawns of San Marino
Charles Bukowski smiles
across the main exhibition hall of the
Huntington Library at
William Shakespeare
under glass

Hank dead center of the centuries
shoulder to shoulder with other
quiet giants of arts & letters

blistering wisteria drip like warm wax in the
Southern California sun

Jacarandas announce the lavender spring

as pools of splashing laughter erupt from the suburbs
as the advancing city sings a strange fire that never dies

as I promise you

this will never
happen
again

A.D. WINANS

Poem for all the Kids Who Wrote Poems for Bukowski

These kids could never
Get enough of him
Not in books or magazines
Or on rare occasions in person
They wrote poems for and
About him
They bemoaned the fact
He hadn't been accepted by
The academics
As if this were somehow a liability
They flailed away at the establishment
Supposedly on his behalf
But I suspect getting
Their names in print
Had more than a little to do with it

Some chastised him
For not using punctuation
But were quick to forgive him
Because he was a genius
And a genius can do whatever
He wants to do

To his credit
When fame came knocking at his door
He quit writing hate poems
To those who had befriended him
And if success can do this to you
She can't be half the whore
We make her out to be

For a man who lived alone
Most of his life
He did remarkably well
And if he conned the small
Press editors and publishers
It was only because
He had the stamps to do it
And selling your soul
To the post office all those years

Was no easy task
I know, I have been there

And the readings never came easy
Puking his guts out backstage
Or in a barroom toilet stall
Or that one time in San Francisco
On the side of Ferlinghetti's van
But fate was kind to him
It gave him Linda Lee and
A new lease on life
A home in San Pedro
& how many years she tacked on
To his life we'll never know

He would have been the first
To tell you he was an asshole
And he was and so are you and I
Sometimes more so
Sometimes less
But rarely with as much class

He would have been the first
To admit he was a hustler
& a con man and he was both
And he did it with style
Which is more than you can say
For most of us

What he wouldn't tell all those kids
Was what they wanted to hear the most
That yes they were poets
That yes their work was dynamite
That yes they too could make it
If they flooded
The littles with their work
For the next twenty years
And fate was kind to them
Failing that
There is always suicide
Or a job with the post office

AMEN
Rest in peace.

SCOTT WANNBERG

People Just Aren't

The lengthy purple-prose eulogy in the *L.A. Times* called
Bukowski the poet laureate of lowlife L.A.
Well, I shouldn't expect too much I suppose from something
like the *L.A. Times*.
Linda, my colleague at work, hit it on the proverbial right
head when she said why not simply call him the poet laureate
of L.A. life.
Years ago I saw him do a wonderful reading in San
Francisco in one of those dignified downtown historical
type buildings. The same evening they were having a 100
dollar a plate dinner to kick off the new opera season.
Those of us there to see Buk were waiting on line and
those of them going to do up the opera were in their own
rhythm and we sort of looked across a large room at one
another and superficially sized one another up.
Later that night in his reading, Bukowski hit us with
a piece saying People Just Aren't Good To One Another.
It was a fine piece and I thought about the looks
we gave the opera folks and vice versa as if there
was an abyss between us that no language could ever
hope to heal.
Language is a tricky river. You may feel you are saying what
it is you think you want to say. Sometimes however
you don't say all that much.
It's a trickster dance floor, language.
You should be able to back it up by having fun.
I feel Bukowski had fun in writing.
He wrote so much.
He wrote in the tradition of Whitman and Woody
Guthrie.
He wrote about everything in his life and worldview,
a lot of it trivial, a lot of it profound.
One can't simply sit back and say I Will Choose Only
To Write The Big Poems The Important Poems The
Majestic Poems.
Bukowski taught me a very important thing when I was
beginning.
You can write what you see and you can see what you
write and you can write anything,

there is no taboo subject matter.
You can write about having to love a person's farts
just as much as their perfume if you are really going
to back up your love.
I said a few lines back he was in the same vein as
Woody. Woody would take out his guitar when the whim hit
and write about anything passing through him.
He once went to work on building the Grand Coulee Dam
but was so taken with the scenery he had to quit and
took his guitar up above where it was being built and
sat down and wrote a song.
Bukowski saw a lot, backed it up in his feeling by
not shying away from anything that a lot of
respectable people might consider worthless or
minor.
William Carlos Williams said once after someone praised him
for being the poet of the antipoetic
there is no anti-poetic. By writing the poem about it
whatever it is
it becomes poetic
by the choosing of it
whatever it is
to be the poem itself.
Someone told me a story once about how when Bukowski was up
in San Francisco reading with a lot of big Northern California
poets, including Ginsberg
(although we know Ginsberg is really East Coast)
a bomb threat rumor invaded the gig and
Bukowski jokingly claimed All I Need To Do Is Stand Behind
Ginsberg, And I Will Not Be In Danger Because
Ginsberg's Karma Will Protect Me.
I did attend a major poetic blowout in Santa Cruz back
in 1975 and Kenneth Rexroth got into a difference of
opinion with some women or a woman,
(I was sitting too far back to see which)
and Rexroth said Don't Hiss At Me I Come From Two Generations
Of Feminists.
Finally, he said, Don't Hiss At Me
You Wouldn't Want Bukowski To Come Down Here, Would You?
I think I was the only one in this vast room
this auditorium of listening
that got that one
and laughed in appreciation.

Cheap writers can try and pigeonhole Bukowski.
Well cheap writers will pigeonhole anything
classify everything
in specious classifications
I won't.
Bukowski was a human who wrote.
He left a lot of pages to go back to
if one feels the urge.
That's all you can ask for,
that a writer simply writes.
A writer shouldn't be out all the time being seen or
even seeing those who are being seen.
A writer belongs where a writer is needed the most,
in the moment and act of writing.
Bukowski once said it all begins here and
pointed to this typewriter.
It all begins and ends here,
in the moment.
Whatever Bukowski might be in the long run
to those who write articles and books and
purple prose obits
like the one in the Times,
he is always and foremost
a writer who
lived in the moment of
the passionate sacred act of
writing.
He taught me to stay home and
pay attention to
the words,
even when I nod off
and try and be lazy.
In the end
if you don't pay attention to
the words
you will trip and break your bones
and nobody will
invite you in
for coffee.
For Bukowski
who gave me many
days of pleasure,
the coffee is on,

it might even go down good.
The process is where we live,
the process is where we always dance.
For Bukowski
a dancer
who graced Los Angeles and
the world
with his music.
Sleep well, friend.

Previously published in
Malpais Review and as a Lummox Broadside

HARRY CALHOUN

Pictures of Bukowski

pictures of Bukowski juxtaposed on the Website
one the young man with a beer
in an alley—
well, young in Bukowski years,
like me he started late—
but with a satisfied smile

another of him old, in a dressing gown
hair tousled like Einstein, eyes
like wormholes staring straight
at death. He looks frightened
but even in fear is truth.
I don't believe that he was more

than human but I don't believe
he ever flinched.

I wrote a poem about my grandmother dying
many years ago, about how my parents
could see death more clearly
because of her passing. My mother's death
put me in the same position.

So I look into Bukowski's hollow eyes
and I look at the satisfied man in the alley
and I wish for all of us
that they could somehow have met in the middle
and come to some terms before
all there was to do was

sit and wait for death

Previously published in
Abbey and *I knew Bukowski like you knew a rare leaf*
(Trace Publications, 2009)

Mark Erickson

Around Hollywood

On my last day of class
I had some time to kill
so instead of heading home
thought I'd check out Hollywood Boulevard,
go by Music Man Murray's
and look at some records
or maybe head up to the tower
and watch the city roll along down below,
before I knew it I was on the Boulevard
tooling towards Highland
when I spotted an old light-colored 1960s Volkswagen
up ahead a block or so,
I decided to catch up with it
you have to move fast around Hollywood,
this was a game I had played before to no avail
the slippery writer always seemed to get away,
the Volks was weaving in and out of traffic
the guy knew what he was doing,
every time I was almost close enough to see who was driving
he sped up and caught a light and bolted ahead
seemingly fluidly being part of road,
then he hooked a fast left
I hit the turn soon after
bounced over the curb and slowed down
and there was the Bug parked
but no one inside,
how could it be
the ghost had flown the coop,
I looked up and down the sidewalk
not a soul walking
had he ducked into a store?
I drove slowly by, peering into the car
had I missed my chance?
as I passed a half dozen car lengths
in my rearview mirror
I saw a head pop up in the driver's seat
and the Volks lurched out of the space
spun quickly into the lane
and made a fast U-Turn

making a mad right back onto the Boulevard
and was gone,
I smiled knowing it was over this time
that crafty ol' Bukowski had escaped again.

DONNA HILBERT

Swimming with Bukowski

He looks up from swimming laps
waves me into the water
puts his arm around my waist
and we swim like upright frogs.
His backyard pool meanders
through palm trees, overlooks San Pedro.
Pool's more than fifty feet long, girl,
what d'you think of that?
His breath is a rosemary cloud
not the mothballs
I'd expected.
His skin is soft and clear again
as sleek as water-smoothed stone.
Inside the house John Martin speaks
to the dark-haired woman
who'll soon be in charge.
In front, a white stretch-limo waits
to drive Hank over the bridge
to the other side of the harbor.

Originally published in
Das ist Alles: Charles Bukowski Recollected
(Pearl Editions, 1995)

NOTES FROM THE CONTRIBUTORS

SHERIL ANTONIO: I welcome the opportunity to engage with new or different works, especially when recommended by friends, colleagues, or my students. Thus, when Karen Finley asked if I was interested in writing about the film *Barfly* for the Silver Birch Press *Bukowski Anthology,* I jumped at the chance. Filled with anticipation and excitement as I had not seen the film and knew little about Charles Bukowski's work, I set out to discover both. After completing the essay that describes my journey, some of Bukowski's phrases stayed with me, and I was still curious about which of them rose to the level of urban legend and were still being disseminated in the world. This led me to search for more his quotes on the web. I found quite a few that felt like the man I had just met. I decided to continue my relationship with Bukowski on Twitter and one of my first tweets went like this: "Went outside my 'expertise' on *Barfly*—'so it's always a process of letting go, one way or another' Charles Bukowski." Since then, I have been tweeting Bukowski quotes to my students and here are some of my favorites: "I remember awakening one morning and finding everything smeared with the color of forgotten love." "Real loneliness is not necessarily limited to when you are alone." "I wanted the whole world or nothing." "An intellectual says a simple thing in a hard way. An artist says a hard thing in a simple way." But by far the one that got the most response from followers was: "Do you hate people? I don't hate them…I just feel better when they're not around."

DAVID BARKER: My short story "One Match Left" was written in 1987, but, as far as I can tell, I didn't do anything with it until 2009, when it was accepted by Jan Hallers for use in the planned second issue of his excellent magazine, *Buk Scene.* To my knowledge, *Buk Scene 2* never materialized and the story lay idle until 2010 when Canadian artist and small press editor Jocelyne Desforges published it under the imprint of her Purple Glow Press as a limited edition mini-chapbook. What makes this little book so incredible is that Jocelyne designed the binding so as to resemble an oversized version of the matchbook from Charles Bukowski and Linda Lee Beighle's wedding, even down to the iridescent, multicolored covers which she hand painted, making each copy a unique work of art. The front cover flips up, just like on a book of matches, and the text is stapled in where a clump of paper matches would be in a real matchbook. Furthermore, she applied the title on each copy by hand using rub-on lettering, each in a different font and layout, adding to the uniqueness of each copy. I can't thank Jocelyne enough for creating such a beautiful edition of this short work. Every time I see it, I smile.

HARRY CALHOUN: I think the essay on my experiences with Bukowski speaks for itself. I still have several letters, a postcard, and what I think to be an original, unpublished poem of his in my files. Some of my greatest treasures. "Bukowski, fame and me" is a sad musing that I'll probably be more known for publishing Bukowski than for my own poetry, while "Pictures of Bukowski' was inspired by photos of the man on the bukowski.net website. I searched through Bukowski's works for the quote I used in the poem "An insomniac thinks of Bukowski" ("Try not to think of the liver, and maybe the liver will not think of you"). Couldn't find it. Then one day I was reading through his letters to me. Boom! The actual line in the letter was, "I don't want to think about my liver; maybe it won't think about me." The poem ends by referring to the irony that after all of Bukowski's heavy drinking he died, not from liver disease but leukemia. Also, during my *Pig in a Poke* and *Pig in a Pamphlet* days, I published writers nearly as famous as Bukowski, such as Jim Daniels, Lyn Lifshin, Louis McKee, and others (including chapbooks by Daniels and McKee). The online version of *Pig in a Poke* is currently inactive, but anyone wanting to take a look can go to www.piginpoke.com/currentissue.html.

RENE DIEDRICH: I consider Bukowski my literary poppa. I loudly proclaimed Buk the most important writer of our time while in college, earning the wrath of gender fetish professors and feminists with earth shoes. They all spat blood as I teetered on heels, regaling old men and impressionable undergrad stories from my days as an L.A. stripper. They laughed when I saw that Hank had much in common with Chaucer. But Bukowski now sits beside the scatological genius who brought us the wife of Bath.

MARK ERICKSON and **BIRGIT (KATY) ZARTL:** We had been on a tear of reading Bukowski books for a quite a few months. I was rereading many and Katy was reading them for the first time. She digested them quickly, enjoying every novel and short story. I reread *Post Office* and *Women*, maybe for the third time. *Hollywood* and *The Captain Is Out to Lunch and the Sailors Have Taken Over the Ship* followed quickly. *Pulp*, that one for the first time I realized. I loved it, laughed all the way through. I had started it years before, and I had stopped. I cannot recall why. This time, it went down easy, truly a great last novel, with that hilarious ending. We read more and, around that time, we felt we had to do a Bukowski poster, a strong graphic image we could enjoy and be proud of. The piece was born on his writings and lived by his incredible stories and wit. The image of him smoking a cigarette just nailed it. I spent extra time on the ash and the burning ember at the end of his cigarette. The trail of smoke circles around and leads you back to Bukowski.

PAUL FERICANO: Ever since the mid-1970s, I've used The Three Stooges as inspirational subject matter to add a satiric kick to certain work. I would place the Stooges in contemporary settings with pop culture or historical figures to reveal some truth about the absurdity of modern life. My poem, "The Three Stooges Meet Charles Bukowski in Heaven" came about as I was working on a draft of another poem titled, "The Three Stooges Roll Dice with Jesus." Unhappy with the direction the poem was taking, I took a break to check my emails and discovered a thoughtful invitation from Silver Birch Press asking me to consider submitting poetry to an anthology the publisher was putting together on Charles Bukowski. That was all I needed. I gave the poem a new title and finished it within the hour.

JACK FOLEY: I wrote my "Bukowski" poem in response to a poem in Charles Bukowski's book, *Mockingbird, Wish Me Luck*. The words in the first, third, fifth, etc., lines are Bukowski's poem; the words in italics are by me. When I perform the poem, I speak the Bukowski portion in my "normal" voice; I speak the words by me in a whisper. I call this way of responding to a poem "writing between the lines." My poem, contrapuntal with Bukowski's, is meant as a kind of portrait.

ANGGO GENORGA: "For the Record" sort of wrote itself after the first entry that I submitted for the *Bukowski Anthology* was rejected. The poem was conceived ten years ago, a few months after I got my hands on a couple of Bukowski's poems—thanks to a friend who responded to my constant egging to print me the poems from the Internet. Back then, you could never find a Bukowski book in any library or bookstore in Manila. I was into Beat poetry at that time and getting disenchanted with reading into metaphors and was looking for straightforward writing—something that would hit closer to home. The crazy part is that I carried the idea for the poem over the years and almost forgot about putting it down on paper. Words and verses, even other poems, meandered inside my head along with this idea, and I realized that I hadn't written anything official about Charles Bukowski until I read the invitation for the Silver Birch Press *Bukowski Anthology*. It's my testament to the essence of Charles Bukowski. It's quite a delight to write the poem for the man and be featured on a collection solely dedicated to his legacy, and it's my first high-profile gig. Goddamn, Long Live Bukowski!

MARJORIE GILBERT: I turned ninety-one on July 17, 2013, and what a surprise getting all this attention—first an article in the *Los Angeles Times* [by Richard Verrier on February 14, 2013] and then a request from Silver Birch Press about my poem. I am most happy to include "The Night Bukowski Read His Poems" in the Silver Birch Press *Bukowski Anthology*. It is a hobby of mine to write about highlights in my life, and seeing and hearing Bukowski was one of those highlights. Thank you for your interest in my "life line," as I call my poems. Regarding my attendance at Charles Bukowski's reading at Cal State, Los Angeles, during the 1970s [as quoted in the *Los Angeles Times*]: "It was quite an evening. I didn't even know who Bukowski was, so I sat there not knowing what to expect. Here he was with a beer can in one hand and he's got these pages in the other hand and he's reading to us like he couldn't care less. He'd sip his beer than throw his page on the floor. He sounded very honest, like he was telling it like it is. I knew he lived a life I would never know, so I was intrigued."

DONNA HILBERT: Sometime during the week that Bukowski died, I had the vivid dream that became the poem "Swimming With Bukowski." I never met him, but living or dead he is a looming presence in literary culture, particularly in Long Beach. Had we met, I doubt we would have had much in common outside a few mutual friends, but I am grateful that he lived and worked nearby, expanding the universe of what can be said in a poem. I wouldn't have mined taking a swim with him.

RODGER JACOBS: "Was Céline Céline or was he somebody else?" L.A. private eye Nicky Belane muses in Charles Bukowski's *Pulp* (Black Sparrow Press, 1994), the last novel that the poet laureate of the damned and dispossessed would write before succumbing to leukemia at the age of seventy-three.

"Sometimes I felt that I didn't even know who I was," Belane continues. "All right, I'm Nicky Belane. But check this. Somebody could yell out, 'Hey, Harry! Harry Martel!' and I'd most likely answer, 'Yeah, what is it?' I mean, I could be anybody, what does it matter? What's in a name?"

In the spring of 2008, I began penning a series of surreal and humorous short and flash fiction pieces for my author website at the time, *Carver's Dog*, collected under the title *Mr. Bukowski's Wild Ride*. The protagonist of the Los Angeles-based stories was not Charles Bukowski but a writer named Mr. Bukowski who dwells in an alternate universe version of the City of Angels, where cartoon characters like Popeye and Woody Woodpecker are flesh-and-blood beings, typewriters can talk, and a famous producer of family fare for film and TV considers making "animated fare for adults only...[stories] that involve pimps and whores, grafters and boozers, gamblers and sinners, except instead of people they'd be represented by furry little woodland creatures."

The "Mr. Bukowski" tales were not only written for my amusement and that of my readers, but they furthered my deconstructive study of the mechanics of experimental fiction (at the time I was writing a popular literature column for Pop Matters called "The Deconstruction Zone," so it can be said that deconstructive analysis was on my mind a lot in those days). But there was more lurking beneath these comic tales than meets the eye; as L.A. journalist and author Joseph Mailander wrote in the introduction to the 2008 book publication of *Mr. Bukowski's Wild Ride*, the collected works were "understated masterpieces[s] about the kind of angry, midlife sexual trauma that afflicts post-millennial, aging America."

Apparently post-millennial aging Americans do not care to read about themselves; when Don Campana, a friend and sales associate at famed City Lights Bookstore in San Francisco, offered to place copies of a "Mr. Bukowski" book up for consignment sale at the retail store if only I would publish it, I collected the pieces in a single slim volume—printed via Lulu Press—and shipped the limited edition of forty-seven copies to San Francisco. The books sold out in less than a year and, Mr. Campana reported at the time, almost all of the sales were to European tourists with an appreciation for Bukowski.

"Mr. Bukowski and the Red Socks" and "Mr. Bukowski and the Movie Star" are, I think, representative of the book but also are two of the more "tame" pieces. A new edition, *Mr. Bukowski's Wild Ride: 38 Stories about a Writer Named Bukowski*, was published in 2012 by The Book Motel.

MICHAEL LIMNIOS: For my generation (born 1969) in Greece, Charles Bukowski HAS (not was) a special relationship. His books were in our rooms with Muddy Waters & Co., Charlie Parker & Co., Grateful Dead & Co., and Bob Marley & Co. records, with Che Guevara and Easy Rider posters, and Tom Robbins, Jack, Allen, Gregory, and William books. Charles had a Zen Taoist influence on us: we are what we read in his books or we did what we read. Charles is our friend, our uncle who told us stories. *Yammas, Cheers, Slainte, Saludos Hank !!!!!!*

GERMA MARQUEZ: I don't remember when I started to paint; I only know that my favorite toys when I was a little girl were the colored pencils and the drawing blocks. Since then, Art is my life and my profession and, more than that, a form of communication with other people. I also have a great interest in anthropology, the human being in many aspects, and maybe that's why I've focused my interest on the human figure and portraits. As a portraitist, I have always been attracted by faces that reveal a story, and Bukowski's face is a gift for me. To explore that is as exciting as reading Bukowski's "Bluebird" the first time. A true adventure.

AUSTIN MITCHELL: I wrote "Things I Whisper on Bukowski's Grave" in college after receiving a prompt to write about a celebrity, or from the perspective of a celebrity. This was supposed to be a quick exercise and not a poem to be workshopped in class. As a result, I didn't put in the same effort that I did for my workshopped poems. My professor said it was the best poem I had written all semester. I reluctantly agreed with her and realized the truth in Bukowski's well-known phrase, "Don't try."

JEFFREY MORGAN: Charles Bukowski was the writer that dared me to go all the way, be constant, contend, endure, never sell out, stay true to the art (despite the worst odds)—because it's worth it. He is still my comrade, my anchor, and my endurance coach. When it's tough, I remember the champ. Thanks, Charles.

GERALD NICOSIA: "Notes on My Fourth of July with Bukowski" comes out of my one and only meeting with Bukowski. In the early 1990s, my first wife Marcia Vincent was a good friend of Linda Bukowski's, and Marcy got to go over to their house in San Pedro all the time. Marcy wasn't a writer—she was a lawyer and arts promoter—and I was jealous that she was getting to spend so much time with Bukowski, and I'd never met him! It turned out Bukowski only socialized one day a year—on the Fourth of July—when they would throw a big barbecue in San Pedro. So Marcy got me invited to the Fourth of July barbecue in 1991. I spent a good half-day there—one of the most memorable days in my life. Barbet Schroeder was there, so was Seymour Cassel. I liked Buk a whole lot. He was a great storyteller, but also filled with sadness then, a sense that his life was ending. Indeed, he died less than three years later. I made a ton of journal notes about it, but only one creative piece resulted, a short poem entitled "Fourth of July with the Buk in San Pedro."

For a long time, I resisted doing anything with those dozens of pages of notes. The notes remained buried in my journal for twenty-two years. At first, I didn't want to put them into a full-length piece because Buk was still alive and it would have seemed too invasive. Then, as time went on, they just got buried under so much new experience, and if I thought about them at all, I couldn't figure out what I should do with them, where they might be published. It all came together when Silver Birch Press asked for something longer (and preferably new) about Bukowski. The actual writing of the piece flowed rapidly in May 2013. Rather than invasion, it now felt like a goldmine of history that needed to be mined and preserved. The dialogue is just as I wrote it down a few hours after the party had ended, and the insights are more or less word-for-word as I put them down the next day. What I added was a little connective tissue, a few transitional passages. I also rearranged a few things, since I sometimes commented to myself on one incident in several different places in the journal. Also, I tried to make the narrative a little more coherent by gathering Buk's remarks on a particular topic—such as women—in one or two places, rather than throughout the whole evening, as they tended to come. That is to say, Buk would ramble a lot from topic to topic, and one or two hours later might finally get back to the end of a story he had begun several beers earlier. Other than those minor touch-ups, what is printed here is more or less an evening with Bukowski preserved in amber.

BART PLANTENGA: The original impetus for "Contemplating Charles Bukowski" was our fascination with how Bukowski managed to overcome, survive, and ultimately thrive despite and/or because of his handicap: being less than classically handsome or, in fact, being considered plug ugly. This was our vision of a pre-writing-success confrontation he may have had with prejudice. Wild child meets conformist-insistent society. His ability to not only overcome his "affliction" has come to embody the struggle that the unempowered worldwide encounter on a daily basis. It also spoke to the unjustly ignored writers among us. Bukowski managed to transform this "affliction" into empowerment, converting this currency based on perseverance, survival, raw talent, ruthless vision, and compassion into a body of work that continues to inspire people worldwide, even in later years becoming himself a kind of inside-out sex symbol as straight society scrambled to make sense of it all. This is a specially condensed version of the original twenty-seven-hundred-word short story. Find the complete story at: www.inotherwordsmerida.com/2012/09/13/fiction-by-bart-plantenga-and-co-author-black-sifichi/

DAVID S. POINTER: My poetry shows the continued influence of Charles Bukowski's work on my work. Of course, I've moved on to many other influences over the years, but Bukowski is still in the room like a stack of leaking collector oilcans in a tabled corner. "The Superhero Zone" is a crazy tale of what takes one person up brings another person down. The reading and TV public seem to constantly line up to see what's happening next.

ALVARO POZO: Each line is a new creation, a solitary process, slow and at times painful, I seek to use all force enabling the strokes, to give my work an identity, a desire, a story. It is never too late to create, although everything is a big lie.

D.A. PRATT ("Encountering Bukowski—Some Canadian Notes"): As the twenty-first century progresses through its second decade, I have become intrigued by the challenge of how we pass along to a new generation of readers our enthusiasm for the books and the writers we have found engaging, especially given that younger readers now have what we call "the social media" at their fingertips. The ways we discuss and write about our favourite books have to take this into account. Shorter essays, almost mini-essays, about our "great moments" in reading could be the way to make an impression. It also strikes me that it is now time to rescue from the academics writers like D.H. Lawrence, who has been an important author to me, if he is to be read by new readers in this century. On the other hand, the approaching twentieth anniversary of the death of Charles Bukowski emphasizes to me that there will soon be a new generation of readers of his works—this new generation will approach him and his writing differently. My thoughts about this are reflected in my piece for this collection.

RAYMOND KING SHURTZ: During my last year in high school in 1975, I lived with my aunt, Linda King, in Los Angeles, where Bukowski was often a resident. I remember him as the poet who took me to the races, the boxing matches, and wanted to fight me on occasion. He was just starting to achieve some rise to fame, but I didn't really care. I was seventeen, having my own adventures, and living every day as if it were my last. I also remember him coming to my school play, where I had the lead, and giving me a standing ovation. I loved poetry, and loved his, but didn't much care for the wild parties that were happening under the roof where I lived, as they kept me up too late.

JOAN JOBE SMITH: Charles Bukowski has been an inspiration to me as a writer and woman since 1973, when I first read his *Days Run Away Like Wild Horses Over the Hills*. As a writer, I was inspired by him to write from the true, real heart—"walk through the fire"—about Life. As a woman, I was inspired to not be overwhelmed by or afraid of "the fire" that had been and still was my strange and hectic life. Ultimately I learned, just as Bukowski had learned: "The world has shaped me, and I shaped what I could." Bukowski, c'est moi. Vive Bukowski!

MARK TERRILL ("The Art of Victory"): Although John Martin's hundred-dollar-a-month subsidy allowed Bukowski to quit his job at the post office and concentrate on writing, it was a long time until wealth and fame finally caught up with him. During that time, Bukowski lived in a sort of hand-to-mouth, precarious yet comfortable poverty, in which the pleasures were few and far between, often of a strictly transitory nature. It was while thinking of these fleeting moments and their capriciousness that I wrote "The Art of Victory," for those are indeed the moments that make life worth living and give it its meaning. Those of us who are capable of realizing this are the real winners.

FRED VOSS: Someday, when academia finally wakes up, Charles Bukowski will be recognized as the Shakespeare of 20th Century L.A.'s real people in the streets and bars and factories. Fortunately, when Buk was still alive, I didn't need academia to tell me that I lived across the L.A./Long Beach harbor from a great living poet.

ABOUT THE CONTRIBUTORS

CHRISTOPHER R. ADAMS is an illustrator, printmaker, and builder of objects living in Corvallis, Oregon. His art feeds off an interest in the flora and fauna of his immediate environs of the Pacific Northwest, his background in architecture, and the world at large, as well as an omnipresent attraction to the underlying currents of absurdity running through this world like so many whimsy-filled veins & arteries.

SHERIL ANTONIO: Dr. Antonio is the Associate Dean, Kanbar Institute of Film & Television and the Clive Davis Institute of Recorded Music at New York University's Tisch School of the Arts. She is a frequent lecturer whose more recent presentations include: a live online debate about the movie *Precious* with Stanley Crouch; a webchat on America.gov about democracy and film with filmmakers at the American Embassy in Bogota, Colombia; *The Double Down Film Show*; The Other in Bush World USA; and Black Representations and Media. Dr. Antonio serves as an advisor and lecturer for various projects including: The William H. Cosby Future Filmmakers Workshop, the Ghetto Film School, The Cinema High School, and the NAACP. She has been interviewed for television, radio, and print, including: *Studio 360: Girls on Film*; WNYC 93.9FM; Orpheus: to Hell and Back; and Carpe Diem a magazine show produced by Montclair State University for Comcast and Cablevision. She is the author of *Contemporary African American Cinema*, 2001. Her other published works include: *Do Hollywood Films Truly Reflect Life in America* in *You Asked* "living book" on America.gov; a feature essay for the inaugural issue of *Black Camera: The Urban-Rural Binary in Black American Film and Culture*, Indiana University Press Volume 1, Issue 1; *New Black Cinema: When Self-Empowerment Becomes Assimilation,* Bertz Verlang, 2006; and *Matriarchs, Rebels, Adventurers, and Survivors: Renditions of Black Womanhood in Contemporary African American Cinema*, Sight & Sound, Supplement, July 2005.

RD ARMSTRONG (Raindog) has been a lifelong fan of Buk's since he was in high school and used to read his column in *Open City*. Never in his wildest dreams did he ever think that he would follow in Buk's footsteps into the literary underground of Los Angeles, but that's how it happened. RD started his current incarnation as a poet around the time that Buk was entering his final lap. RD has published two anthologies devoted to Buk, the most recent is *LAST CALL: The Bukowski Legacy Continues* (Lummox Press, 2011). Raindog lives in Long Beach, California, and even though there are days where he feels like he is entering *his* final lap, he continues to serve the small press as best he can. Find him at lummoxpress.com.

THE ART WARRIORS (ANTONIO GAMBOA) was born in 1984 in Málaga, Spain, and has lived in Madrid since he turned eighteen. He holds an undergraduate degree in advertising and a master's degree in creativity, and currently serves as creative director at Arena Quantum. In his free time, he works as art director and illustrator and with The Art Warriors and makes anything that requires a head and two hands—from graffiti to books. He always has ten thousand projects in mind, but hardly completes all of them. He's a straight Christian that believes more in hell than in church. Those who know him well know that he loves classic horror films, good books and comics, tattoos, graffiti, and of course art. He considers himself a very open-minded person. What he reads inspires him, and what he listens to inspires him too.

DAVID BARKER'S short stories and poems have been published in dozens of small press chapbooks, little magazines, and anthologies in the U. S. and Europe since the early 1970s. In 2011, Bottle Of Smoke Press published his novel, *Death At The Flea Circus*, and another novel, *Stella Vero,* has been accepted by the same publisher. *Opal's Trails,* a book of short poems about nature diarist Opal Whiteley was published in the United Kingdom by Pig Ear Press in 2013. He is best known among Bukowski fans for his short 1982 memoir *Charles Bukowski Spit In My Face*, which has been reissued as a Kindle ebook.

WILLIAM BARKER is a poet and novelist born in New Jersey, where he currently lives with his wife, Robin, newborn son, Gavin, and black cat, Eleanor Rigby. A prose writer most of his life, he took an interest in poetry after discovering the works of Charles Bukowski, Jim Morrison, and the Beat Poets during college. Currently he has self-published a full-length volume of poetry entitled *Shards* (poems 2007-2010) and a chapbook, *The Writing Must Leap Upon You Like A Wild Beast,* whose title is derived from a line in a Bukowski poem.

BLACK SIFICHI is a spoken word artist and writer who was born in New York City and lives in Paris. He has recorded albums with a multitude of artists, including The Black Dog and Ez3kiel. Find him at blacksifichi.com.

HARRY CALHOUN has had work published in various poetry journals and more than a dozen books and chapbooks over the past three decades. His career has included Pushcart nominations, a Sundress Best of the Net nomination, and publications in *Abbey, Orange Room Review, Faircloth Review, Thunder Sandwich, Lily,* and others. In 2011, Flutter Press published his chapbook *The Insomnia Poems*. The year 2012 was an exceedingly good one, with the publication of the limited-edition chapbook *Maintenance and Death*, the collection of poems from the 80s and 90s called *Retro*, and the chapbook of love poems, *How Love Conquers the World. Maintenance and Death* is in the process of going to a second edition and a full-length poetry book is in the works. Harry lives in Raleigh, North Carolina, with his wife Trina and his dogs Hamlet and Harriet.

DAVID STEPHEN CALONNE was born in Los Angeles, earning a BA in Ancient Greek at UCLA and PhD in English at the University of Texas at Austin. He is the author of *William Saroyan: My Real Work Is Being, Buddhist Bebop Ecstasy: Saroyan's Influence on Kerouac and the Beats,* and, most recently, *Charles Bukowski* (London: Reaktion, 2012). He has edited *Charles Bukowski: Sunlight Here I Am, Interviews & Encounters (1963-1993),* as well as three Bukowski titles for City Lights: *Portions from a Wine-Stained Notebook* (2008), *Absence of the Hero* (2010), and *More Notes of A Dirty Old Man* (2011). He has taught at the University of Texas at Austin, the University of Michigan, and at the University of Chicago, and presently teaches at Eastern Michigan University. He has lectured internationally at the Bukowski Gesellschaft in Andernach, Germany, as well as in Florence, Paris, London, Berkeley, Columbia, Harvard, and Oxford.

JARED A. CARNIE is a writer in his twenties currently enjoying the freedom of the Outer Hebrides. He can be found at prettyneet.wordpress.com

NEELI CHERKOVSKI: Emerging from the Los Angeles underground of the sixties, Neeli Cherkovski is a poet, painter, and literary biographer. He has written ten books of poetry, including: *From the Canyon Outward*, the award-winning *Leaning Against Time*, and *Elegy for Bob Kaufman*; two acclaimed biographies, *Bukowski: A Life* and *Ferlinghetti: A Biography*; his book, *Whitman's Wild Children* (a collection of critical memoirs), has become an underground classic. In the late 1960s, he co-edited the poetry anthology *Laugh Literary and Man the Humping Guns* with Charles Bukowski. The forthcoming James Franco biopic of Bukowski is based on his biography. He's currently completing a memoir of a life in poetry and a new collection of poems, *When the Crow and I Are Alone*. His papers are housed at the Bancroft Library, UC Berkeley.

KIM COOPER is the creator of 1947project, the crime-a-day time travel blog that spawned Esotouric's popular crime bus tours, including *Haunts of a Dirty Old Man: Charles Bukowski's Los Angeles, Pasadena Confidential, the Real Black Dahlia,* and *Weird West Adams*. Her collaborative L.A. history blogs include *On Bunker Hill* and *In SRO Land*. With husband Richard Schave, Kim curates the Salons of the Los Angeles Visionaries Association (LAVA). When the third generation Angeleno isn't combing old newspapers for forgotten scandals, she is a passionate advocate for historic preservation of signage, vernacular architecture, and writers' homes. Kim was for many years the editrix of *Scram* (a journal of unpopular culture). Her books include *Fall in Love For Life, Bubblegum Music Is the Naked Truth, Lost in the Grooves,* and an oral history of *Neutral Milk Hotel*. For information about tours, visit esotouric.com.

ABEL DEBRITTO's new book is *Charles Bukowski, King of the Underground*.

HENRY DENANDER was born in 1952 and lives in Stockholm, Sweden. An artist and a poet, his latest book *The Accidental Navigator* was published by Lummox Press. Visit Henry at his website, which features poetry and art, at www.henrydenander.com.

JOCELYNE DESFORGES, painter, co-publisher and co-editor of Purple Glow Press, lives in Lachine, Quebec, Canada. Inspired by all colours. Never saw one that didn't tell me a story. Words, songs, and dance are also great storytellers. My works are recollections of what I heard, read, or saw. Bukowski's work ethics have inspired me more than I can say. Bukowski's poem "Roll the Dice" gave me all I needed to keep going. "If you're going to try, go all the way. Otherwise, don't even start."

RENE DIEDRICH, a teacher with the Los Angeles Unified School District, is a poet an artist. She is currently working on a memoir and a novella that pays homage to Nathaniel West. She edited the anthology *How Dirty Girls Get Clean* (2011).

JOHN DORSEY is the author of several collections of poetry, including *Teaching the Dead to Sing: The Outlaw's Prayer* (Rose of Sharon Press, 2006), *Sodomy is a City in New Jersey* (American Mettle Books, 2010), *Leaves of Ass* (Unadorned Press, 2011) and *Tombstone Factory* (Epic Rites Press, 2013). His work has been nominated for the Pushcart Prize. He may be reached at archerevans@yahoo.com.

MARK ERICKSON was born in Hollywood, California, and lives along the West Coast of United States, near the surf breaks and the sand dunes. After growing up in Hollywood, his family moved to Germany and Italy. He later settled in the Bay Area to study painting and art history at the San Francisco Art Institute and the San Francisco Art Academy. Mark paints in his studio in California and exhibits in galleries around the United States. He continues writing poetry and short stories that often are inspiration for his paintings. He has self-published numerous books on painting, photography, and poetry in collaboration with Katy Zartl of Katworks Graphics in Vienna, Austria. He is presently working on a photo book, *The Man From Painted Woods,* of his father's exploits in World War II. You can view Mark's work at markerickson.com.

DAN FANTE is the author twelve books: Novels, poetry, plays, and short vision. His work is published in eight languages. His latest novel, the thriller *Point Doom,* arrived in May 2013.

PAUL FERICANO is a poet and satirist and co-founder (with Elio Ligi) of the first parody news syndicate, *Yossarian Universal News Service* (1980). His work has appeared in *The Wormwood Review, The New York Quarterly,* and *Projector,* and his books of poetry include: *Commercial Break; Sinatra, Sinatra;* and *Loading the Revolver with Real Bullets.* In the forthcoming year, *The New Yorker, The Atlantic Monthly,* and *The Paris Review* are all expected to reject his work. Visit Paul at www.yunews.com.

KAREN FINLEY is an artist, author, and performer. Finley exhibits, performs, and lectures worldwide. She has written seven books, most recently *Reality Shows* published by Feminist Press. Finley is an Arts Professor at Tisch School of the Arts, New York University.

JACK FOLEY is a widely published, innovative California poet. He has published twelve books of poetry, five books of criticism, and *Visions and Affiliations,* a chronoencyclopedia of California poetry from 1940 to 2005. His radio show, *Cover to Cover,* is heard on Berkeley, California, radio station KPFA every Wednesday at three; his column, "Foley's Books," appears in the online magazine *Alsop Review.* In 2010, Foley was awarded the Lifetime Achievement Award by the Berkeley Poetry Festival, and June 5, 2010 was proclaimed "Jack Foley Day" in Berkeley. The Fall 2012, Vol. 5, No. 1 issue of the online *Tower Journal* is a Festschrift for Foley: www.towerjournal.com, go to archive. *EYES,* Foley's selected poems, is forthcoming from Poetry Hotel Press and a chapbook, *LIFE,* from Word Palace Press. With his wife Adelle, Foley performs his work (often "multi-voiced" pieces) frequently in the San Francisco Bay Area and elsewhere. Their performances can be found on YouTube.

FRANCEYE (FRANCES DEAN SMITH): Born in San Rafael, California, in 1922, FrancEyE was a poet whose works include *Snaggletooth in Ocean Park* (1996), *Amber Spider* (2004), *Grandma Stories* (2008), and *Call* (2009). Mother of Charles Bukowski's only child, Marina Louise Bukowski (born 1964), FrancEyE passed away in 2009.

ED GALING, at age ninety-six, still writes every day. Ed has been widely published in the small press and was recently featured in *Rattle* magazine as a poet of the "Greatest Generation." He is the author of over fifty poetry collections, including *Tiddly Winks* (2003), *Rooftops* (2007), and *Pushcarts and Peddlers* (2011). Visit his blog at edgaling.blogspot.com.

JOAN GANNIJ began her career in Southern California in 1973 as a writer/photographer, rock and roll disc jockey, and creator of two syndicated radio talk shows, "Culture Shock" and "Off the Record." Born in New York City, raised in Hollywood, she worked on both coasts before relocating to Amsterdam in 1987 to edit magazines, write books, and shoot pictures. She is the author of three poetry chapbooks, a book on Dutch designer Hester van Eeghen, two prize-winning children's books *Elusive Moose* and *Hidden Hippo* (Barefoot Books), numerous travel guides on The Netherlands, Finland, Norway, and Iceland, and is also a writer of pop and jazz lyrics. "In Hollywood, I had gotten tired of photographing movie stars and rock musicians (from Marty Feldman to The Rolling Stones). After the fateful demise of my 'Frigid Air' project (A Book of Famous People and Their Refrigerators) in 1976, I realised that I had gotten burnt-out on the celebrity scene in L.A., which is why shooting literary figures like Charles Bukowski and Henry Miller, and, later, my reportage on a homeless woman in San Diego was so gratifying. There was something deep and soulful behind their eyes that the camera picked up. An integrity of spirit, which I also wanted to reinforce in my own life as well as in my work—-and which ultimately motivated me to leave America for Europe." After taking an "early retirement" of almost twenty years from photography to focus on her writing, Gannij returned to making black and white portraits of "interesting people, not necessarily famous" in 1998. Her photographs have been exhibited in galleries in London, Helsinki, Amsterdam, in the Huntington Library in Pasadena, and Huis Marseille (photography museum) in Amsterdam. She still shoots proudly with an analogue camera.

ANGGO GENORGA was born and raised in the Philippines and is now doing a nine to five gig in the United Arab Emirates. Up until now, he hasn't owned any Bukowski books but has copies of the poet's writings printed from the Internet. He's currently writing poems dealing with his concept of poetry and hopes to get the book published.

MARJORIE GILBERT was born in Racine, Wisconsin, in 1922 and in July 2013 celebrated her ninety-first birthday. During WWII, she served in the WAVES (the women's branch of the U.S. Navy) until her husband was released from the U.S. Army. A mother of two, Marjorie went to work as a secretary in the History Department at California State University, Los Angeles, where she worked for over twenty years. During her retirement years, Marjorie has traveled throughout the world. An art lover, she volunteered for sixteen years at the Norton Simon Museum in Pasadena, California—a city where she currently resides.

JEFFREY GRAESSLEY lives in La Puente, California. His poems can be found in the upcoming volumes of *Emerge Literary Journal* and *RCC MUSE Magazine*. His first chapbook, *Her Blue Dress* will be published in the Silver Birch Press *Chapbook Anthology* (Fall 2013). His recent discovery of the Beat generation has prompted loving and longing thoughts for that simple, drunken, far-gone time in American history.

S.A. GRIFFIN: Husband, father, Vietnam-era vet, and Carma Bum, S.A. Griffin lives, loves, and works in Los Angeles. Recent books include *Greatest Hits* (Pudding House), *They Swear We Don't Exist* (Bottle of Smoke Press), and *Numbskull Sutra* (Rank Stranger Press). In 2010, he created The Poetry Bomb, a seven-foot-tall former Vietnam-era practice bomb converted into an art object and filled with poetry from around the world. He then took Elsie on a five-week tour of the U.S. for his *Poetry Bomb Couch Surfing Across American Tour of Words 2010* in an effort to inspire civil disagreements. Editor of *The Outlaw Bible of American Poetry* (Basic Books, Firecracker Award), he is presently editing Scott Wannberg's next book *The Official Language of Yes!* for Perceval Books.

WIN HARMS is a poet living in France with her professor husband. She hails from the state of the cowboy poetry contest, but she has lived pretty much everywhere, including many psych wards, and considers herself a survivor of the struggle. The chaos has ceased and now she spends her time doing needlepoint and laundry, but longs to share her words with the world. As of last year, she left her roaring twenties, and is now feeling fecund and free.

DONNA HILBERT's latest book, *The Green Season,* World Parade Books, a collection of poems, stories, and essays, is now available in an expanded second edition. Donna appears in and her poetry is the text of the documentary *Grief Becomes Me: A Love Story*, a Christine Fugate film. Earlier books include *Mansions* and *Deep Red* from Event Horizon, *Transforming Matter* and *Traveler in Paradise* from Pearl Editions, and the short story collection *Women Who Make Money and the Men Who Love Them* from Staple First Editions (published in England). Poems in Italian can be found in Bloc notes 59 and in French in *La page blanche*, in both cases translated by Mariacristina Natalia Bertoli. New work is in recent or forthcoming issues of *5AM, Nerve Cowboy, Pearl,* and *Poets & Artists.* A new collection, *The Congress of Luminous Bodies,* is forthcoming from Aortic Books. Learn more at donnahilbert.com.

RODGER JACOBS' first novel, *The Furthest Palm* was published by Silver Birch Press in 2012. His most recent publication, "Nazi Noir: The Ghost of the Prophet of Fascism," is online at *L.A. Review of Books*, and an original work of short fiction, "The Air Down There," is featured in *Green: An Eclectic Anthology of Poetry and Prose* (Silver Birch Press, 2013). His short story "No Style, No Grace, No Mercy" will appear in the print edition of *Underground Voices* in December 2013. Rodger's writer website is silverlakeadjacent.wordpress.com.

LINDA KING is a poet, playwright, and artist working in painting and sculpture who was immortalized in the poetry and prose of her former love Charles Bukowski. During the 1970s, King edited the little magazine *Purr*. She also has had her poetry published in a wide variety of magazines, including *The Bukowski Review* and *Wormwood Review*. Her most recent works are the memoir *Loving and Hating Bukowski* and the novel *Mad Ouija*.

HARVEY KUBERNIK is the author of the books *This Is Rebel Music* (2004) and *Hollywood Shack Job: Rock Music In Film and On Your Screen* (2007). Kubernik has been an active music journalist since 1972, and a record producer since 1979. A former West Coast Director of A&R for MCA Records, Kubernik is a music historian and pop culture archivist and researcher and has credits in over one hundred and fifty books and television programs. Kubernik also develops strategic marketing and media campaigns for filmmakers, musicians and entertainment companies.

DANA LAINA is an artist who lives in Chicago. Find Dana on deviantart at ~danalaina.

LAUTIR (FABRIZIO CASSETTA) was born in 1971. He lives and works in Limbiate, near Milan, Italy. His credits include serving as a cartoonist on the magazine *Intrepido* and working as an illustrator for school textbooks. He's also worked as an airbrush artist and designer of motorcycle helmets and is a licensed tattoo artist. His style has evolved from figurative to poetic-mysterious, as demonstrated in his portrait of Charles Bukowski.

SUZUKI LIMBU: Biographies aren't really that interesting until the person is in the limelight or dead and Suzuki is neither. She is a psychology undergraduate, her star sign is Scorpio, and her personality type is INFJ. She never intended to write poetry until she came across Bukowski's "Cause and Effect."

MICHAEL LIMNIOS started his career as a road manager at Blues and Jazz concerts in Greece with Junior Wells, Albert King, Phil Guy, B.B King, Louisiana Red, and more. He has worked as a DJ as well as a writer at travel magazines, newspapers, European music magazines, and in the website of The Museum of American Poetics. In Blues Foundation's magazine, Mike has written about the connection of Blues music with Greeks. His radio broadcasting (Blues: "The Rose of Music") was the first daily show around Europe. His articles are inspired by his journeys around the world—from Papua New Guinea to Africa and from Latin America to the Himalayas—and his concern about the local culture of tribes. He is also working on a special project about the connection between Music and poetry.

GERALD LOCKLIN is a professor emeritus of English at California State University, Long Beach, where he taught full-time from 1965-2007, retains his office and contact information, and still teaches an occasional class as needed. He has published fiction, poetry, essays, and reviews prolifically in periodicals and in over a hundred and fifty books, chapbooks, and broadsides. Recent or upcoming books include a fiction e-Book, *The Sun Also Rises in the Desert,* from Mendicant Bookworks; a collection of poems, *Deep Meanings: Selected Poems, 2008-2013,* from PRESA Press; three simultaneously released novellas from Spout Press; and a French collection of his prose, *Candy Bars: Le Dernier des Damnes* from 13e Note Press, Paris. Event Horizon Press released new editions of *A Simpler Time, A Simpler Place* and *Hemingway Colloquium: The Poet Goes to Cuba* in 2011; Coagula Press released the first of two volumes of his *Complete Coagula Poems;* and *From a Male Perspective* appeared from PRESA Press. In February 2013, Silver Birch Press published *Gerald Locklin: New and Selected Poems (1967-2007),* originally published by World Parade Books (2008). Contact: gerlocklin@gmail.com, www.geraldlocklin.org, or www.facebook.com/geraldlocklin.

SUZANNE LUMMIS has served on the executive board of Beyond Baroque Literary/Arts Center, is one of the co-directors of its new imprint, Pacific Coast Poetry Series, and the literary director for the Arroyo Arts Collective, which in 2014 will place Los Angeles poems in the storefronts along Figueroa, Northeast L.A. In 2011, she received Women in Theater's Red Carpet Award for her activity as playwright, actor, and performer. Her poems have appeared in the Knopf "Everyman's Poetry Library" anthologies *Poems of the American West* and *Poems of Murder and Mayhem* (the "Noir" section), and in the Heyday Books anthologies *California Poetry from the Gold Rush to the Present,* and *New California Writing 2012,* and in major literary magazines across the country.

MARVIN MALONE received a BS in Pharmacy from the University of Nebraska in 1951, an MS in Physiology/Pharmacology in 1953, and in 1958 a PhD in Pharmacology. In 1958, Malone joined the pharmacy department at the University of New Mexico, transferring to the University of Connecticut in 1960, and to the University of the Pacific in 1969. Malone was a dedicated researcher, publishing more than two hundred and forty scientific papers, a Fellow of the American Association for the Advancement of Science, and affiliated with more than twenty professional and honorary societies. Although Malone was a scientist by profession, his first loves were literature and art, especially the avant garde. Married to an artist, Shirley, who encouraged his artistic expression, Malone early turned to painting, woodblock printing, and assemblage. When the Malones and their two small daughters moved to Connecticut in 1960, Marvin discovered an upstart small-press poetry journal called the *Wormwood Review*. After financial ruin threatened the press, he took over the publication, editing, designing, and publishing quarterly issues by himself up until his death in 1996. Though small, unpretentious, and nonprofit, the *Wormwood Review* was one of the most influential and long-running poetry publications in the U.S., publishing the work of a wide range of writers, including Charles Bukowski, William S. Burroughs, Gregory Corso, Paul Fericano, Linda King, Gerald Locklin, Jack Micheline, Henry Miller, Joan Jobe Smith, and Fred Voss.

ADRIAN MANNING writes from Leicester, England. His poetry and articles have appeared in numerous chapbooks, magazines, and on-line sites around the world. He is also the editor of Concrete Meat Press and a massive fan and collector of Charles Bukowski works.

DEAN MARAIS is an artist and a writer who lives in the Southeast United States. He draws deep satisfaction and inspiration from many artists, poets, and thinkers, including but not limited to Thoreau, Whitman, Kerouac, and of course Bukowski.

GERMA MARQUEZ, born in 1966, lives and works in Frankfurt, Germany. She is a graduate in fine arts from Seville University (Spain) and specializes in portraits and the human figure. While living in Spain, she worked as an art teacher. Now she is a commissioned portrait artist with clients around the world. She has exhibited her work in Belgium, Spain, Portugal, and Germany. Find her at: germamarquez.blogspot.de/ or via email: germaniamarquez@yahoo.com.

CATFISH MCDARIS's most infamous chapbook is *Prying with Jack Micheline and Charles Bukowski*. His best readings were in Paris at the Shakespeare and Co. bookstore and with Jimmy "the ghost of Hendrix" Spencer in NYC on 42nd St. He's done over twenty chaps in the last twenty years. He's been in the *New York Quarterly, Slipstream, Pearl, Main St. Rag, Café Review, Chiron Review, Zen Tattoo, Wormwood Review, Great Weather For Media*, and *Graffiti* and been nominated for fifteen Pushcarts, Best of Net. He won the Uprising Award in 1999, and won the Flash Fiction Contest judged by the U.S. Poet Laureate in 2009. He loves cats better than dogs, he misses the New Mexican Mountains, but loves the green of Wisconsin. He retired after thirty-four years at the Main Milwaukee Post Office. He's married to a beautiful Mexican lady and they have a daughter with a tree-climbing dog.

ANN MENEBROKER lives in Sacramento, California, and has been writing and publishing since the late 1950s. A longtime member of the Sacramento Poetry Center, she has published over twenty books and chapbooks, has had her work on broadsides, been in anthologies, edited literary publications, taught in prisons, and her poems have appeared in a college textbook, *Literature and Its Writers*. Her last publication is *The Measure of Small Gratitudes*, 2011, from Kamini Press, Sweden.

HEATHER MINETTE is from Texas. Her poems and stories have been published in numerous magazines and ezines, including *Backhand Stories, Up the Staircase, Frost Writing, The Blue Hour,* and *Bayousphere*.

AUSTIN MITCHELL: Born 1986 in Rocky Mount, North Carolina, Austin Mitchell is a writer, musician, and aspiring actor. He studied at the University of North Carolina in Charlotte and also in Wilmington, North Carolina. After toiling around the American south for a quarter of a century, he has plans to relocate to Los Angeles to toil there.

RICHARD MODIANO: Executive Director of Beyond Baroque Literary Arts Center, Richard Modiano is a writer, curator, and member of the Industrial Workers of the World. In 2007, he produced Beyond Baroque's On the Road 50th Anniversary marathon reading, and in 2009 he produced another marathon reading of William Burroughs' *Naked Lunch* for its 50th anniversary publication.

JON MONDAY is an American producer and distributor of CDs and DVDs across an eclectic range of material including work by Aldous Huxley, Christopher Isherwood, and Charles Bukowski. Monday directed and co-produced with Jennifer Douglas the feature-length documentary *Save KLSD: Media Consolidation and Local Radio*. He is also President of Benchmark Recordings.

JEFF MORGAN is an artist. Find him on Facebook at ipaintlive.

PAUL NEBENZAHL is a writer, musician, and painter living in Evanston, Illinois, and in Sleepy Hollow, New York. As a performing multi-instrumentalist and composer, Paul has created works for film and television, and has performed extensively in theater, stage, and club settings, most recently as Karen Finley's musical director. Paul's poem *"Gusen Station"* was published in English, Italian, and German in 2012 by the *International Committee for Mauthausen and Gusen*. His poetry collection *Black Shroud with Rainbow Fringes* will be published by Silver Birch Press during 2013.

GERALD NICOSIA, born and raised in Chicago and transplanted to the San Francisco Bay Area in his late twenties, is a poet, fiction writer, biographer, historian, and playwright. He is best known for his biography of Jack Kerouac, *Memory Babe*. Long associated with the Beat and post-Beat writers, he has organized and taken part in hundreds of poetry readings, including a recent Beat reading at Bob Weir's Sweetwater Music Hall in Mill Valley, California, that drew over three hundred people and celebrated the release of the movie version of *On the Road*, on which Nicosia worked as a consultant. He has also spent a good part of his life studying, helping, and chronicling the story of Vietnam veterans; his book *Home to War* on their struggle to heal and readjust was picked as one of the "Best Books of 2001" by the *Los Angeles Times*. He is currently at work on a biography of Ntozake Shange, and his fourth book of poetry, *Night Train to Shanghai*, is forthcoming with Creative Arts Books. He has also taught and lectured extensively on the Beats, the Sixties, and modern literature.

MICHAEL O'BRIEN enjoys native and edible plant landscaping, timely spontaneity, outdoor art, nature, moving things around, good philosophy, practicing qigong and tai chi, learning, neighborliness, writing, art (including photography), helping others, and hunting—for sustenance—mastodons with a bow and arrow. He loves the work of Gelek Rimpoche, Charles Bukowski, Cesar Millan, Harlan Hubbard, Maurice Merleau-Ponty, Paul Cezanne, Dr. Yang Jwing-Ming, and Bill Roberts. His dislikes include false pretense, gas-powered lawnmowers, hunting for sport, chemical pollutants, overexploitation, and the idea of adults joining clubs/groups/unions/parties/etc. He strives to make work that is worth its weight in deforestation.

BART PLANTENGA is the author of *Beer Mystic*, a novel that circumnavigates the globe in a unique pub crawl. He is also the author of *Wiggling Wishbone*, *Spermatagonia: The Isle of Man*, *Paris Scratch*, and *NY Sin Phoney in Face Flat Minor*. His books include *Yodel-Ay-Ee-Oooo: The Secret History of Yodeling Around the World* and *Yodel in HiFi*. He has been the DJ of *Wreck This Mess* in NYC, Paris, and now Amsterdam since 1986. He was a founding member of the NYC-based literary alliance, the Unbearables. He lives and hopes in Amsterdam with his partner Nina and daughter Paloma Jet.

DAVID SCOTT POINTER joined the underground in 1990. Recent poetry collections include *Sundrenched Nanosilver, The Psychobilly Princess, Warhammer Piano Bar,* and others. Recent anthologies include *Proud to Be: Writings by American Warriors, Poe-It, Grave Robbers, Science Gone Mad, Hell Whore*, and many others. David is an advisory panel member at "Writing For Peace," and has been publishing in the small press for twenty-three years. When he started publishing in the little mags, Dave Church, Catfish McDaris, Alan Caitlin, and others were all over the scene and he thought they were the Charles Bukowskis of literature—though he soon discovered that Henry Chinaski was Charles Bukowski. David kept plugging away. Recent publications appear in *The Southern Poetry Anthology* Series for the state of Georgia and Tennessee. His most recent poetry book is entitled *Oncoming Crime Facts*. David can be reached at dspointer@hotmail.com.

ALVARO POZO was born in Santiago, Chile, in 1975. His studies in Visual Arts at Universidad and his experience in publishing projects, virtual platforms, and personal and collective exhibitions have developed his artistic work in drawing, painting, and illustration. Currently, Alvaro serves as Artistic Forensic at Criminalistics Laboratory at Policia de Investigaciones de Chile.

D.A. (DAVID) PRATT was rescued from what was being imposed upon him in school as "literature" when he read D.H. Lawrence's *Lady Chatterley's Lover* during his late teens and, since then, he has often said that reading "Lady C" changed everything. From that first encounter with "real reading," he has maintained a "common reader" interest in a wide range of the world's literature while working for what now seems like "far too long" in the field of taxation policy for the Government of Saskatchewan. One day, at a bookstore near his workplace, he encountered the writing of Charles Bukowski and this transformed his view of what poetry could be. He's now had a few poems published here and there. With a twinkle in his eye, he considers one of his articles in *Nexus: The International Henry Miller Journal* to be the definitive study of the two versions of Miller's *The World of Sex*.

WENDY RAINEY's works have appeared in *Chiron Review, Carnival Literary Magazine,* and several other journals. She has read her work at Hotel Cafe in Hollywood, Grand Performances in Los Angeles, Mount San Antonio College Literary Festival, and San Gabriel Valley Literary Festival. She is the founding poetry editor of *Cultural Weekly*, and in 2012 was nominated for a Pushcart Prize.

STEVE RICHMOND was a poet who enjoyed a forty-year friendship with Charles Bukowski, Richmond's mentor during the 1960s. His memoir, *Spinning Off Bukowski,* was published by Sun Dog Press in 1996. He died in 2009.

DAVE ROSKOS is the editor of *Big Hammer* magazine and Iniquity Press/Vendetta Books. Most recent chapbook is called *Intensive Care* (Black Rabbit Press, 2010). Other chapbooks include *Lyrical Grain, Doggerel Chaff & Pedestrian Preoccupations & Fall & All*. He has supported himself as a factotum most of his life, but presently works as a Life Skills Specialist in the Mental Health Field, working with the MICA community.

DR. ROSS T. RUNFOLA is a poet, professor of sociology at Medaille College in Buffalo, New York, and an attorney who started writing real poetry in the Bukowski genre after discovering his muse. He also became an avid collector, until recently when he decided to share Buk with others, including the University of Buffalo poetry collection.

RICHARD SCHAVE has been at various times an art historian, a mason, an independent film producer, a computer programmer, and the director who transformed the Downtown Los Angeles Art Walk into a nonprofit organization. With wife Kim Cooper, Richard founded Esotouric, which has allowed him to fuse his otherwise exclusive experiences into a very special view of Los Angeles. Richard's tours include his celebrated Raymond Chandler and Charles Bukowski excursions, the occasional John Fante's Dreams from Bunker Hill, The Birth of Noir and the California Culture series. When he's off the bus, Richard is the host of the LAVA Literary Salon series, named Best L.A. Literary Salon by *Los Angeles Magazine*. He also curates an ongoing series of forensic science presentations for LAVA, including "Cracking the Case," "TRACE" and "The Science & Art of Forensic Investigations." Visit Richard at esotouric.com or lavatransforms.org.

RAYMOND KING SHURTZ has written over thirty plays, three published with Samuel French and Anchorage Press/Dramatic Publishing. The Founding Artistic Director of Playwright's Workshop Theatre in Phoenix, Arizona, Raymond produced eighty new plays in his twelve-year tenure with the company. In 1998, he began teaching theatre, film, and humanities at Metro Arts, a high school for the performing and visual arts in Phoenix, Arizona, where he taught and produced another ten years' of new theatre. His play, *Blue Baby, A Memoir* won the Playwriting Fellowship in 2003 from the Arizona Commission on the Arts. Since 2008, he has worked as a freelance director, actor, writer, and musician. In 2009, Raymond produced and performed his one-man show *Bohemian Cowboy* at The Elephant Theatre, "pick of the week" in *LA Weekly*, and subsequently performed the show approximately seventy-five times in Los Angeles, San Francisco, and Southern Utah, with another twenty-three shows in Austin, Texas.

JOAN JOBE SMITH, founding editor of *Pearl* and *Bukowski Review,* worked for seven years as a go-go dancer before receiving her BA from CSULB and MFA from University of California, Irvine. A Pushcart Honoree, her award-winning work has appeared internationally in more than five hundred publications, including *Outlaw Bible, Ambit, Beat Scene, Wormwood Review,* and *Nerve Cowboy*—and she has published twenty collections, including *Jehovah Jukebox* (Event Horizon Press, US) and *The Pow Wow Cafe* (The Poetry Business, UK), a finalist for the UK 1999 Forward Prize. In July 2012, with her husband, poet Fred Voss, she did her sixth reading tour of England (debuting at the 1991 Aldeburgh Poetry Festival), featured at the Humber Mouth Literature Festival in Hull. In November 2012, Silver Birch Press published her literary profile entitled *Charles Bukowski Epic Glottis: His Art & His Women (& me)*. In 2013, World Parade Books will release her memoir *Tales of an Ancient Go-Go Girl*. Her literary magazine *Pearl* will release its fiftieth edition in 2013—find out more at pearlmag.com.

BEN TALBOT graduated with a BA in TV/Film from California State University, Fullerton. Currently, he makes his living as a caterer in Los Angeles and lives on his own at the base of the Hollywood Hills. Over the past ten years, he has published articles for *Kern County Family Magazine*, collaborated on screenplays for features, TV shows, and web series, and he continues to write album reviews for the music webzine *WORDKRAPHT*. His personal writing includes a finished a memoir, and he is now working on a second book.

MARK TERRILL shipped out of San Francisco as a merchant seaman to the Far East and beyond, studied and spent time with Paul Bowles in Tangier, Morocco, and has lived in Germany since 1984, where he's worked as a shipyard welder, road manager for rock bands, cook, and postal worker. He is the author of *Bread & Fish* (The Figures), *The United Colors of Death* (Pathwise Press), *The Salvador-Dalai-Lama Express*, (Main Street Rag), *Superabundance* (Longhouse), *Laughing Butcher Berlin Blues* (Poetry Salzburg), and several other collections of poetry, prose, memoir, and translations.

DIRK VELVET is a Poet/Writer of Songs from Muskego, Wisconsin. His writing has been featured in *Beggars and Cheeseburgers, Pearl, Re)verb, Nerve Cowboy,* and *Milwaukee Renaissance.*

MELANIE VILLINES is a novelist, playwright, screenwriter, television writer, biographer, editor, and ghostwriter. Her published work includes the novel *Tales of the Sacred Heart* (Bogfire Press), the family memoir *Reason to Fight* (co-written with Hiram Johnson), a celebrity biography *Beyond Hollywood* (co-written with J. Herbert Klein), *Anna & Otto*, a novel for children (Inklings Press), and a variety of ghostwritten books and screenplays. A founding member of Chicago Dramatists, she is the author of twenty plays. Her original screenplays include *Calling Oz*, finalist in the Austin Film Festival and many other screenwriting competitions, and *Just Say the Word*, top-10 finalist in Illinois-Chicago screenwriting competition. She co-wrote the critically acclaimed ninety-minute drama *Crime of Innocence*, based on the life of Emmett Till, for the NBC affiliate in Chicago. Her play *Bernice* (co-written with Hiram Johnson) had a February 2013 workshop production in Dallas and her story "Windy City Sinners," an excerpt from her upcoming novel of the same name, will appear in the *Chicago Quarterly Review* (Fall, 2013).

FRED VOSS, a machinist for thirty-two years, has had three collections of poetry published by the U.K.'s Bloodaxe Books. He is regularly published in magazines such as *Poetry Review* (London), *Ambit* (London), *Rising* (London), *The Shop* (Ireland), *Atlanta Review,* and *PEARL*, and has twice been the subject of feature programs about his poetry on National BBC Radio 4. In 2008, he was featured at The Ledbury Poetry Festival, and in 2011 he and his wife, poet Joan Jobe Smith, were featured readers at the University of Pittsburgh and, in 2012, were featured at The Humber Mouth Literature Festival (Hull, England). His latest book, *Hammers and Hearts of the Gods* from Bloodaxe Books, was selected by U.K. newspaper *The Morning Star* as one of the Top Seven Books for 2009. In 2011, he was featured poet in a hardbound limited edition of *DWANG* (London, England), and in 2013 World Parade Books will publish his first novel, *Making America Strong.*

SCOTT WANNBERG: A prolific poet and American original, Scott Wannberg was born in Santa Monica, California, in February 1953. A big man with an even bigger presence, he attended Venice High School and then went on to receive his Master's degree in Creative Writing from San Francisco State University, where he studied with Stan Rice and Daniel J. Langton. Scott spent his life working as a sales clerk and book buyer for independent bookstores, most notably Dutton's Books in Brentwood, California, where he held court and worked the stacks for almost twenty-five years, becoming a legendary and iconic figure in the process. From 1989-2009, he rode shotgun with The Carma Bums on the road and off. His book *Nomads of Oblivion* (Lummox Press) made the *L.A. Times* bestseller list in 2000, and in the late 90s *Los Angeles Magazine* named him one of the "Top 100 Coolest People" of L.A. No longer able to keep up with the increasing cost of living in his native Southern California, in 2008 he relocated to Florence, Oregon, where he died too soon at the age of fifty-eight in August of 2011. Scott's two most recent titles, *Tomorrow Is Another Song* (Perceval Press) and *All Your Misplaced Utopias* (Bottle of Smoke Press), were both released shortly after his passing in September and October of 2011 respectively.

VANESSA WILKEN was born in Cincinnati, Ohio, in 1977. She works predominantly in acrylic paints, but also dabbles in oil paint and collage work preferring portraiture in fauve. Vanessa is a (mostly) self-taught artist from a family of artists, journalists, and writers. She has contributed to shows at the University of Washington (Seattle) and The Station Cafe and Gallery (Seattle). Her work has also been featured in online magazines such as *The Commonline Journal* and the *International Journal of Radical Critique* (IJRC). Vanessa sells original pieces in her online shop at venture77.etsy.com. She lives and works in Seattle.

A. D. WINANS, an award-winning native San Francisco poet and writer, edited and published the acclaimed *Second Coming Press* for seventeen years. He worked for the San Francisco Art Commission from 1975-80, and during that time produced the 1980 Poets and Music Festival honoring the poet Josephine Miles and blues legend John Lee Hooker. His work has been published in over fifteen hundred poetry magazines and anthologies, including the *Outlaw Bible of American Poetry*. He is the author of over fifty books of poetry and prose, including *North Beach Poems* and *Drowning Like Li Po in a River of Red Wine: Selected Poems 1970-2010.* In 2002, a song poem of his was set to music and performed at New York's Alice Tully Hall. In 2006, he won a PEN Josephine Miles Award for excellence in literature, and in 2009 PEN Oakland awarded him a lifetime achievement award.

BRADLEY WIND is an artist and author. He spent a good deal of his twenties reading Bukowski's work. He owes Charles Bukowski a debt that can never be repaid so he drew a picture in his honor. Find him at bradleywind.com.

ERIK WOLTERSDORF considers himself a native Hawaiian trapped inside the body of a New Yorker. A product of New York City, Erik was born on August 17, 1969. Erik worked as a truck driver, dispatcher, and shipping clerk before moving on to the art of music production. He has worked in sound design, touring logistics, and all other facets of the music industry. He graduated from The City University of New York, where he focused on writing and English literature. He has since been accepted to a prestigious program at New York University for a select group of aspiring novelists. Erik began writing poetry four years ago at the age of forty and is currently finishing work on his first novel. Erik lives in Jackson Heights, Queens.

PAMELA MILLER WOOD, a native Californian, has lived in the Los Angeles area most of her life. For over thirty years, she has enjoyed a successful career in the Southern California real estate industry, garnering many awards for outstanding achievement along the way, including Top Producer in Los Angeles County for ten consecutive years. *Charles Bukowski's Scarlet* is Pam's first full-length book—a memoir of her multi-year relationship with legendary author Charles Bukowski—a true tour de force.

EDDIE WOODS, born 1940 in New York City, is a native alien as opposed to an expatriate. Although an American writer ("The language is far too rich to ever let go of it," he says), Eddie definitely does not see America as 'back home.' For him home is wherever he happens to be. Which, after having traveled and lived in many parts of the world both East and West, since 1978 has mainly been Amsterdam, the Netherlands. It was then that he and Jane Harvey launched *Ins & Outs* magazine and later founded Ins & Outs Press. Always with numerous irons in the literary fire, Eddie regularly appears in various online and print publications. The most recent of his books and spoken-word CDs is *Tsunami of Love: A Poems Cycle*. His website is http://eddiewoods.nl

TIM YOUD is a Los Angeles-based artist, whose work regularly incorporates text and literature. Youd is represented by Coagula Curatorial gallery. His work has been shown extensively in the United States and he has two upcoming solo museum shows.

BIRGIT (KATY) ZARTL: Born in Vienna, Austria, Katy Zartl studied psychology at the University of Vienna and worked in the Neurological Department of the Hospital Lainz (Vienna). She received additional training in Cognitive Behavioural Therapy and art therapy, which included courses in painting/drawing techniques as well as in the study of chromatics. Since 2000, she has worked as a self-employed psychotherapist, photographer, and painter.

your life is your life.
know it while you have it.
you are marvelous
the gods wait to delight
in you.

Charles Bukowski
from The Laughing Heart

Collage by S.A. Griffin

www.ingramcontent.com/pod-product-compliance
Lightning Source LLC
Chambersburg PA
CBHW071454170626
46811CB00007B/2579